Taming the Beast

Taming the Beast

*Wall Street's Imperfect
Answers to Making Money*

Larry Light

WILEY
John Wiley & Sons, Inc.

Published by John Wiley & Sons, Inc., Hoboken, New Jersey.
Published simultaneously in Canada.

For general information on our other products and services or for technical support,
please contact our Customer Care Department within the United States at
(800) 762-2974, outside the United States at (317) 572-3993 or fax (317) 572-4002.

Wiley also publishes its books in a variety of electronic formats. Some content that
appears in print may not be available in electronic books. For more information about
Wiley products, visit our web site at www.wiley.com.

Library of Congress Cataloging-in-Publication Data:

Light, Larry, 1959–
   Taming the beast : Wall Street's imperfect answers to making money / Larry Light.
     p. cm.
   Includes bibliographical references and index.
  ISBN 978-0-470-60215-7 (hardback); ISBN 978-1-118-08418-2 (ebk);
ISBN 978-1-118-08419-9 (ebk); ISBN 978-1-118-08420-5 (ebk)
  1. Investments. 2. Portfolio management. 3. Speculation. 4. Investment
analysis. I. Title.
  HG4521.L654 2011
  332.6–dc22

                                          2011002033

Printed in the United States of America

10 9 8 7 6 5 4 3 2 1

Contents

Acknowledgments

As a journalist, I've written and edited a cornucopia of stories about finance. The topic always has fascinated me. During the financial crisis, it was like having a ringside seat at the Apocalypse, at once thrilling and scary. In the aftermath, the task of making sense of the rubble was a daunting challenge. Throughout my career, I have had the good luck to work with many astute business and editorial minds.

I want to thank my agent, Cynthia Manson, for urging me to write this book about the investing arena. She had shepherded my mystery novels through to publication.

My superiors at the *Wall Street Journal*, Nikhil Deogun, Ken Brown, and Neal Templin, gave me guidance and encouragement from the outset. Another colleague at the paper, Jason Zweig, was excellent at pointing me in the right direction vis-à-vis Benjamin Graham and behaviorism; he is an expert on both topics.

Bill Baldwin, my boss at *Forbes* magazine, and Dave Wallace and the late Chris Welles, my editors at *BusinessWeek*, were key influences in shaping my financial thinking. So were the superb columnists I edited at *Forbes*, including Gary Shilling, John Rogers, Lisa Hess, Jim Grant,

Ken Fisher, David Dreman, Marilyn Cohen, and Laszlo Birinyi and his intrepid research director, Jeff Rubin.

I want to thank Steve Shepard (former head of BW) and Steve Forbes for running two world-class magazines that allowed me to hone my craft, and for being great guys.

Writing a book like this one requires a torrent of information. Thankfully, Nadine Youssef at Morningstar and Mike McNamee at the Investment Company Institute were wonderful and generous at providing crucial data.

My brilliant wife, Meredith Anthony, who also is a mystery novelist, edited and advised me as I prepared this book. My friend, Terry Rooney, was there for me as always to help me see this project through.

At Wiley, Laura Walsh and Judy Howarth were the perfect editors, smart and incisive.

Taming the Beast

Prologue

The Rosetta Stone

Modern investing began when the world was burning down. Benjamin Graham, a celebrated financier who was in the middle of the flames, invented a systematic process of evaluating investments and popularized it during the Depression-ridden 1930s. It was a way for ordinary people to rebuild their decimated holdings.

Before, there had been no widely used investing systems. The capital markets were like wild frontiers. They too often operated on cronyism and outright fraud; they were swept by manias and laden with onerous debt. Cornelius Vanderbilt concocted a massive stock slide in 1869 by flooding the market with shares from his railroads, as a means of thwarting rival Jay Gould.

Ben Graham taught that investors must be analytical, flexible, and diligent about choosing and managing their holdings. He provided an orderly method of evaluating stock and bonds.

Hand in hand with that insight was the strategy he invented, called value investing, which aims to find cheap, underappreciated stocks. Inspired by his example, other investing systems later sprouted. Some extended Graham's thinking; others were in opposition to it. All sought to tame the unruly market beast, which was capable of bringing both destruction and riches. It's significant that the symbols of Wall Street are both animals: the bull (optimistic) and the bear (pessimistic). Graham taught that people should be careful when dealing with such powerful, dangerous creatures.

Taken together, the approaches created by Graham and his various successors form the foundation of investing in the 21st century: indexing, behaviorism, growth investing, hedging, and on and on. But here's the rub. While the adherents of each often swear by their preferred system as the one true path, all these approaches have deep flaws. Graham's beloved value investing has a pretty good track record, except when it doesn't. Value investors were big underperformers in the late 1990s' tech boom, and were devastated by the bear market that erupted in 2008 because what looked cheap and reliable—financial outfits like Lehman Brothers and Fannie Mae—were the first to fall when the credit crunch occurred.

Hidebound notions are obstacles to clear thinking, Graham argued. Stretch that concept, and you see that smart investors should be free to dip into any number of investing styles, provided they have done their homework. It made no sense to stay out of growth stocks during the tech boom. From 2002 until 2007, real estate plays were very smart. Investing in a private hedge fund can be quite lucrative, provided that it is the right fund. Amaranth Advisors collapsed in 2006 when its managers bet the wrong way on energy futures. Its investors lost most of their money. Graham disagreed with some of the more complex investing ideas that rose after World War II.

No one system works in investing. It's wise to know the strengths and weaknesses of each. Ordinary investors, after doing some studying, can figure out how to use any of the bright ideas that animate modern personal finance. Usually, hedge funds (which focus on trading securities) and private-equity funds (they buy all or part of a company, and hope to sell it after improvements) are the turf of the rich. You need $1 million in net worth just to be allowed inside their hallowed doors.

But there are instruments available that permit regular investors to play even in these arenas.

Successful investors have an ambidextrous ability. They don't put all their chips in one pot. While Graham is considered the avatar of value stocks, he also advocated owning a large slug of bonds, for safety's sake.

★   ★   ★

Graham had an innate ability at math. He devised a formula, perhaps dated today, to figure out what a stock's "intrinsic value" was—in other words, the price at which it should be selling, based largely on its earnings growth. To Graham, stocks selling for much less than the intrinsic value were cheap and should be purchased—or, at least, given a good hard look. Those fetching much more than their intrinsic value were overpriced and usually best avoided. Math, however, had its limits in Graham's book. Any investment-related math beyond arithmetic or simple algebra was suspect, he believed. "Whenever calculus is brought in, or higher algebra," he wrote in a 1958 article in the *Analysts Journal*, "you could take it as a warning signal that the operator was trying to substitute theory for experience."

As in baseball, statistics have long ruled markets. Small wonder, then, that with the advent of computers, exceedingly complex math has crept into the investing world. Indeed, a school of thought has developed over time that statistics can actually divine the market's path ahead, that the beast can be tamed by numerical intelligence. The underlying philosophy here is that the stock market isn't very wild at all. Rather, the market is a rational entity, and humans can decode it. The seeds of this idea were planted centuries ago. In his classic 1776 book, *The Wealth of Nations*, economic philosopher Adam Smith declared that an "invisible hand" drove economies and markets, a collective consciousness that harnessed individual strivings and produced bounty for the good of all.

In 1906, a Yale economist named Irving Fisher published a seminal book, *The Nature of Capital and Income*, which took the Adam Smith concept a step further. By Fisher's reckoning, it was a statistical certainty that the early-20th-century market was a sort of nirvana, a blessed place of perpetual wealth expansion. After his death in 1947, other academics refined that to come up with the "efficient market hypothesis," or EMH. The proposition here is that the combined knowledge of market figures, from analysts to money managers, is distilled to ensure that stock prices were what they should be. It was virtually impossible to try to beat the market, hence why try? Leading EMH advocates rode this to great renown. Several of them won Nobel Prizes.

Missing in these formulations is the powerful influence of ignorance, emotions, and herd mentality. To a Graham follower, reading bird entrails is more enlightening than any mathematical forecasting method since what's ahead is unknowable. Yogi Berra was wise on this subject, saying, "I never make predictions, especially about the future." Some investors do make great market calls. Charles Merrill, the bon vivant founder of Merrill Lynch, figured that the Jazz Age bull market was getting out of hand, largely because investors were borrowing heavily to get in on stocks. Back then, investors could take out huge margin loans, with just 10 percent down in cash (today it is 50 percent) and use paper gains to purchase still more shares. In early 1929, Merrill advised his brokerage clients to sell at then-high prices and thus decrease their stock exposure. But Merrill's foresight was an exception.

The first decade of the 21st century boasts a dubious distinction: it has had two huge market meltdowns that seemed to come from nowhere. The first was the 2000–2002 tech bust; the second was the housing-related slump that hit hard in 2008.

Both smashed markets worldwide. Nassim Nicholas Taleb's fascinating book, *The Black Swan: The Impact of the Highly Improbable,* had a captivating name to describe catastrophic events such as the twin market busts blighting the century's start. While everyone knows that swans are white, he writes, a black one occasionally appears. And when it does, in the market if not the pond, the impact can be devastating. Francis Bacon, the British philosopher, pointed out 400 years ago that humans, by their nature, strive to find order when none exists in a random universe. They are thunderstruck when disastrous disorder inevitably surfaces.

Since nobody can predict the market, timing its mood shifts is not in the ambit of mere mortals. If only you knew ahead of time that Lehman Brothers was going to fail in mid-September 2008, and that its collapse would freeze up lending worldwide, then you could have exited the market or shorted it.

But Nostradamus does not work on Wall Street. In early 2009 on his program *The Daily Show*, comedian Jon Stewart chastised CNBC investing guru Jim Cramer for failing to correctly predict the market's demise for his viewers, and absurdly implied that Cramer saw what was coming. "You all knew," Stewart told the abject Cramer, a normally loquacious fellow too cowed by the razor-witted Stewart to defend himself. If Cramer knew, he would be among the richest people in the world. No one knows.

While you can't win all the time, with sufficient study and nimbleness, you can make enough good calls to prevail in the end. Often a buffoon on his TV show, Cramer emphasizes lots of trading, which may be unhealthy for your portfolio since all the activity saddles you with a noxious abundance of fees and taxes. Still, give him credit for peering deeply into the innards of the stocks he recommends.

Chance plays a role in investing—who could forecast in early 2008 that major Wall Street banks would end up as wards of the state in late 2008? But chance is hardly the only factor. "It is generally agreed that casinos should, in the public interest, be inaccessible," wrote the great British economist John Maynard Keynes, a contemporary of Ben Graham. "Perhaps the same is true of stock exchanges." Keynes was wrong to compare gambling and investing. Unlike gambling, investing is a continuous process that allows time for analysis and, more importantly, the odds investors will win are often better than 50-50. Most of the time, markets do go up, whereas in a casino the odds favor the house.

Probabilities, rather than chance, rule markets. Calculated by historical returns, probabilities are a helpful, albeit hardly infallible, guide to what may come. On a macro level, the past has shown us a few things. One is that small-capitalization stocks, generally those with market value below $3.8 billion, lead the rest out of a downturn, because investors have been hiding in the relative safety of large-cap stocks and see the small-fry as a bargain once the weather clears.

Another lesson from history is that bear markets, at least since World War II, do not last long—an average 13 months. After its 2008 drubbing, when the Standard & Poor's 500 stock index lost a punishing 37 percent, stocks in March 2009 began a strong rally.

Yet what's vexing is how thoroughly the market can humble even its smartest students. Ben Graham knew that timing when patterns will kick in was impossible. Consider capitulation: the point where a sell-off has routed the weak investors, allowing the strong survivors to mop up and begin a new rally. Capitulation is determined statistically by examining days of heavy selling and comparing them to past downturns.

Pinpointing it is frustrating. Google, the search powerhouse, has shown strong revenue and earnings for years, even in the Great Recession. Its technology and business model seemed superior to competitors. So it is reasonable that Google stock has been a good long-term play, and that the market should reward its growing dominance.

But from its high point in November 2007, at $725 per share, to its low point a year later right after Lehman's bankruptcy filing, the market had sliced two thirds off its value. When even a sterling stock like Google had tanked that badly, capitulation would surely be at hand around November 2008.

After a brief bear-market rally, though, the market resumed free-falling, hitting a new bottom in March 2009. Almighty Google fell right along with it. Why? Investors were stampeding for the exits and didn't trust anything outside of U.S. Treasuries, whose default risk was zero since they are backed by the government's taxing power over what still is the richest economy in the world. In such a mad panic, great stocks like Google will suffer, too.

★   ★   ★

The 1929 crash wiped out a lot of speculators and regular investors alike. In October 1929, the market lost 25 percent of its value in two days. Then big bankers like Charles Mitchell and Albert Wiggin of Chase National Bank stepped in to buy stocks and halt the decline. For a while, they succeeded, and by April 1930, stocks had recovered almost half what they had lost. But by autumn, the market slid anew. It later turned out that Mitchell and other bank executives benefited from a National City fund that gave them no-interest loans to buffer their losses. And Wiggin even shorted his own bank's stock.

As the Great Depression began, Graham got a painful reminder of what can go wrong by not paying sufficient attention. Here was a man who knew Wall Street, how to measure its moods, how to navigate it with the pluck and skill that had worked so well for him before. But despite this deep expertise, he made a terrible mistake one year after stocks plunged. Unlike Charles Merrill, he turned bullish. Based on little more than gut feel, Graham decided that the worst was over. In 1930 he made big bets on a brighter future, buying stocks both for himself and for his clients at his Wall Street brokerage, Graham-Newman. He borrowed heavily to magnify the excellent returns that he was sure awaited. The madness, he told clients, had passed. Painfully, he soon found out that it hadn't.

★   ★   ★

From 1929 through 1932, Graham's firm lost 75 percent. A short fellow with a daunting intellect, a fishlike face, and dancing blue eyes, who usually saw life as an endless well of fun, Graham now was distraught. As the debacle ground on, he dragged himself to his office in the now-desolate canyons of lower Manhattan and flipped through Graham-Newman's woebegone books. His clients were fleeing the firm in legions, pulling out what remained of their money. With a heavy heart, he concluded that closing the business was the only alternative. Graham reluctantly relented only after his partner, Jerome Newman, announced that his father-in-law would invest some money to keep them going.

Graham glumly soldiered on. He took no salary for four years. He moved his family out of its palatial apartment overlooking Central Park into a less grand space nearby. His wife, a former dance instructor, went back to work. Graham turned into a miser, hoarding dimes and quarters, riding the subway instead of a taxi. Where once he had treated his mother to weekly dinners at fine restaurants, now he took her to cheap Chinese eateries. He wrote later about "the feeling of defeat and near-despair that almost over-mastered me." His eyes were no longer alight.

From Wall Street to Main Street, the shimmering, can't-lose aura of the 1920s had vanished. The bright, Gatsby-esque days of flowing champagne and ever-climbing stock prices were a bitter memory. Bread lines of shabbily dressed people stretched along the streets of America. Weedlike, shanty towns popped up everywhere. Once-prosperous folk saw their life savings vanish as banks collapsed and investments shriveled. Much as with the bear market that started in 2007, fear and despair hung in the air like a foul fog.

Amid all this malaise, the supremely rational Graham sat back and did what he did best—he examined the situation. He knew he had gone wrong in 1930, trusting his optimistic instincts when more reasoned examination might have steered him away from the abyss. He had learned to be a careful investor, with a rare eye for financial detail, but in 1929 he had veered from his own personal philosophy. He realized that the methods he originally had used to build his now-decimated wealth in the 1920s still applied, more than ever. Not only that: he should share them with the world. And so even with his considerable assets in tatters, he became curiously upbeat. His eyes began to dance anew.

This was the perfect time, he figured, to write a book that would tell people how to build wealth by their own wits and perseverance, by examining stocks minutely, in search of flaws and opportunities. What investors needed, he realized, was a system that they could use to pull themselves out of their personal financial mires and build new portfolios, based on an investing discipline.

The result appeared two years later, in 1934, when he published *Security Analysis*. The book codified the lessons he had been using for a class he taught part-time at Columbia University. With a ready supply of humor and steadfast reliance on statistics, he told his eager young students how to evaluate stocks and bonds by delving into companies' financial reports. He and his teaching partner-cum-coauthor, a Columbia professor named David Dodd, distilled this wisdom for the book. The lanky Dodd, who sat in the back of Graham's Columbia seminar taking notes, recorded the puckish sayings and piercing investment insights of the Wall Street savant.

★   ★   ★

The lessons of *Security Analysis* took a while to catch on. Few in the depths of the Depression were open to Graham's thoughts about investing success. The prevailing mood was best summed up by the celebrated humorist of the day, Will Rogers, who said he preferred playing the lottery to the stock market because, with the lottery, "you don't need

as much money and you have more of a chance to win." Even investment pros had lost hope. Robert Lovett, part of the old WASP-y Wall
Street establishment, wrote in the *Saturday Evening Post* that good stocks
were virtually impossible to find: "[T]he only permanent investment is
one which has become a total and irretrievable loss." Burned so very
badly, not many people wanted to invest. Turnover, the rate at which
shares are traded, in the 1930s at the New York Stock Exchange was
20 percent of the yearly clip in the buoyant 1920s.

In the mighty councils of government, no one thought canny
investing was any kind of answer. Under the New Deal, Wall Street
found itself saddled with a welter of new rules. Some were overdue,
such as banning trades using insider knowledge of yet-to-be-released
corporate results. Others were harmful, like curbs on short selling,
a technique that ferrets out bad stocks before they blow up and
hurt investors.

All over the globe, as the Depression spread, governmental answers
were grand in scale, and individual efforts counted for nothing. In
Washington, the answer was more public-sector spending, a host of
new social programs, and tighter regulations on business. In Berlin, the
answer was a dictatorship that would rearm its military, impose draco-
nian order, and scapegoat Jews. Everywhere, the answer was to jack up
tariffs to support domestic industries by shielding them from foreign
competition. The Washington answer took a long time to work, the
Berlin answer led to epic bloodshed, and the higher worldwide tariffs
only deepened the Depression.

Security Analysis offered an individualistic redemption. Graham
never intended for it to cure an entire society. But he figured that investors could improve their sorry lot by intelligently investigating what
stocks and bonds they should buy, and what ones they should avoid.

For those open to its lessons, Graham's book benefited from a
sudden advantage; his technique had just gotten a big boost from one
facet of Washington's regulatory crackdown. The new Securities and
Exchange Act mandated that corporate financial data, previously released
sporadically or not at all, and with dubious accuracy, now must be
disclosed quarterly and completely. Fudging, like inflating reported
earnings, was punishable by law. Suddenly, investors had more tools to
analyze securities, if only they would use them.

An organized system, Graham's approach was revolutionary to the investing public. It instructed investors to dissect corporate finances with a biologist's care. The core of Graham's value investing is a search for hidden jewels—stocks that had been beaten down because their companies were out of fashion for the moment or had made a strategic mistake, yet were basically sound and would rise anew once the market woke up to them.

A typical, and now rather quaint, example from *Security Analysis* is something called Hamilton Woolen Co., a textile maker in Massachusetts. In the late 1920s, Hamilton's stock was priced at around $13 per share. But Graham saw that its net current assets—what's left over after subtracting liabilities like payments and interest due within a year from current assets like cash and receivables on hand—amounted to $38.50 per share. In other words, the company was worth more than the value the market had placed on it. Hamilton's problem was it suffered from lousy management, and it was often in the red. With new leadership and revamped operations in place, Graham figured it was a buy. Within a year, the stock rose to $40. Investors who bought at the previous, lower price had tripled their money.

Of course, no investing system could banish all the market's old ways, where stocks often were bought and sold via clubby connections, *sotto voce* tips, and hucksterism. There were precursors of the $50 billion Ponzi scheme of Bernard Madoff, sentenced to a long prison term in 2009. Graham, who early in his career got bilked himself, showed how to spot the scammer. He advocated a healthy skepticism toward what someone wanted to sell. That even included registered stockbrokers who supposedly had customers' interests at heart, but who might be tempted to peddle an iffy stock simply to garner a transaction fee. As Graham wrote: "Since his business is to earn commissions, he can hardly avoid being speculation-minded."

Over time, as America's economic health recovered from the Depression, Graham's books became bibles. *Security Analysis* has been reissued five times. The companion volume, *The Intelligent Investor*, written without Dodd, came out in 1949 and also has had multiple reprintings. It benefited from better timing than *Security Analysis* encountered in the 1930s. America's grand postwar economic surge was starting. The Dow Jones Industrial Average, at a low ebb for two decades, returned to its 1929 level in 1952. More and more people began to look to Wall Street again as a crucible of wealth. Today, half of American households are exposed to stocks, many of them via 401(k)s and similar retirement programs.

⋆   ⋆   ⋆

At the heart of investing is the concept of risk. What are the odds that your venture will be successful? To Graham, investing could never be an exact science with predictable outcomes. Yet investment decisions could be made that increased the chances of success by doing careful prep work.

One thing that made Ben Graham such a canny investor was his ingrained sense of fate's nasty side, driven into him at an early age. Born in London as Benjamin Grossbaum, Graham was one year old when his family immigrated to New York to expand its china and pottery importing business. Unfortunately, Ben's father died when he was young and the importing business failed. His mother opened a boarding house, only to see that fizzle, too. To make matters worse, she tried to recoup by buying U.S. Steel stock on margin (that is, using borrowed money). The Panic of 1907 wiped her out. As World War I started, the family changed its name to Graham to avoid the stigma attached to German-sounding monikers. That was the only bet that worked: no one persecuted them for suspected affiliations with Kaiser Wilhelm.

Young Ben was mentally gifted. He had an extraordinary memory and learned to read in six languages. He was at the top of his high school class and won a scholarship to Columbia. Most of all, Graham had a real knack for mathematics. When he graduated, he was offered Columbia teaching positions in English, philosophy, and math. He chose to go to Wall Street, where he figured the odds were good he could use his numerical abilities to gain the financial security that had eluded his parents. He quickly rose through the ranks at a firm called Newburger, Henderson & Loeb.

But once there, he learned about Wall Street's perils the hard way. He made a big mistake when he invested in a company called Savold Tire. Automobiles were the hot new industry right after the Great War. He and friends in 1919 put $60,000 into Savold stock, or $765,000 in today's dollars. It turned out the company didn't exist. Graham and his friends lost their stakes. That taught him to look very closely at anything he invested in and not be swept up by a stock's seeming glamour, lessons that became core principles of value investing.

Graham preached that people should be investors, not speculators, as he had been, to his shame, with Savold. He tirelessly told students, readers, and clients his basic tenets: Don't take things at face value, look for long-term performance before committing, be prepared for rough patches, and don't follow the herd.

To illustrate the perils of risk, Graham whimsically invented a fellow he called Mr. Market, who embodies all the collective behavioral foibles of investors. As one of Graham's celebrated protégés, Warren Buffett, described this fellow in a letter to shareholders of his Berkshire Hathaway conglomerate, Mr. Market is a manic-depressive. Sometimes, he is euphoric and names a very high price for a stock, fearful that you will lowball him and deprive him of his well-deserved gains. Other times, he is depressed and pessimistic. At that point, Buffett writes, Mr. Market "can see nothing but trouble ahead for the business and the world." Then, Buffett goes on, Graham's Mr. Market "will name a very low price, since he is terrified you will unload your interest on him."

Knocked about by tides of emotion, pulled one way by fear and another way by greed, Mr. Market has a tendency to humble even the most brilliant investors. Buffett, who has many times topped *Forbes* magazine's list of the world's richest, himself got slammed in 2008 by such moves as investing in two Irish banks that later went south, and by buying energy stocks when oil prices seemed to be headed for the stars instead of the mud, where they ended up as the recession tamped down energy demand.

Their own human foibles, Graham contended, were an ever-present danger to investors. Buffett's misadventures with oil and bank stocks and Graham's ill-fated exuberance in his 1930 investments show it always is possible for even the most clear-eyed investors to stray disastrously from their own strategies. By going, in current Wall Street parlance, "out on the risk curve," investors may be setting themselves up for a fall.

Graham's answer to combating risk was to invest using his three-word motto: "margin of safety." In other words, figure out what a stock truly is worth, then try to buy it at a cheaper price. Odds are, Graham declared, the stock eventually would spring back to its correct price. And by buying a number of these stocks, the odds increased that enough would be winners to yield a result that Graham with characteristic understatement termed "very satisfactory." Since Graham's time, other savants have their own answers to offsetting risk.

Regardless of their beliefs, all market pros know that vast economic trends can sink the best-laid plans. Even if Graham had been more prudent in 1930, the incredible market meltdown would have hurt him to some degree. Before the tech crash, bulls contended that the rules had changed this time and that growth stocks would soar ever higher. Then, silly companies like eToys.com ran out of money when they didn't attract enough customers. Before the next crash, there were smug assurances circa 2007 that the subprime mortgage mess was under control because Wall Street geniuses had parsed risk so expertly that nothing would truly blow up. Too bad they were dead wrong.

★　　★　　★

In bear-mauled 2008, almost every asset class (chief exception: ultra-safe but low-paying U.S. Treasury bonds) suffered. The thoroughness of the wipeout was breathtaking. Of the almost 5,000 U.S. mutual funds specializing in stocks, only one was in the black. Forester Value fund eked out a 0.4 percent total return for 2008. At the same time, the average return for stock funds was minus 39 percent.

Markets are vexingly cyclical. Graham and numerous commentators have long warned that the past is no guide to the future—and that the future is certain to dish up unexpected and unpleasant surprises. Even growth adherents, who are typically very bullish, acknowledge that nasty things can happen to the economy, although they are the first to declare the danger is past. Growth-minded strategist Laszlo Birinyi foretold stocks' 2008 collapse based on the gathering financial storm, but at year-end he was advising investors to get in on shares while they were cheap.

In the twilight of his life, Ben Graham dined out often on being the father of modern investing. His firm, Graham-Newman, disbanded in 1956 and he moved to California, where he continued to teach, at UCLA. He also had a home in France. Although technically retired, he had a big public presence, often giving lectures and interviews, fawned over by adoring fans. Steady streams of pilgrims visited him, seeking guidance.

Among the investing systems that, post-Graham, took form as entrenched beliefs are those aimed at diversifying holdings widely so they are better protected (now known as asset allocation), divining the influence of crowd psychology on the market (behaviorism), unmasking inept or fraudulent companies and betting against them (short selling), focusing on index funds that track the broad market instead of picking individual stocks, and investing overseas where hidebound Americans tend not to look for terrific opportunities. Hedge funds have come to the fore, using mind-numbing math called quantitative analysis to find targets or to traffic in complex new securities like derivatives.

Certainly, a number of these ideas have been kicking around for a long time, yet merely in a minor sense. Nowadays, they are championed by hordes of professional adherents.

Example: Diversifying assets, so all of them don't get slammed at once, is simple common sense that wise souls have long followed. Graham, in *Security Analysis,* advised people to spread their holdings "to minimize the influence of luck and to allow maximum play to the law of probability." Lately, though, an intellectual discipline has appeared to guide that diversification. An entire industry of financial planners has arisen, using sophisticated tools such as the computerized Monte Carlo simulations, which crunch hundreds if not thousands of scenarios for your portfolio to see what the odds are it will last through retirement.

By the same token, people have been shorting stocks for centuries, although only now does a real discipline exist, with experts solely dedicated to ferreting out weaknesses and exploiting them. The accounting forensic work of big-shot short sellers like James Chanos, who exposed the rotten insides of Enron, is new under the sun. Graham himself at times sold short, betting on the decline of stocks his own probes had shown to be overhyped losers.

Some of these ideas, such as the hedge funds' quant approach, went in overly complex directions that Graham likely would have disdained. The quant wizards believe they can divine market directions or exploit trading anomalies via extremely intricate calculations, possible only on computers. The quants slice up funky bonds, packaging them into supposedly safer creatures with names like collateralized debt obligations. Also, the quants cobble together bafflingly complicated derivatives, which are phantom securities that are based on the behavior of actual securities. While wide use of computers for investing didn't exist until Graham was elderly and retired, he likely would have considered the quants too abstruse. He believed that the math needed to get a good picture of a stock's true value was accessible to anyone with brains and dedication. Buffett, his disciple, is leery of derivatives, which he labeled in 2002 as "financial weapons of mass destruction."

Two latter-day ideas we know Graham disliked are growth investing, the notion that rising stocks should be snapped up because they surely will continue to rise, and the efficient market hypothesis, which holds that trying to beat the market overall is silly.

Growth investing was very popular in the 1920s, although no one had a name for it. Growth investors usually don't much care about whether a stock is any good; they only care if its price is rocketing. A market commentator named Gerald M. Loeb, whose book *The Battle for Investment Survival*, appeared around the time *Security Analysis* first did, counseled that investors should buy when a stock is hot, regardless of the price, then sell on any weakness. But without examining stocks' fundamentals, Graham said, that kind of investing is sheer folly. Such a strategy calls on someone to be ahead of the crowd, often an impossible task. A growth strategy, he wrote, "is largely a matter of A trying to decide what B, C, and D are likely to think—with B, C, and D likely to do the same."

At the end of his life (he died in 1976), Graham took time to lambaste the fashionable idea of EMH, a then-new academic theory contending that a stock's price is the summation of all publicly available knowledge. Thus, the theory says, with hordes of investors scrutinizing the market every day, it is doubtful that a stock can be mispriced for long.

As a result, according to EMH, investors can't beat the market overall, and their best bet is to buy an index fund that passively mirrors it, such as the Vanguard 500. The stocks in such a fund are preselected by dint of their index membership, without need of much human intervention. And that seems like a pretty good idea. Indeed, from 2004 through 2008, Standard & Poor's found that its S&P 500 index (covering large-capitalization stocks) did better than 72 percent of large-cap actively managed mutual funds, meaning those that pick stocks. The S&P MidCap 400 beat 76 percent of actively managed mid-cap funds, and the S&P SmallCap 600 did better than 85 percent of small-cap funds.

Graham's argument against EMH was that ignorance and emotions are powerful factors in stock pricing, which prevent markets from operating anywhere near efficiency. Thus, stock values, he said, are typically skewed higher or lower than they should be. Individual investigations of a stock's true worth may show it is temporarily undervalued, hence a bargain waiting to be exploited. Under the Graham approach, smart managers who have the tools to delve into the innards of corporate finances can be among the 28 percent of actively managed large-cap funds that beat the index, and the same goes for the 24 percent of mid-cap funds and the 15 percent of small-cap ones that best the market.

This book is not simply a how-to for investors, nor is it merely a history. It explores the evolution of the prominent investing approaches that animate today's financial world—and it analyzes their strengths and weaknesses. No one approach is a panacea. You need to know about each of them: Where they came from, where they are headed, and whether they can take you where you need to go.

In the end, Ben Graham had one revelation that investors of all stripes can agree with: a lot of investing is done badly, which benefits those who do it well. "It is fortunate for Wall Street as an institution," he said, "that a small minority of people can trade successfully, and that many others think they can." Graham knew well that taming the beast of investing is hard, brain-challenging work.

Chapter 1

Tarnished Gems:
Value Investing

Warren Buffett is the modern-day heir of Benjamin Graham. Buffett knew Graham and his thinking very well: he took Graham's fabled class at Columbia University. Later, Buffett worked at Graham's Wall Street firm, Graham-Newman. He has eclipsed his mentor in one respect: Buffett has his own idolatrous sobriquet, the Sage of Omaha (he went back to his native Nebraska after tiring of New York). Graham is not so lucky. Some have called him the Father of Security Analysis, but that one never caught on.

The discipline of value investing has changed since Graham's time. Buffett learned from the master, then went on to refine his teachings to suit the current, more complex era. And while Buffett, like Graham, was never one to follow fads, he became one of the world's richest people by keeping an ear to the ground and adjusting his methods.

Graham, although well off, never achieved Buffett's stellar wealth. Since Buffett is still alive and ultra-rich, he has replaced Graham as value investors' role model.

The financial world Graham worked in, from the end of World War I through the mid-1950s, was a simpler place. The upheaval of the Great Depression aside, capital markets were rather staid during his career, at least in terms of how they operated. Institutions and rich people bought and sold most of the stocks and bonds. Brokerage commissions were fixed. Except during the occasional panic, trading activity was at a genteel pace. Buffett's long career, which started in the 1950s, has spanned a time of gut-wrenching change. Since the Eisenhower Era, America has been transformed into a nation with a much wealthier population and a much larger, more intertwined marketplace, one that takes more intellectual effort to comprehend. Buffett is the man who has bridged the gap between Graham's time and now.

At present, a huge amount of the U.S. population is involved in the market; fully one half of all American households are invested, mainly due to 401(k) retirement accounts or individual retirement accounts (IRAs), which have sprung up to replace old-style, employer-provided pensions. The level of homeownership has rocketed. Thanks to easy credit, Americans have taken on enormous debt loads. For a small fee with an online service, anyone can trade stocks from the comfort of his or her den. No one needs a broker anymore. Investing information, once hard to access, is widely available. The average person can glean news, corporate financial ratios, and stock performance from the Internet.

To a dizzying degree, the advent of electronics has speeded up trading. A stock can be bought in a nanosecond. The importance of the financial industry to the economy has expanded enormously as a result of all this. In Graham's time, financial services' share of the S&P 500 was in single digits. Now, even after the 2008 financial crisis, it is around 20 percent. A mind-bending array of new financial instruments has invaded the scene, from credit default swaps to structured products. Companies do business all over the globe, indulging in foreign currency swap strategies whose intricacies only a PhD could master. The swaps have evolved into exotic permutations that defy Graham's dusty analysis.

In the Graham fashion, Buffett has made a point of doing extreme due diligence before buying. But he goes beyond Graham in analyzing a company's products, prospects, and, above all, its operations. Graham, never a gregarious sort, confined himself to financial statements to tell him what he needed to invest in. Buffett feels it is vital to know the management of companies. Graham avoided this, fearing executives would try to snow him.

In late 2009, Buffett bought Burlington Northern Santa Fe for $26.3 billion after a conversation with Matthew Rose, the railroad's chief executive officer. Buffett, who had owned a minority chunk of Burlington stock since 2006, knew Rose personally and had stopped by for a courtesy visit when he popped the question about buying out the railroad.

Often, Buffett examines a possible investment through a macroeconomic lens. Buffett's strategic reasoning to buy the rail carrier was based on his reading of broad transportation trends. Burlington is part of a four-railroad oligopoly that has divided up the country, meaning competition is sparse and barriers to new entrants insurmountable. That, coupled with the likelihood that energy prices are likely to trend upward over time, shows that Burlington has a future as a freight hauler, Buffett reasoned. After all, rail had proved itself to be better at transporting heavy cargo than trucks. Read any of Graham's books and you'll be struck by how seldom he looks at the macro picture when weighing an investment.

Graham rarely owned and operated entire companies, something Buffett routinely has done through his conglomerate, Berkshire Hathaway. Berkshire runs insurance companies, a candy maker, and myriad other entities—and also functions as a massive quasi-mutual fund with minority amounts of stock in traditional titans of business such as Procter & Gamble and Wal-Mart Stores. Berkshire holdings, whether they are minority or majority positions, usually are true to Buffett's dictum that they have a "moat around them." This means that, like Burlington Northern, they possess strong franchises that rivals have trouble breaching, the ability to raise prices, and steady revenues that build wealth.

Another difference with Graham is that Buffett is willing to take a flier occasionally on a questionable company, one perhaps beyond the likelihood of redemption all value investors look for. Consider the insurer Geico, which both Graham and Buffett controlled at different times. Geico, one of the few companies that Graham actually had a hand in running, was in solid shape, yet valued at less than book, when its majority owner approached him in 1948. The weak stock price was a fault of market misperception, not of the firm's business model or management. Wall Street didn't understand its strategy of selling low-cost auto insurance to military families using direct mail, and sidestepping insurance agents. Coverage always had been sold by those friendly guys in insurance offices on Main Street.

Seeing a bargain with promise, Graham took over the company and served on its board, getting heavily involved in its inner workings. The insurer went on to prosper. But then it went awry. Almost 30 years later, during the ruinous 1970s inflation, a much larger Geico was teetering on the edge of bankruptcy due to poor claims management and pricing problems.

Graham, who had sold most of his Geico shares by then and left the company's board, never had an appetite for any business lacking his prized "margin of safety." By the 1970s, Geico had become very unsafe. Had Geico been in such sorry shape in 1948, Graham surely would have shied away. Buffett was different. Seeing a bargain where others saw nothing but disaster, he bought control of the insurer in 1976, installed new management, and eventually turned it around. Geico, he explained, suffered from a "local, excisable cancer."

Also in contrast with Graham, Buffett has been more willing at times to trust his gut, and occasionally more than he should. In recent years, he looked around and noticed that Ireland was booming and needed bank loans, spotted an explosion of arcane Wall Street products spurring demand for credit ratings, and saw oil prices spiraling ever higher. So he bought stock in the two Irish banks, in financial rating firm Moody's, and in oil giant ConocoPhillips.

These moves ended up costing Buffett dearly in 2008. The financial crisis battered Ireland's economy, vaporized financial exotica, and sent oil prices plunging. Gazing back in his 2009 letter to Berkshire shareholders, he admitted he had screwed up big time, especially buying the oil stock when petro prices were at a peak. "Pessimism is your friend, euphoria the enemy," he wrote in one of his shareholder letters.

One thing that separates value from growth investors is patience: the value folks say they will wait for a good stock to turn around, and some will stay with that good stock even after it does, expecting more upside. Unlike the unsentimental Graham, Buffett developed an almost unshakeable attachment to some holdings. Buffett famously has contended that a proper holding period for a stock was "forever." Graham regularly took profits when a stock had gone up. At one point, he advised selling after a stock had climbed 50 percent.

In fairness, Buffett is not a purist about "forever." He has culled his portfolio from time to time. Periodically, he sold because he realized he had made a mistake. He once thought buying USAir shares was a good idea, and shelved one of his core beliefs in the process. The airline hardly had a moat around it. Air travel is punishingly competitive. In the mid-1990s, tired of losses, fare wars, and other turbulence at USAir, he dumped the stock.

Many of the stocks that he married multiplied in value over the long haul, such as Coca-Cola (first share purchase was in 1988), Wells Fargo (1990), and the *Washington Post* (1973). Coke was the leading soft-drink maker, Wells the premier bank in expanding California, and the *Post* the circulation leader in the nation's capital. When these companies ran into tough times later, Buffett hung on.

To be sure, Buffett enjoys advantages that few other investors or money managers possess. He doesn't have to worry about meeting his kids' college tuitions or paying his way into a retirement home. His grip over Berkshire, his vast fortune, and his huge reputation give him a lot of leeway others don't have. In today's volatile markets, people get very antsy. Should any Berkshire investors whine to Buffett about a particular investment that is doing poorly, he could easily ignore them.

In January 1998, Buffett bought 130 million ounces of silver at an average cost of $5.88. In April 2006, he sold that stash for a little more than double what he paid, for an annualized gain of 13.6 percent. Not a bad haul after eight-plus years. But for the first few years he owned the metal, silver prices kept dropping. At one juncture, they were down 18 percent. His position didn't cross into the black until 2003. As financial consultant Laszlo Birinyi put it: "If I, and most managers, held a position for five years and the position was down that much, clients would not have been very tolerant."

Buffett usually has hewed to his core credos. One was that a holding should be understandable. So Buffett was dismayed in 2002 when he learned that one Berkshire asset, General Re, a large reinsurance firm he acquired in 1998, had a large tangle of derivatives, those complicated instruments that are tied to the value of other things like bonds. Derivatives are good at protecting against financial risk, unless there's a big systemwide crash, which is what later ended up happening to kick off the Great Recession. Buffett uses them sparingly, to hedge, never for speculation. Hedge funds often deploy them like gambling chips.

Buffett compelled General Re to unwind 23,000 derivatives contracts over five years. Thus, when the world blew up in 2008, and many derivatives were swept away, General Re was in relatively good shape. In his 2009 shareholder letter, Buffett wrote about the dangerous interconnectedness of derivatives, the risk that the other side of a contract will endanger your own position: "It's not whom you sleep with, but also whom they are sleeping with."

By the same token, Buffett has usually avoided technology stocks because he does not understand their businesses. At first blush, he was wise to be skeptical of the Web stocks that took flight in the 1990s and then spectacularly crashed. Many of those were built on dreams, not hard business realities. Graham also was suspicious of tech, which had started to rise toward the end of his life. In the late 1960s, he observed that the success of IBM was sure to inspire the founding of many other tech firms that had poor prospects.

For Buffett and Graham, the worst sin of tech stocks is that they tend to be growth oriented. In other words, their revenues—or at least their projected revenues—were expanding rapidly, and so were their stock valuations. Since value investors want to buy cheap, investing in such issues is heresy. A lofty price-to-earnings ratio (P/E), the measure of whether a stock is cheap or expensive (the stock price divided by the past four quarters earnings on a per-share basis), is a badge of dishonor to a value aficionado.

But Buffett's broad-brush dismissal of tech likely is short-sighted and shows the limitations of the value credo. Interestingly, Microsoft, which went public in 1986, always had a high P/E. Up until the 2000–2002 tech crash, the software maker's price had risen exponentially. Those who had invested early on became very rich, even after the price ebbed some in the new century. Had Buffett gotten heavily into Microsoft, he would be even richer.

Buffett developed a friendship with Bill Gates, Microsoft's chief and a fellow billionaire, who regularly has traded places with Buffett as the world's richest person, by *Forbes* magazine's tally. Aside from their wealth and a passion for bridge, the two share a background: they had been smart and gawky youngsters. The two men sometimes appear together in public forums and discuss the issues of the day.

Buffett donated a bunch of his wealth to Gates's charitable foundation, but never became a big Microsoft investor. To be polite, he owns a smattering of his friend's shares. Value guys usually don't go there.

$$\star \quad \star \quad \star$$

Like Graham, Buffett started out in life as a geeky, numbers-obsessed type. Neither man was much of a looker, but they more than compensated by their brains and drive.

Buffett's father, Howard, was a stockbroker. Hanging out in his father's Omaha office, the younger Buffett became fascinated with stocks and took to charting their movements. Howard also served as an arch-conservative Republican congressman in the 1940s. From Howard, Buffett learned the value of independence. Howard was a staunch opponent of organized labor and the New Deal—an unpopular stance in the Age of Roosevelt. Attending a baseball game with his dad, Warren marveled at Howard's nonchalance when the crowd booed him. The man believed in enhancing "liberty," and the hell with what the rabble thought.

After a couple of years at Penn, young Warren felt he wasn't learning much, so he returned home and finished at the University of Nebraska. After reading *The Intelligent Investor* and hearing about Graham's fabled class, Buffett went to Columbia University for graduate work. One of 20 students in Graham's class, many much older and some working on Wall Street, Buffett quickly became the star. His hand regularly shot up. Discussions between the kid, barely out of his teens, and the professor dominated the proceedings. Graham gave Buffett an A-plus, reputedly the only one he ever awarded.

Buffett drank deeply from Graham's wisdom and even bought some of the stocks that the Graham-Newman firm owned. He learned not to follow the Wall Street herd. He learned that, to Graham, the stock market was not a "weighing machine," where value was determined precisely, but rather a "voting machine," which a lot of people used to register their opinions based on both logic and emotion. He learned that great opportunity could be found in cheap stocks, characterized by Graham as "cigar butts." He learned that stocks had an "intrinsic value," their true worth, not the market's sometimes benighted assessment.

Once Buffett graduated in 1951, he naturally asked Graham for a job. But the master, who had been born Jewish, turned him down. Roger Lowenstein, in his superb *Buffett: The Making of an American Capitalist*, writes that, at the time, "Jews were locked out of gentile firms, and Graham preferred to hold his spots for Jews." It never occurred to the gentile Buffett to work for anyone else on Wall Street. So he went back to Omaha and started at his father's brokerage firm. This was unsatisfying for the young Buffett, who specialized in research, yet found many of his clients unappreciative.

He kept in touch with Graham via letters, and eventually his old teacher offered him a job. Back he went to New York with his new wife and rented a cut-rate apartment in the suburbs, even though he could now afford more opulent digs.

At Graham-Newman, Buffett learned even more. After a time, though, he chafed under Graham's cautious stewardship. Lowenstein recounts how Buffett and Graham argued about Buffett's practice of visiting companies. Plus, Buffett thought Graham was sitting on too much cash, when he should have put more of it to work.

Come 1956, Graham had gotten tired of Wall Street, so he folded the firm and moved to California to teach. Rather than stay on in New York, whose pace wearied him, Buffett decided to return home once again. By this time, he had amassed a decent wad of capital himself, and he could go into business solo. No more working for his dad or his intellectual dad, Graham.

At his new firm, Buffett began to dazzle as he bought value stocks that went on to vault in price. One such investment was in American Express, which had gotten embroiled in a scandal involving a subsidiary that stored salad oil, and used it as collateral for loans. There was very little salad oil in the AmEx division's storage tanks. Fraud arrests ensued, and the subsidiary filed for bankruptcy. The stock of parent AmEx took a dive.

Buffett saw opportunity. People, he observed from visits to stores and to restaurants, were starting to use the company's charge cards in droves. In 1964, Buffett bought lots of American Express shares. And he has kept them to this day. The stock, which has suffered ups and downs through the years, has been a net winner for him.

Along the way, Buffett acquired an ailing textile maker in New England, known as Berkshire Hathaway. The stock was tantalizingly inexpensive—and in a dying industry. Buffett didn't care that Berkshire had no moat because he had little interest in textiles. He used Berkshire as a vehicle to get into areas that were more promising, like insurance. And he closed its mills, which consumed capital with little chance of a turnaround. Graham would have been appalled at this audacity.

Graham-Newman was a public company, so one wonders what the thrifty Graham would have thought of Berkshire stock. The Berkshire A shares have topped $100,000 each; the more affordable B shares were more than $3,000, until they were split to a much lower price, under $100, after the Burlington deal. (The Burlington takeover payment was partly in Berkshire stock, which thus needed to be sliced into smaller, cheaper units.) Graham-Newman stock went for $30 in 1949, which is around $260 in current dollars. Not cheap, but not unreachable either.

Also, Graham's company paid its investors dividends. Buffett never has, preferring to hoard the cash so he can deploy it as he wishes. Berkshire stock has a P/E of around 16, comparable to that of the broad market. That sounds affordable, but not when you look at the six-digit price of the A shares. Value investors may love Buffett, but there's an irony if they own his pricey, non-dividend-paying shares.

★   ★   ★

Buffett's down-to-earth Midwestern persona has an unspoken message for investors: regular folks can aspire to be like him. Here is a guy who, with his folksy manner and unpretentious ways, could be your neighbor. You might bump into him at a fast-food outlet or the mall. He doesn't drive a flashy car or live in a palace. His house is unassuming, located in a pleasant if unfancy neighborhood. Like many Americans, he could stand to lose a few pounds and has a weakness for junk food— ice cream, Cherry Cokes, cheeseburgers.

This aw-shucks personality masks someone who, like his mentor, enjoys the limelight. The Berkshire shareholders' meeting is a massive gathering whose main purpose is his veneration. He from time to time appears on CNBC, always treated with deference. Anything he does or says makes news. His takeover of Burlington Northern was splashed on newspaper front pages worldwide. If Henry Kravis, the private equity king, had bought the railroad, the news stories would have gotten less play. Buffett got a lot of notice supporting Barack Obama for president, and again when he complained that the Obama administration's agenda was too ambitious. In public appearances, Buffett—as a young man, so terrified of appearing before crowds that he took a Dale Carnegie course—has the poise and warmth of a master politician.

Buffett has fostered the image of an approachable demigod. Listening to Buffett talk and reading his ideas, you get the impression that investing is a matter of common sense. Hard work is involved, obviously. But his special genius is to show that everyone can do this. Maybe not everyone can become a billionaire. They can come out ahead, nonetheless.

★   ★   ★

Value investing is not the sole path to salvation. It just happens to be Graham's and Buffett's path. The question for growth investors is: will this stock keep soaring? The question for value investors: is it a cheap, underappreciated stock that is good enough to someday take off? Growth investing is a sprint; value investing is a marathon. Stock prices are supposed to reflect future earnings. For value types, the key is divining what has staying power. And to do that, there are math methods to assess earnings potential.

Philosophically, they all spring from the formula that Graham devised to find the "intrinsic value" of a stock—in other words, its true worth. Maybe a stock is selling at $20 a share, pulled down because its industry is out of fashion or its earnings suffered a hiccup due to a temporary problem. The classic Graham formula may show that the true value of the stock is $50. So if you buy this "cigar butt" now, you get a bargain, and can patiently sit back until the market wises up to its actual worth. That's assuming the market ever does, but more on that in a minute.

Graham's intrinsic value formula is:

$$E (2R + 8.5) \times 4.4 / Y$$

Here, E is a stock's earnings per share, R is its projected growth rate, and Y is the average interest rate on high-grade corporate bonds. As to the numbers, 8.5 is the P/E for a company with no growth, a sort of a baseline, and 4.4 the bond yield (interest rate as a share of price) in Graham's day. Few stock strategists still use this formula, which mainly is geared toward a world where the overwhelming number of stocks were cheap, during and after the Depression. Remember that the market didn't fully recover from the 1929 crash until the early 1950s, a few years before Graham left professional investing. Nowadays, U.S. government bonds are the benchmark most often used, since they presumably are free of default risk. And the 4.4 number may not do justice to current interest rates. High-end corporate bonds and Treasury bonds usually yield more than that, albeit the Treasuries were below 3 percent in the aftermath of the Great Recession as investors flocked to them for safety.

Various market thinkers have concocted new formulas to find a 21st-century intrinsic value. One of the most widespread is the so-called PEG ratio, which is the current P/E divided by a company's earnings growth rate. Some use the company's past growth rate, which carries the risk that its best days are behind it. Many use earnings estimates, which give the assurance (perhaps misplaced) that the future is knowable. In any case, a PEG ratio below 1.0 is considered cheap. The higher you go above 1.0, the pricier the stock. The PEG ratio, lamentably, never tackles the question of a company's quality.

Joel Greenblatt, a managing partner at New York hedge fund Gotham Partners, attempts to do that. His investing choices are guided by what he calls the "magic formula." This approach, which he outlines in his *The Little Book that Beats the Market,* argues that the best way to cull out the most promising value plays is to focus on earnings yield and return on capital—his yardsticks for whether a stock is cheap and good quality.

Earnings yield, which is the P/E inverted, is a gauge of how much earnings a company throws off in relation to its price. If the earnings yield is high, it likely shows that the business is a good profits generator and yet the stock trades at a bargain price. Return on capital measures how much earnings are generated by a company's factories or stores or whatever marks its tangible worth. Greenblatt likes stocks with high scores on both counts. He takes 3,500 stocks available for trading in the United States and makes two separate rankings using his two measures. Then he combines them to find the best overall scorers. Greenblatt contends that his method has had an extraordinary record. In late 2009, he launched an online money management service using his strategy.

The point of these formulas is that the average person can suss out intrinsic value. This is simple math. Of course, other considerations enter into the mix. Graham wanted a stock whose P/E was 0.4 of the highest P/E it had hit in five years, meaning its price was on the downswing. In his quest for a company with low debt, he insisted that the debt be less than tangible book value, which is the amount that you would get by liquidating all the business's assets. Those investing metrics remain reasonable. Old Ben still has much to teach us, after all.

★   ★   ★

But other Graham measures haven't fared well, perhaps unjustifiably. He put a lot of store in dividends, a notion some today view as antiquated. Tech and other growth companies usually disdain these payouts to investors, reasoning that growing businesses are best served by keeping all the money to expand and improve operations. Graham liked a dividend yield (the dividend divided by the stock price) that is two thirds the yield of a high-grade corporate bond. Anything higher than that, in his view, was too risky: A company might have trouble paying a lofty amount and end up cutting it, which would hurt the stock price. Or a very high dividend might signal that a stock price is too low for a reason—the market correctly surmises that the stock is lousy.

Buffett has been less vocal about dividends, but only a handful of Berkshire's holdings don't offer them. Many value buffs these days remain keen on dividends, which tend to be paid by reliable stalwarts lacking in flash. Industries that customarily award dividends, such as utilities and consumer staples, typically are less expensive than the broad-market S&P 500 stock index.

A sizable overlap exists between dividend-oriented and value investors. Money manager David Dreman, a celebrated voice in the value community, wants stocks with solid and growing dividends—that is, the company keeps increasing the payouts at a consistent pace, year in, year out. He calculates that steady dividend raisers do well in stock-price terms over the long haul.

After all, they tend to be blue chips with strong balance sheets, a comfort to investors. Their key advantage is that they pay investors to own them. Standard & Poor's has a list it calls the Dividend Aristocrats, showing companies that have raised payouts 25 years in a row. This gilded roster has outpaced much of the market for a long time.

During bear markets, Dreman notes in his book *Contrarian Investment Strategies: The Next Generation*, dividend-paying stocks hold up better than nonpayers in downturns. Payers on the S&P 500 index were badly mauled in 2008, when they dropped an average 39 percent. Nevertheless, stocks with no dividends were hurt even worse then, down 45 percent. Reason: They lacked the cushion that dividends provide.

Since 1972, reckons Ned Davis Research, companies that increased or started paying dividends have returned 9.5 percent yearly on average. Investors tend to punish those that pared or eliminated payouts. Such moves are seen as admissions of internal woes. These stocks lost 1.8 percent annually since 1972. Those that never paid a dividend gained only 1.2 percent. In 19 of the past 30 years, S&P data show, payers' shares did better than nonpayers'.

Nonpayers' stocks have done best when technology issues are popular, like in the late 1990s—since few tech firms pay dividends—or they outperform in the immediate rebound from a bear market, when relieved investors regain a zest for riskier stuff. So for much of 2009 nonpayers were ahead, up 56 percent, with the likes of Amazon.com, Starbucks, and Tenet Healthcare more than doubling in price. The last year where nonpayers did better was 2003, in the snapback from the tech bust.

The trouble with dividends is that fewer companies offer them of late. And during the Great Recession, many payers either eliminated dividends or slashed them badly. In late 2008 and early 2009, payout cuts were rife in financial stocks, once a dividend cornucopia. As huge banks teetered on the brink, it made sense to pare dividends to bolster waning capital. In 2007, Bank of America paid $2.40 per share yearly in dividends, yielding more than 5 percent. That was clipped to four cents a share. Meanwhile, the stock fell from $44 to $3 in March 2009, and has moved up again—but only to around $14 in early 2011. Its current yield is a microscopic 0.3 percent.

With corporate cost-cutting all the rage after the Great Recession, many companies started hoarding cash rather than sharing it with investors. Aluminum giant Alcoa Inc., which boasts $1.1 billion in cash and cash equivalents, shrank its dividend 82 percent in early 2009. After a string of losses, the savings helped it return to the black.

All that said, Dreman reasons, high-yielding stocks are a better place to be than bonds if there is a rise in interest rates, the bane of bond prices. For every 1 percent increase in interest rates, a 30-year bond will fall 12 percent in price.

Odds are that stocks will be less affected by rate boosts. Often, but not always, a slump in bond prices is good news for stocks, especially if the stocks raise their payouts. "Dividend payments go up over time," he writes, "interest payments on bonds do not."

★　★　★

David Dreman is a mild-mannered fellow whose Dreman Value Management sits in Wall Street West, the cluster of financial firms in Jersey City that's a subway ride away across the Hudson River from the celebrated district in Lower Manhattan. But he has a fierce devotion to value investing and loves to defend it against all comers. In early 2000, as the tech craze neared its apogee, Jim Cramer, later of CNBC fame, wrote in TheStreet.com investor site that Dreman was a stodgy type unwilling to chase the hot stocks of the moment. Dreman fired back promptly. "In a great market for Internet stocks," he wrote in his *Forbes* column, "a day trader who is fond of them can make money—for a while." I edited this column at the magazine, and I marveled at how feisty Dreman became on the subject. "Cramer is full of hot air," he told me with atypical annoyance.

With the hot-eyed certainty of a tent revival preacher, Dreman insists that value investing is better than growth investing. He crunched some numbers to prove it, using a broad group of stocks called the Compustat 1500. Sure enough, he found that from 1970 through 2008—an era that encompassed stagflation, two roaring bull markets, and two horrendous busts—value trumped growth. That was true regardless of how big the stocks were. For those with market values over $10 billion, value grew at 12.3 percent annualized, while growth dragged across the finish line at 6.7 percent. For small stocks from $250 million to $1 billion, the story was much the same—a 17.4 percent advance for value versus a mere 10.5 percent for growth.

Hmm, aren't these numbers a tad suspect coming from one of value's staunchest champions? Well, it turns out that Dreman is right, using other metrics. Russell Investments, which is a pretty fair broker in this debate, keeps two indexes, one for value and the other for growth, measuring even more stocks than Dreman does, 3,000 for each. While the results aren't as stark, they do show that value prevails over the fullness of time. For the 10 years to the end of 2009, for instance, the Russell 3000 Value Index was up an annualized 2.97 percent, and the Russell 3000 Growth Index was a negative 2.28 percent. And that was so despite superior earnings from growth. The growth index had an earnings expansion of 16 percent and the value list just 3 percent. Yet, as always, the numbers show that growth stocks can be, well, overvalued. The growth index had a price/book ratio—often the best way to measure valuation since earnings more easily can be erratic or manipulated—twice that of its value cousin.

Dreman styles himself a contrarian because his stocks often are out of favor. The reason value triumphs in price performance, he argues, is that when the market wakes up to the true worth of these bargain stocks, it showers them with love. However, investing in a growth stock means you are paying a lot for something whose run may soon peter out. The go-go tech stocks of the 1990s are a prime example. Pets.com seemed like a really good idea, allowing customers to order dog food deliveries, until the sizzling stock burnt out and its ashes spiraled into oblivion. "At times, no price seems too high for aggressive growth stocks," Dreman writes in his book. "Investors repeatedly pay through the nose, and just as repeatedly get stung." Instead, he counsels, go for the "blue chip stocks that widows and orphans traditionally choose."

Stocks, Dreman preaches, will always do something called "regress to the mean." That is, if the market shoots up to an extraordinary degree, it eventually will fall back to its customary pattern. The average P/E of the S&P 500 over time is 16. During the dot-com boom, that number rose above 30. Once the bubble popped, it fell back to its usual level. "Don't be seduced by recent rates of return for individual stocks or the market when they deviate from past norms," he writes. "... If returns are particularly high or low, they are likely to be abnormal."

★   ★   ★

As Buffett has shown, the best value investing nowadays ventures beyond the confines of a financial statement. That means focusing on who is in charge of companies, delving into their strategies (whose merit may not be obvious yet), and detecting who is riding incipient trends.

Nowhere are the skills of a chief executive as important as in a turnaround situation, where a company has gotten itself into a jam and needs to be fixed. The market has given up on the stock and written off the company as yesterday's news. For a value manager, the trick is to find a floundering enterprise whose basic business is sound. It's the execution and strategy that are at fault. Not everyone has the skill and moxie to correct problems. Being sure that the right person is in command of the turnaround is no easy task.

Lloyd Khaner is the sort of value investor who keeps an eye on executives. That's one reason that his hedge fund, Khaner Capital, has had an extraordinary run since it started in 1991, even though it doesn't take on lots of debt, which is a hallmark of many hedge operators. In 2008, a horrible year for almost everyone, when the S&P 500 dropped almost 40 percent, he succeeded in holding Khaner Capital's losses to just 14 percent. He looks for companies with manageable debt loads and good cash flow, yes. He avoids those in dying industries, yes. But the question of who is in charge is the real key. As Khaner puts it: "Decision making is critical. New computers, machines, and business models are worthless without the right people using them."

Khaner's 2005 investment in Campbell Soup is an example. The company, founded in the late 1800s, had been a laggard contender in the food arena for too long. The firm went 10 years without any new core products and ritually jacked up prices by 10 percent annually. Then Campbell brought in a new chief named Doug Conant, formerly of Nabisco, who was determined to shake things up. Khaner, knowing Conant's reputation, was intrigued. Conant was the sort of person who writes dozens of thank-you notes daily to employees, suppliers, and customers. He had a firm grasp on the simple, yet often overlooked, concept of leadership—that it is often a matter of getting people behind you.

Khaner recognized that Conant had something valuable to work with in Campbell. Its brands still were iconic and widely used—the typical U.S. household often had several of its cans in the pantry. How to get it moving again? Conant booted 300 of its top executives, and he sold noncore products like Godiva chocolates. Most important, he revved up morale by telling employees that the company's low state was not their fault, and set about enlisting them to help him to locate and implement ideas. A rush of new products appeared, emphasizing convenience. Campbell introduced a microwaveable soup package, for instance. Conant marveled that the microwave had been invented in 1948 and was ubiquitous in American homes, yet Campbell hadn't caught up with that. Soup sales surged. So did the stock. So did Khaner's returns. Revenue and earnings did later dip due to the recession, and so did the stock, only to recover in 2009.

For a true value investor, discerning when a company has found a good new strategy is not easy, especially when the news around the company is negative. Kian Ghazi of Hawkshaw Capital Management zeroed in on a supplier for convenience stores that was dominant in the western United States named Core-Mark Holdings. Thus, it had a Buffett-style moat. Trouble was, Core-Mark's key product, cigarettes, was suffering from declining sales. Historically, tobacco has made up one third of convenience store revenues. The stock price reflected that unpromising reality, and the shares changed hands for a mere six times earnings. Ghazi saw that the company had a smart plan to move past that obstacle. Core-Mark was betting on a move into fresh foods like salads, sandwiches, and fruit cups. With gross margins on those items ranging from 15 to 25 percent, versus 4 percent for cigarettes, the new strategy had the trappings of a winner. The stock at last began climbing in 2009 on the strength of the new strategy.

Then there's identifying companies that are riding trends. As the Great Recession dragged on and consumers sat on their wallets, veteran value manager Chuck Akre figured out ways to invest in stocks less tied to people's everyday spending. "The consumer is strapped and I am cautious," he said in late 2009. Wise value investing has carried him far through the years. His mutual fund, FBR Focus, lost less than the market in 2008, and in the century's first decade, it racked up an 11 percent annual return, at a time the S&P 500 had essentially gone nowhere. In 2009, he split from FBR Capital to form his own fund, Akre Focus, employing the same insights.

What kinds of companies, he asked himself, would do well in an age of muted consumer demand? Figuring that usage of cell phones would remain robust, he favored American Tower, which owns the towers used in cell transmissions. He admired the company for carrying half the debt to EBITDA (a measure of earnings that doesn't subtract interest, taxes, and intangible accounting charges) of rivals. Although advertising was in the dumps, he believed that billboards would fare better since they were harder to ignore—as they line the roadside, you can't fast-forward or flip past them. Lamar Advertising, a big presence in this area, was his choice. Another plus, in Akre's eyes, was Lamar's bold push into digital billboards, which made it a very flexible player. While earnings lagged during the recession, the company was able to keep revenue up, portending a brighter future.

Amid lame auto sales after the financial crisis, Akre decided that a good company selling auto parts would thrive. His thinking: with people keeping their cars longer, repairs would become a bigger industry; and demand for auto shops and do-it-yourselfers would leap. That trend was helped along by the closing of many auto dealerships as the Detroit Big Three contracted in size. He was right, investing in O'Reilly Automotive, a parts retailer. These three Akre picks responded as he hoped. His system worked.

★   ★   ★

Unfortunately, value investing as a whole has endured long spells of subpar performance and, for some individual value stocks, horrible disasters. The late-1990s, when the tech boom roared, and the Great

Recession were not good to certain value stocks like financials, to say the very least.

True-blue value buffs, certainly, tried to ride out these bad times cleaving to the old teachings. Graham counseled that an investor should hold up to 30 securities to provide the safety of diversification. He realized that not all the holdings in a value portfolio, even a meticulously researched one, could be winners. The goal was that, on average, the entire grouping would rise, with winners overpowering losers. An important coda, often championed by Buffett, was that patience was needed. Value investing is no place for someone who needs instant gratification. Panicky investors, who had bought expensive shares during the 2002–2007 bull run, dumped their stocks amid the March 2009 market nadir—the exact wrong step, buying high, selling low—and later suffered for it.

Diehard adherence to the value creed, however, can lead even the smartest investors into something called a "value trap." That is a stock whose low P/E seems to signal a great bargain. Some stocks deserve a low valuation. Citigroup, the giant bank, teetered on the edge of oblivion during the financial crisis. But since Washington judged it too big to fail, massive federal help righted it. The stock, which had been at $35 in 2007, cratered to $1 in the depths of the bear market. Later in 2009, as financial issues rallied, it climbed back to $5. Still, it continued to be saddled with many problems, from rotten assets stinking up the balance to a clumsy structure that consumed executive time and energy.

John W. Rogers Jr. has a fund company called Ariel Investments, whose symbol is a turtle. Rogers is fond of quoting Leo Tolstoy: "The strongest of all warriors are these two, time and patience." The turnover rate of his flagship Ariel fund is very low, usually around 20 percent per year or less. Rogers studiously works out the intrinsic value of stocks that interest him, and after he buys, embraces them with a near-religious fervor. Sticking with his most beloved stocks is ingrained in him.

Habitual behavior is his hallmark. According to Lauren Young, writing in *SmartMoney* magazine, every day he eats the same food for lunch (a McDonald's burger, fries, and Diet Coke) and wears a charcoal gray suit (he has a rack of identical ones). Young quotes his ex-wife,

Desiree, who went on to a job in the Obama administration, saying: "You try living with that, honey." One of the most prominent African-Americans in finance, a long-time supporter of fellow Chicagoan Barack Obama, and despite the diet, almost as trim as he was when playing basketball for Princeton, Rogers owes much to his diligence and consistency.

Rogers has an enviable 10-year record, with returns that easily best those of the S&P 500. But he had a very bad 2008, when Ariel slid a sickening 48 percent, far worse than the market. One cause was his steadfast ownership of newspaper stocks. Even before the Great Recession hit, circulations had been declining because people could more easily get their news from the Web. Not helping were expensive consolidations in the field, paid for with worrisome amounts of debt that became harder to service as ads fled. In a 2006 *Forbes* column (which I edited), Rogers argued that newspapers should be fine over time, since Google and the like could never match their local coverage. Plus, he noted, many papers had started successful web sites.

The weakness of this argument was that the Internet became an even more formidable competitor to the dead-trees industry. Digital media have the advantage of much lower fixed costs—no costly union contracts, newsprint purchases, and delivery truck fleets to maintain. And newspaper web sites couldn't charge as much as the print versions, hence they weren't the papers' saviors. The descent of newspaper stocks was harrowing. The worst was that of Tribune, owner of big-time names like the *Los Angeles Times* and the *Chicago Tribune*, which swash-buckling Chicago financier Sam Zell had bought with the aid of too much debt and no notion of what it took to turn the enterprise around. Tribune careened into bankruptcy court.

Patience, so often touted as a value-investing virtue, sometimes ends up as an investor enemy. According to data from Financial Research Corporation, the average large-cap value mutual fund turned over its portfolio in 2009 by 75 percent. The average growth fund had a 112 percent turnover. The numbers mean that growth managers were more eager to cash in on gains and move to the next hot prospect. The value people were much more cautious, and at times waited too long to ditch losers.

One of the worst hurt by misplaced patience was Bill Miller, the venerated value guru who oversees investing at fund house Legg Mason, and manages its vaunted Value Trust. Like Rogers, Miller usually has a very low turnover, around 20 percent.

What happened to Miller in the 2008–2009 bear market bordered on tragic. His Legg Mason Value Trust outpaced the S&P 500 each year from 1991 through 2005, a record no one has equaled. He developed a yen for financial stocks, favoring them when they were under the most pressure. In the early 1990s, amid the savings-and-loan crisis, financials were at a low ebb—hence, Miller bought a lot of them cheaply. When they recovered, his portfolio soared. As the financial crunch began in 2007, he also discerned a buying opportunity in financials. Although two Bear Stearns hedge funds had collapsed that summer, he loaded up on Bear. As financial stocks kept dwindling, he kept buying: Merrill Lynch, Freddie Mac, Wachovia, Washington Mutual. These turned out to be a roster of the damned. Even after Bear blew up in spring 2008, he got deeper and deeper into financials.

After a small loss in 2007, his fund plunged a harrowing 55 percent in 2008. Investors scrambled to get out, and Value Trust shrank from $20 billion in assets at its peak to a mere $4 billion. Big corporate and pension-plan investors, a sophisticated group, were no exception. "I served on boards where they said, 'Get rid of Bill Miller—now,'" recalls fellow value manager Rogers. Miller rode the storm out, and in 2009, with the market recovery and a renewed appetite for surviving financials, again outperformed the market. Yet he faced a long climb to recover what he had lost during the bad season.

Say this for value managers like Dreman, Rogers, and Miller: They have the courage of their convictions. Dreman had a stellar record with a fund called DWS Dreman High Return Equity, which he ran for its parent Deutsche Bank. He had a fervent belief in Fannie Mae and stuck with its stock during an earlier accounting scandal. Amid the financial crisis, the government took over the mortgage firm, and its stock sank. After Dreman's fund clocked a 45 percent loss in 2008, the bank canned him as a manager and renamed the fund.

Explaining the problem later, Dreman says, "Investors overreacted to events." When they do, value stocks are a scary place to be.

Walter Schloss: At the Master's Table

In his mid-90s, veteran value investor Walter Schloss is alive with memories of his career working at Benjamin Graham's firm, alongside a young up-and-comer named Warren Buffett. Schloss, who now lives in a swanky Park Avenue apartment with a lofty view of Manhattan, managed money for private clients until the early 2000s. In 2001, a rotten year in the market, he says his accounts were up 12 percent.

"You may lose at times, like in 2008," he says with a toothy grin. "But it pays to be an optimist. My father died at 103. I want to beat him."

By Schloss's reckoning, in the five decades as a solo investment manager after leaving Graham, he averaged 16 percent yearly, versus 10 percent for the S&P 500. After dissolving the firm he ran with his son in 2003, he continued to invest his own multimillion-dollar portfolio, using Graham principles. In a famous speech at Columbia in 1984, entitled "The Superinvestors of Graham-and-Doddsville," Buffett cited Schloss, along with legends like William Ruane of the Sequoia fund, as exemplars of value that good investors should emulate.

"Ben Graham changed my life," Schloss says, recalling how he came across *Security Analysis* as a young man in the 1930s. Schloss, living in near-poverty in Depression-stricken Brooklyn, was an ill-paid runner at a Wall Street firm, meaning he was the gofer who carried stock orders and documents around the office. He took a class that Graham ran at the New York Stock Exchange, a version of his celebrated Columbia sessions, and impressed the great man. After World War II service as a code cracker, Schloss landed a job at Graham-Newman.

Schloss owns no computer and follows the market with the help of the daily newspaper and Value Line investment reports. He also makes sure to stick to the Graham verities. He wants stocks with low price-to-book and very little debt. Plus, he knows that disappointments litter a value investor's path. One of his stocks, a compressor maker called Tecumseh Products, had fallen from $35 in 2008 to $8. Schloss can rattle off all

Walter Schloss: At the Master's Table *(Continued)*

manner of stats about the company. And as he rolls through the bad ones about Tecumseh, he grimaces. By late 2010, it had only recovered to $12. "That one is a shame," he says.

The real test for a value investor: "A stock has lost half, and you go in and buy more. That is not easy. People will think you are crazy."

Summary

- Warren Buffett, the modern-day heir of Benjamin Graham, has updated the master's concepts of value investing. In addition to Graham's devotion to fundamentals, Buffett wants to know a company's management, sometimes applies macroeconomic analysis, and will take an occasional flier on a dubious-seeming investment. Sometimes, he lets his gut guide him—as it did, to his sorrow, when he invested in Irish banks.
- Buffett, though, still hews to such core beliefs as: an investment should be understandable to the investor. That's why he normally shies away from tech issues and derivatives.
- Graham's notion of "intrinsic value," which seeks to find a stock's real worth, has been refined. Value money manager Joel Greenblatt, for instance, uses the nexus between earnings yield and return on capital.
- Dividend-paying stocks, another time-honored value favorite, have had their problems but they still win the plaudits of value icons like David Dreman. Studies still show that these stocks outpace nonpayers over the long pull.
- Value stocks, by many analyses, do better over time than do growth stocks. One reason is that they have higher to rise and are innately strong, not just fads.
- But value stocks have weaknesses. They have endured bad times, too, as during the tech boom. Also, there are such problems as the "value trap," where cheap stocks only get cheaper, hurting investors. That happened to financial stocks, a value stalwart, during the 2008–2009 bear market.

Chapter 2

Eternal Equities: Stocks Do Best?

Jeremy Siegel is the very picture of the mild-mannered professor, the tweedy fellow who gently tells the brash student loudly dominating the seminar that he must get the facts straight. With his low-key manner, high forehead, shaggy gray hair, and spectacles, Siegel comes across more like Mr. Chips than a false prophet out to trick the masses into believing a hazardous heresy that will seal their financial doom.

Siegel, an economist who lives the life of the mind amid the graceful old walls of the University of Pennsylvania, is a divisive figure whose thinking is regularly denounced by some in the wake of the 2007–2009 stock market meltdown. In financial circles, his name stirs up intense reactions, much like Nancy Pelosi's or Glen Beck's do for political ideologues. Jeremy Siegel, a gentlemanly academic, inspires passion, outrage, and no little envy. He is adored by many, and he is pilloried by others.

"Jeremy Siegel, wrong," writes Henry Blodget, on his Business Insider web site. "Jeremy Siegel is brilliant, uplifting, and just plain wrong!" chimes in Vitaliy Katsenelson, research director at Investment Management Associates in Denver. "Jeremy Siegel is a dangerous individual," adds the financial site, passionsaving.com, some years ago.

The Wizard of Wharton, as his many admirers call him, brings forth vivid reactions because he is the largest voice for an enormously important financial philosophy. He is the long-standing champion of the stock-o-centric credo, the belief that holdings in equities will do better than anything else over time. His hugely influential *Stocks for the Long Run* was first published in 1994 and since has been updated, with the fourth edition appearing in 2008. Hailed as a financial classic, this very readable book forms the foundation for how much of the public invests its money. To his detractors, Siegel is a villain because he shrugs off or at best downplays the very real danger that stocks can disappoint, and for a long time. Those cozened by Siegel's entreaties into concentrating on equities will eventually rue that decision, the critics contend.

Siegel, who carries the august title of the Russell E. Palmer Professor of Finance at Penn's Wharton School, summons the full sweep of U.S. history to support his view. By his interpretation, over the past two centuries, despite ups and downs, stocks in America have been the best-returning investment of them all, and likely will remain so into the future. Siegel's research concludes that stocks have gone up around 7 percent annually on average, after inflation, since 1802. In spite of the market catastrophe that erupted shortly after his fourth edition came out, Siegel held to his sunny thesis. In numerous articles and debates, some televised, he has kept insisting that a bet on stocks will be amply rewarded in coming years. Stocks' recovery since the March 2009 low seemed to bear him out.

In truth, the Great Recession didn't have its roots in the stock market, as the late 1990s' tech bubble did. The economic near-apocalypse was caused by too much crazy debt, mostly focused on real estate. Still, stocks rode the housing boom, and got crushed when it ended. The stock market's downward spiral, which began in late 2007, was terrifyingly epic in scope. It slashed the portfolios of many investors in half or worse. Stocks are wagers on corporate earnings, which in turn are linked to economic growth. Should growth falter, for whatever reason, stocks will, too.

Back in the 1990s, when Siegel first popularized his treatise, stocks seemed peerless. The conventional thinking was that the market worked like a well-engineered machine, Wall Street had a special genius, and corporations sought to maximize their earnings for the good of investors. Bill Clinton, a centrist Democrat, pushed deregulation of financial markets, preparing the path for even more loosening from his successor, George W. Bush. Next, the 2000–2003 dot-com bomb exploded. Venerated companies like Enron and WorldCom were revealed to be vile constructs of Potemkin accounting. Web companies that raised huge sums in the stock market, like Webvan.com, shriveled away for lack of profits or prospects.

But then came the 21st century's big housing boom, which took form partly due to the Federal Reserve's low interest rates designed to lift the economy out of the tech wreck. For many investors, all was forgiven and forgotten. Stocks soared anew. When the market took its 2007–2009 groin kick, just a half-decade after the last one, a lot of investors began wondering whether they had been euchred. Money invested in the S&P 500 at the beginning of the decade lost, by one measure, around 1 percent annually. Stocks for the long term? Ten years is the long term, right? Some began to wonder about Siegel's credo.

A lot was at stake. The bulk of Americans' investments in 2007 were tied up in the stock market, on the assumption it was an enchanted grotto where growth was guaranteed. From 401(k) retirement accounts to individual portfolios, most investment dollars were concentrated in equities.

Thanks to the financial calamity of 2007–2009, many investors trimmed their equity holdings. Yet the prominence of stocks in American life hardly disappeared. Equities remained the asset of choice.

That's most apparent in mutual funds, where most Americans stash their nest eggs. In 2007, according to the Investment Company Institute, bond funds constituted 37 percent of stock fund assets, $2.4 trillion versus $6.5 trillion. The next year, when equity valuations had shrunk radically, bond fund assets were 40 percent of stock funds'—$1.5 trillion to $3.7 trillion. Stock prices had fallen much further than those of bonds, although the gain in bond funds' share was partly due to investors pulling money out of equity funds. Even in 2009 and 2010, as the stock market had a heady recovery, investors withdrew money from stock portfolios.

All that said, the fact remains that stock funds continued to lead bond funds in assets by a wide margin. One of the most popular investment choices during the recovery was the target-date fund, a mixture of stocks and bonds that shifted from stock-heavy to bond-heavy as the investor's retirement date drew nearer. Just the same, even when a target-date fund hit a person's retirement age, it would keep a decent slug in stocks.

★   ★   ★

No matter where one stands on Siegel, there is one universal truth about stocks: they have a special, almost talismanic, attraction. The reason is that no other widely held asset class has the chance of doubling, tripling, or quadrupling in a short period. The thought that your stocks could make this kind of advance stimulates that universally shared lobe of the brain that houses greed. Enthusiasm for stocks is akin to that for sports. You want your team to win, and when it does, you are very happy. When your team loses, you seldom disown them, or at least not for long.

The periodic bull markets are buoyed by this innate belief that stocks are meant to go up. The faith in stocks' helium-balloon nature reached an extreme in James Glassman and Kevin Hassett's spectacularly overoptimistic 1999 book, *Dow 36,000: The New Strategy for Profiting from the Coming Rise in the Stock Market*, which foresaw such a surge in the ensuing five years or so. At that time, the Dow Jones Industrial Average was a tad over 10,000. The enthusiasm seemed merited: the average price of a big U.S. company had expanded almost 12 times over the previous 20 years. Unfortunately for Glassman and Hassett, their book came out right before the tech mania ended in early 2000. The Dow skidded down to 7,286 by October 2002. For sure, it motored up to 14,165 by October 2007—until it sank anew with the Great Recession's onset. Ten years after the euphoric Glassman-

Hassett forecast, the Dow stood about where it had been when their book appeared.

It's a testament to stocks' enduring popularity that most people never seem to reach a point where they've had a bellyful of the nutty volatility and broken promises. A Vanguard Group study of 3,000 investors in late 2009 discovered that, even after undergoing the bear market's turmoil, they wanted to stick with stocks. Almost three quarters of them said that equities were a risk worth taking.

Indeed, the public turned its back on stocks from the early 1930s until the early 1950s. The effect of a depression and a world war were not easily dispelled. Once prosperity seemed assured in the Eisenhower Era, though, stocks were back in favor. Now, despite the body blow from the Great Recession that broke too many people's lives, the average American benefits from a material abundance that his ancestors couldn't fathom. The relative comfort and security of most American households allow them to keep betting on a better tomorrow, which is what stock investing is about.

The United States, as the largest economy on the planet by far, has been the world's leader in stock market capitalization for a long time. Total capitalization of all U.S. equity markets was 44 percent of global market cap in 2007. No nation comes close to America, where stock ownership is broader than anyplace else.

Given the iron link between economic and market growth, faith in ongoing U.S. supremacy is needed to believe that the nation's stock market will keep delivering. Of course, investing in overseas markets has become an increasingly important trend that we will cover later. For the moment, however, there's a strong argument to be made that American stocks will remain a good venue for your money.

The reason is that America has, since the 1800s, been the earth's leading innovator. Sir Harold Evans, a British journalist and author, writes: "I challenge anyone to get through the day without an innovation that was developed by an American." The entrepreneurial spirit found in the country, he points out, gave birth to "the airplane and the PC, jeans and the cell phone, bio-tech and the sewing machine, TV (and 24-hour news) and the search engine."

One school of critics holds that nothing assures America of holding onto its lead forever. Yale historian Paul Kennedy contends that America is in danger of "imperial overstretch," and he illustrates how European powers went into decline after spending too much on their militaries. The United States certainly spends an enormous amount on the armed forces—deploying, for instance, 11 carrier strike groups, versus two for Britain, one for a handful of other nations, and none for China.

Meanwhile, China's economic growth rate hovers around 9 percent annually, compared to a fraction of that for the United States. By any measure, the United States is the most productive nation and has the largest gross domestic product, at around $15 trillion. By some measures, China has about $5 trillion, a hair more than Japan. China also happens to own the largest number of U.S. Treasury bonds, leading some to wonder whether it can someday use its standing as America's biggest creditor to its advantage, pressuring America to do its bidding on pain of dumping that paper on the market. Pessimists love to harp on how Washington's enormous spending, for the military and entitlement programs like Social Security, has saddled it with debt that dwarfs those of many other nations. However, since the 1960s, many a dirge has been sung about how America is on the way out, a la the Roman Empire. Somehow, this dire scenario never quite seemed to happen.

In the 1980s, it was Japan that was supposed to be the United States' replacement, what with their long-term-oriented conglomerates that had bled American automakers and electronics companies nearly to death. Japanese buyers were grabbing prized American trophies, like the Pebble Beach golf club in California and the Rockefeller Center office complex in New York. Then Japan stumbled. Its industrial genius lacked the innovative spark that had fueled America through the decades. Japan's industrial growth waned. The Nikkei 225, Japan's premier stock index, has tumbled as a consequence, to around one quarter of its towering level in 1989.

Professor Siegel projects that emerging nations like China and India will see their stock markets grow mightily, to the relative detriment of the West. Now, the developed countries have 90 percent of the world's stock market value, with the United States accounting for half of it. By 2050, the developed world's share will shrink to one third, with the United States at 18 percent, he believes. That projection may be overblown, as Japan's one-time inevitable triumph has shown. China and India have massive internal problems, such as widespread poverty and violently disruptive factions. Siegel says people should invest abroad for the best diversification, although he cautions that emerging stocks tend to be expensive.

But the key, under the gospel according to Jeremy Siegel, is that you should be investing in stocks, wherever they are.

★   ★   ★

Siegel begins his book with the cautionary tale of a fellow named John J. Raskob, a General Motors financial executive, whose Glassman and Hassett–like bullish views on the market's assured upward path graced the pages of *Ladies Home Journal*. The article, written by journalist Samuel Crowther, had an arresting title, "Everybody Ought to Be Rich." Raskob opined that people should put a small sum of money into stocks every month, and in two decades, it would blossom into a decent pile of dollars. Unfortunately, just as did Glassman and Hassett, Raskob suffered from hideously bad timing. The article appeared in the summer of 1929. A few months later, the stock market began its operatic plunge. Raskob ended up painted as one of the biggest fools ever to tread the ground.

After recounting the plight of Raskob, Siegel slyly notes that the sum he advised investing—$15 monthly, or $190 in present-day dollars—would have grown to $9,000 by 1949, which translates to $80,000 today. And that was even before the market had finally recovered its balance from depression and war.

The spine of Siegel's argument is *reverting to the mean*. In other words, the average real (inflation-adjusted) return on stocks, which he calculates as around 7 percent per year, is what the market keeps returning to. A sort of elastic tether pulls the market back to that mean after it flies unsustainably high or crashes unsustainably low. This 7 percent standard, he writes, "means that returns can be very unstable in the short run but very stable in the long run."

Siegel marvels how returns "cling" to this trend line over two centuries. Thus, when the market was above trend, such as in the 1960s and late 1990s, it inevitably corrected. And when it was below trend, as in the early 1990s, the stock market then obligingly shot up to its customary place. For Siegel, this phenomenon is remarkable given the enormous changes that have rolled through America since 1802, his favorite start point, since that was when the nation began to move from an agrarian economy to an industrial one. The country later shifted to a postindustrial economy, with emphases on services and tech; it shucked the gold standard and adopted paper money that a central bank can print by fiat; and modern communications accelerated and broadened the availability of market information that investors can act upon instantly. With an awed shake of the head, Siegel declares: "Despite mammoth changes in the basic factors generating wealth for shareholders, equity returns have shown an astounding stability."

After establishing the durable 7 percent growth of stocks, Siegel's book moves on to trash the reverse of equities, namely bonds. Bond returns are anything but stable, he states. By Siegel's inflation-adjusted calculations, in each 30-year period starting in 1889, short-term Treasuries were up more than 2 percent only three times. Long-term Treasuries fared only a little better, never topping 4 percent and rising more than 3 percent just 22 times. That's quite a comedown when you compare those to that golden 7 percent that stocks keep running up. What's the reason? Chiefly, Siegel feels, it was the transition from the gold standard touched off by Franklin Roosevelt, a shift that built an inflationary bias into the economy. During the Depression, when stocks were less popular than Herbert Hoover, Siegel explains, bond returns were plodding because scared investors piled into them, making them costly to buy and holding down yields (which move inversely to prices).

Siegel is hardly the first professor whose research awarded the crown to stocks as the best investment possible under heaven. After studying the matter, Yale's Irving Fisher in the early 1920s countered the then-conventional assumption that bonds were better, and stocks were the playthings of speculators. And Siegel is not the first stock-champion academic to be slammed for his views either. Fisher, like the industrialist Raskob, got a little too enthusiastic during the 1920s boom, and announced in October 1929 that stocks had reached "a permanent high plateau." Pilloried, Fisher encountered big financial reversals and died in 1947 before stocks really took off again. Raskob, a wealthy man, kept busy enough to surmount the ridicule: He went on to develop the Empire State Building.

Siegel has kept his considerable reputation intact by his sober-minded insistence that the long run for stocks really meant that—and warning that nasty downturns were part of the process. In March 2000, right at tech craze's peak, he made the shrewd prophylactic move of penning a *Wall Street Journal* column warning that a market bloodbath lay ahead.

Still, Fisher concluded, and Siegel seconds him, that overall stocks outpaced bonds in inflationary eras. Inflation is poison for fixed-income securities, whose interest payments are steadily eroded; stocks, however, stand to gain ultimately in a time of rising prices since, among other factors, inflation usually means a prosperous economy, where company earnings benefit. The poor performance of stocks in the inflationary 1970s seems to give the lie to Fisher's formulation. Well, maybe it's all simply a matter of public misperception. Later academic work by the likes of Franco Modigliani, Richard Cohn, and others found that investors failed to see what a fine inflation shock absorber stocks are due to what they called the "money illusion." That's where investors confused nominal with real, or inflation-adjusted, earnings and didn't foresee that earnings could grow anymore. Once the 1970s were done, earnings did grow again.

Siegel makes the case that periodic disruptions like the Depression and the Great Recession come along like hurricanes. They happen occasionally, wreak great destruction, and yet never really slow the march of humanity. He derides both hardcore bullish and bearish market forecasters, as tending to make too much of selective evidence, or overreacting to recent events. One of the worst bearish calls of all time was the infamously downbeat *BusinessWeek* cover in 1979 that asked whether equities were dead. As the 1980s proved, they definitely were not. Siegel calls on investors to "avoid these fickle prognosticators."

Beyond catastrophes, though, Siegel laments stocks' tendency to gyrate in price thanks to forces beyond a rational, Ben Graham–like assessment of their fundamental values. Like Graham, he has trouble with the efficient market hypothesis—where stocks are correctly priced based on known information. "The efficient market hypothesis does not say a stock's price is always equal to its fundamental value," Siegel writes. "But the theory implies that it is impossible to tell which stocks are undervalued and which are overvalued without either costly analysis or an innate skill possessed only by a chosen few, such as Warren Buffett, Peter Lynch, or Bill Miller."

Temporary shocks to the system, as in 2008–2009, do indeed make investors jittery after the danger has passed, and subject to overreacting to each piece of news. In 2010, Graham's Mr. Market swung up and down depending on the latest economic indicator. Siegel calls this condition his "noisy market hypothesis." It has led him to a value approach that would do Buffett proud. If you buy a lot of stock that is pulled down by market noise, and not fundamental problems like stinky earnings, he says, then its eventual restoration to grace will be gratifying.

His fascinating answer to minimizing the noise is to invest in funds that are constructed on the very fundamentals he reveres. So he helped set up a value-oriented asset management firm called WisdomTree, whose holdings are weighted using dividends or earnings. The better the earnings or the dividends, the more a stock is represented in a Siegel-style fundamental fund.

Many standard funds are devoted to indexes that allocate stock holdings based on market capitalization, the amount companies' outstanding shares are worth in toto. The S&P 500 and the Russell 3000 indexes, usually cited as proxies for the entire market, use this method. The Dow Jones Industrial Average, which covers only 30 stocks and yet has an iconic presence, uses a slightly different yardstick, employing actual stock prices. Regardless, the biggest and most popular stocks hold the most sway with the traditional indexes, not the ones with the best earnings or dividends, as Siegel prefers.

WisdomTree began offering its exchange-traded funds in 2006, so it's still a bit early to judge how well they will do over Siegel's sacred long run. This was a funky time to be launching something, and the track record of WisdomTree's funds is not illuminating. From its 2007 debut through 2010's third quarter, WisdomTree's Total Earnings fund tied the market's return, losing an average annual 3.5 percent; its Total Dividend, which started in 2006, also was in a dead heat with the market, down a fraction of a percent.

Siegel's research, he says, shows that such fundamentally weighted funds would have outperformed cap-weighted ones during the 2000–

2002 tech bust. The Russell 3000 lost 50 percent then, while Siegel's dividend-weighted variant—had it existed at the time—would have dropped a mere 20 percent.

Whether proselytizing for fundamental indexing or the broader idea of stocks *uber alles*, Siegel is a regular figure on the lecture circuit. He often can be found holding forth before some business association at swanky locales like New York's Metropolitan Club, where he is greeted with awe. His WisdomTree work has helped enhance his cachet. A partner in the company is the renowned investor Michael Steinhardt and its head is Jonathan Steinberg, son of swashbuckling 1980s raider Saul Steinberg and husband of CNBC's "Money Honey," Maria Bartiromo. Wherever he does go, Siegel is greeted as that most delightful kind of human being, the wise man—except by those who think his wisdom is a tree bearing deceptively alluring fruit that will be the undoing of those who taste it.

★　　★　　★

Writing bullish books about stocks is a good tactic to gain popularity, provided the timing is right. A fellow named Edgar Lawrence Smith wrote a best-selling book in 1925 called *Common Stocks as Long Term Investments*, much praised by Professor Fisher. It had a Siegel-like view that stocks did the best over time. The great economist John Maynard Keynes even asked Smith to join the Royal Economic Society. And Smith was onto something. Later academic studies—brought out in 1938, 1953, 1964, and 1976—arrived at the same pro-equities conclusion.

But poking holes in such optimism is deliciously tempting. In spring 2009, right after the bottom of the bear market, a prominent money manager named Robert Arnott unleashed a powerful counterargument to Siegelism in an attention-grabbing article for the *Journal of Indexes*: that 20-year government bonds have taken the lead from March 1969 through March 2009, a 40-year span. In the article, entitled "Bonds: Why Bother?," Arnott, a bearded, bearlike fellow who once edited the wonkish *Financial Analysts Journal*, concedes that stocks do outpace bonds over the very long run. Since 1802, Siegel's start point, Arnott calculates that stocks expanded 4 million times in value, versus just 27,000 times for bonds. But the obvious question arises: what investor has ever lived more than two centuries? Arnott notes that stocks triumphed from 1932 to 2000, which takes in the Great Depression and also the United States' postwar rise. Stocks ran into a quagmire in the new century's first decade, bracketed by the tech slump and the housing mess. That was sufficient to pull stocks' showing down below that of bonds, and to create the phrase "Lost Decade" to describe the sorry period.

In a January 2010 newsletter to investors in his Research Affiliates financial firm, Arnott looks over the wreckage and laments: "The naughts were the worst decade ever for U.S. investors, even after an astounding rebound in the past 10 months of 2009, during which the S&P 500 index surged 55 percent. Yes, worse than the previous two low points, the 1850s and the Depression-riddled 1930s."

To Arnott, the equity-centered mind-set engendered by Siegel (whom he does not name) has had a rotten impact on investors who believed it. Arnott examines the typical retirement portfolio with 60 percent in stocks in the S&P 500 (the rest in bonds) during the Lost Decade. Even with the beneficent influence of the bonds, the portfolio barely earned any money. The S&P 500 itself lost money. Worse, he goes on, investors didn't really learn their lesson from this humbling experience. Corporate 401(k) plans kept their offerings tilted toward stock funds, particularly those that had a history of run-ups. The heads of retirement plans fondly recalled the good record stocks had enjoyed once upon a time and conveniently overlooked the bad spells. Ordinary investors, known as "retail" people, got the hose as a consequence. Arnott finds this outcome to be outrageous since the investors could have reshuffled their holdings away from cement-shoed stocks: "The concept of rebalancing—building on the idea that past is not prologue—is rarely followed in the retail community."

Arnott finds that stocks too often disappoint and don't return as much as Siegel calculates. In his bonds article, Arnott pooh-poohs the often-touted 5 percentage-point historical advantage of stock over bond returns, figuring that the real number is half that (meaning 2.5) over the long pull. Siegel immediately fires back that he never used a 5-point figure, and that stocks' advantage, employing data from 1871 through 2008, is actually 3.2 points per year. Now, this may sound like a lot of quibbling, yet a percentage point or two extra adds up when compounded over time.

In rebuttal, Siegel forecasts that bonds will not do well in the future. There's some logic to this. Bonds have had their own sweet rally since interest rates began a downward trend from lofty levels in the early 1980s. With short-term rates near zero during the Great Recession, it is only logical that they should start creeping up. Higher rates hurt bond prices, so their prospects over time certainly do seem cloudy. Meanwhile, a recovering economy is the main ingredient for a stock rally in the future.

What about the past, however? While stocks do take the laurels, it all depends on what period you are examining. The best span to measure is 40 years, since that envelops the typical length of an active investor's wealth accumulation, beginning in her 20s and ending in her 60s. According to data from Ibbotson Associates, a well-regarded research outfit, stocks and bonds finished in a dead heat for the four decades ending in bearish 2008, 9.0 percent for stocks and 8.9 percent for bonds annually. Our investor here started salting it away in 1968. Bond-harming inflation was just cooking up and would dominate the next decade. Then, in the early 1980s came the rate-reduction trend that goosed bonds. Meanwhile, stocks went on a roller-coaster ride, from the doldrums of the 1970s to the deal-fueled 1980s surge and the 1990s tech run-up, then the housing-fired bull market of the naughts— and the party was spoiled by the tech wreck at the decade's outset and the Great Recession at its conclusion.

Remember that performance hinges on what period you are eyeing. If you narrow the focus a bit, bonds win. Casting back only 20 years from 1988 through 2008 has bonds ahead 10.0 percent to 8.4. Constrict the aperture some more, to 10 years (from 1998 through 2008) and you have pretty much the Lost Decade, where bonds deliver a solid 8.4 percent gain, compared to a 1.4 loss for stocks.

Try this another way. See what a four-decade investing regimen yields for people who retired at different points in the past – in 2003, 1998, 1993, and so on. For people who retired in the 1960s through the early 1980s, stocks were ahead by many lengths. With a 1978 end point, for instance, stocks came in at 9.9 percent annually over the previous 40 years, and bonds a mere 2.7. Later on, due to the fixed-income rally, bonds did much better, although stocks still were comfortably ahead. Example: Someone who retired in 1998 after 40 years of investing garnered 12 percent yearly from stocks and 7.2 percent from bonds.

Arnott has more wide-ranging tastes in investments than Siegel. His firm moves money among different asset classes where he can see an advantage. In 2009, it was high on convertible bonds, corporate bonds, and junk. Research Affiliates, his company, manages a mutual fund called Pimco All Asset Fund, which follows this ambidextrous approach and handily beats the S&P 500.

Siegel, however, seldom has a good word to say about nonstock investments. In 2006, when commodities futures (oil, gold, wheat, etc.) were taking wing, he disparaged the trend. Unlike stocks, commodities don't pay dividends, he wrote; plus, hedge funds and other sharpies were artificially driving up their prices. Don't play their game, he counsels. His alternative is—you guessed it—stocks. "If you want to invest in commodities," he goes on, "it is much better to hold stock in companies that own, mine, and extract these resources.

Tellingly, by Arnott's own admission, certain classes of stocks have held up quite well over time, besting his lauded long-term Treasuries by a wide margin. His newsletter lists how, during the Lost Decade, the best performer was emerging market bonds (10.9 percent increase annually), but real estate investment trusts—which are sold as stocks and mainly represent collections of rent-paying buildings like malls and offices—logged a close second (10.2), with emerging-market stocks not far behind in third place (10.1).

Some of Siegel's detractors come at him from another direction, questioning the methodology behind his assertion that stocks tran-scended everything else going back to 1802. *Wall Street Journal* invest-ment columnist Jason Zweig wrote that the data the professor used for the 1800s is suspect. By Zweig's telling, Siegel relies on the flawed tabulations of two economists, Walter Buckingham Smith and Arthur Harrison Cole, in the 1930s. These two counted only companies that had thrived during the 1800s and excluded those that had failed, Zweig charges in his 2009 column, "The Intelligent Investor." According to Zweig, Siegel depended on an index that ignored 97 percent of existing stocks in the early American stock exchanges: "Never mind all of the canals, wooden turnpikes, rubber-hat companies, and the other doomed stocks that investors lost millions on."

Siegel's response is that another study, by Ibbotson and Bill Goetzmann, backs him up on the 1800s, although Zweig has trouble with Siegel's interpretation of this data, too. Yes, at least nobody disputes that stocks took the honors for much of the last century. As Siegel wrote in a letter to the newspaper, data gathered starting the late 1800s and through the 20th century are very solid and support his stocks-do-best viewpoint, which Zweig does not dispute.

At core, to assume that stocks will continue to be the best investment on earth requires a hopeful anticipation reminiscent of Charles Dickens's Mr. Micawber. A study by two other professors, Lubos Pastor of the University of Chicago and Robert Stambaugh of Wharton, finds that the U.S. market benefited from two centuries of American ascendancy. In a reiteration of the old saw that past performance is no guarantee of future returns, Pastor cautions there is no certainty that "the next two centuries will be as kind to the domestic equity market as the last two."

★   ★   ★

Past patterns are vital tools for economists and market strategists, despite the possibility that they might turn out to be invalid going forward. The seasons change with measurable regularity—until that comet collides with the Earth, casts a permanent winter pall over the sky, and knocks the globe from its axis. Yet Wall Street and the investing public are wedded to market augury, much of it based on what has transpired before. And a lot of the time, the past does set patterns that likely will hold true into the future. Except when they don't.

The relatively bullish Siegel has an ongoing debate with his old friend, Robert Shiller, whom he has known since their graduate school days at the Massachusetts Institute of Technology. Shiller, in his 2000 book *Irrational Exuberance*, called the end of the tech bubble, and later expressed doubts that the housing price boom could keep going. Why? Well, bubbles tend to pop. In 2010, Shiller worried that the housing bust would linger and harm stocks over time. Shiller, who does his own survey of home prices to guide him, reasoned that the real estate morass was too deep, so draining it away would be hard. Siegel decried this pessimism as wrong-headed partly because, in his eyes, the stock market was cheap and positioned for better days. This is an article of faith to bulls: when shares are cheap, they become attractive, and ipso facto, investors bid them up. The result is a rising market. Shiller, for his part, using his own measurements, felt that stocks were not cheap. The larger point here is that the divination of patterns is, despite what the diviners will tell you, a very tricky business.

The stock market does have cycles, but they are not immune from a comet strike that shatters all the past patterns. Between 1946 and 2007, there were 10 bear markets, defined as a slump of at least 20 percent in the S&P 500. Recoveries tend to take a while—around seven years to recoup losses, says the InvesTech *Market Analyst* newsletter. After the tech-stoked bull market began in 2000, stocks didn't return to their peak level until 7.2 years had elapsed. By that rule, the Great Recession's bear-clawed market won't regain its 2007 high until 2014. Ned Davis researchers have concluded that increases in the P/E—that widely used measure of value and affordability—mainly happen in the first six months of a market upturn. But these are hardly immutable laws. Recall that stocks took more than two decades to recover after the 1929 crash. The damage from the housing and credit crunch in the 2000s, bears say, may have been too severe to merit a strong and sustainable bounce-back.

Can past patterns tell us anything? Sam Stovall, Standard & Poor's market strategist, notes that since 1910, no decade had ever had a cumulative loss, with one big exception—this century's first decade. Including dividends, even the 1930s saw stocks up 10 percent from start to finish. Dividends back then were on the order of 5 percent of a stock's price, whereas today they are just under 2 percent, so dividends no longer pack the wallop they once did. The 2000s Lost Decade was the comet-strike departure from the pattern. So what's next? Factoring out dividends to focus on prices, Stovall discovers that stocks have not declined two decades in a row since 1900. But that is no guarantee this particular pattern will hold going forward.

Structural changes have come along that have altered the investing landscape. Rapid-fire electronic trading can accelerate big overall market movements. The 1987 market crash was worsened by automatic sell orders that kicked in when prices dropped to a certain level. Then there's the narrowing of bid-ask spreads, where brokers used to take a nice slice of a stock purchase order and slip it into their pockets—until the Securities and Exchange Commission (SEC) spoiled the fun by doing away with fractions in stock pricing, in an effort to reduce trading costs. A stock used to be priced at, say, 12 and one-eighth dollars. Then the SEC made all prices in pennies: $12.01, $12.02, and so on. For brokers, pocketing an extra penny isn't as lucrative as an eighth of a dollar, or 12.5 cents, multiplied over hundreds of shares. That has made trading stocks less lucrative for brokerages, but has encouraged cowboy trading among people who want to get in and out of a stock quickly. This, the charge goes, has not been helpful to the market's stability or to long-term investors' portfolios.

But through the fullness of time, Jeremy Siegel makes clear, an investor with a stubborn faith in equity investing should triumph. The question is whether stocks are what should make up the bulk of your portfolio for the long run. As Lord Keynes put it: "In the long run, we are all dead."

Ken Fisher, the Historian

One of the premier stock strategists of our time always has an eye on what the past can teach us—and knows its limitations. Ken Fisher got to be one of the richest men in the United States by, among other things, knowing what is a market myth and knowing what isn't. Never shy to offer an opinion, the deep-voiced Fisher, whose Fisher Investments manages billions in others' assets, is an outspoken advocate for saving California's redwoods and for going against the herd.

Like Jeremy Siegel, Fisher is a devotee of owning stocks for the long run. In his 2009 book, *The Ten Roads to Riches*, which appeared amid the aftershocks of the vicious bear market, Fisher calls for getting a 10 percent annual return, despite the reality that this level is one most professionals don't attain, "even though it's not hard." His answer to performing this feat: "Easy—invest in stocks, pretty much all the time ... because they have superior long-term returns." Yet his devotion to equities is not total. In prolonged market downturns, he cautions, moving into cash and bonds may be wise. For the most

(Continued)

Ken Fisher, the Historian *(Continued)*

part, Fisher says you should be diversified globally, using a broad measure like the MSCI World Index as a guidepost.

Along the way, Fisher has some interesting tactical advice, based on the emotion-driven human tendencies of investors. He loves examining market seers' forecasts for the upcoming year, and choosing the one spot they haven't named as the right guesstimate. A good number of times, he is correct. The reason evidently is that the market at large already has cast its bets with the smarties, so the actual outcome will be different. In 2001, most savants saw the market pulling out of its tech swoon. Fisher was bearish, closer than most in his prediction (he said the market would be flat, and it slipped another 12 percent).

Most investors, Fisher observes, harbor beliefs that turn out to be wrong. Example: The widespread belief that years when stocks are expensive turn out to be bad in the end. Not always so, he says. He loves to trash bogus market indicators, such as which team wins the Super Bowl and skirt lengths, and back ones that seem to work, at least a lot of the time. For instance, he finds that the third year of a U.S. president's term usually has a benign stock market. The rationale for that, he says, is that "almost all the big schemes to redistribute wealth or property rights happen in the first half of presidents' terms." Sometimes, of course, Fisher is way wrong, as when he predicted in his January 2008 *Forbes* column that the year would be a good one. Fisher knows, above all, that the market, which he has called the Great Humiliator, dishes out nasty surprises.

Summary

- Professor Jeremy Siegel's book, *Stocks for the Long Run*, is hugely influential. It has helped justify U.S. investors' preference for equities. While the 2007–2009 bear market dimmed stocks' appeal to a degree, they remain the asset class of choice for 401(k) retirement plans and the investment community at large.

- According to Siegel's research, since 1802, stocks have been the single best returning investment, rising around 7 percent on average after inflation—and this trend will continue into the future. While stocks may soar above it or plunge beneath it, they always are pulled back to that 7 percent level, he says. He calls this phenomenon *reverting to the mean*.

- Statistics show that stocks do indeed outpace other investment types, as they are linked to the U.S. economy, which over the past two centuries in Siegel's study has grown exponentially—advancing much more than it has declined. Adjusted for inflation, Siegel finds, stocks beat bonds on an annual basis by 3.2 percentage points.

- But the horrible market results of the 21st century's first decade has cast Siegel's sunny thesis into question. During this so-called Lost Decade (2000–2009), stocks actually lost money, while bonds did better. Critics say that Siegel misled investors who followed his stock-centered advice, and they suffered for it. One critic, Robert Arnott, calls the "naughts" the worst decade ever for investors. Some critics, such as the *Wall Street Journal*'s Jason Zweig, question Siegel's data from the 1800s, when the professor says stocks romped.

- Still, few deny that stocks outperformed in the 20th century. What confronts investment strategists going forward is how much to put in stocks. In fact, some classes of equities, such as emerging market shares, did fine in the Lost Decade. Will stocks in the United States, still the world's largest economy and equity market, bear out Siegel's credo?

Chapter 3

On Autopilot: Indexes

They call him Saint John, some facetiously, some with aching sincerity. Few living persons have statues erected in their honor, but John Bogle has one, on his company's campus outside Philadelphia. Famously cantankerous, this saint is often found speechifying about the righteousness of the faith that he founded. He has a steadfast coterie of acolytes, called Bogleheads. He believes he is on a mission and his cause is just. The company he launched to be the instrument of his vision, the Vanguard Group, has striven for greatness, he says—and he leaves no doubt that he and Vanguard have attained it through virtuous conduct. On Vanguard's investing style, he quotes Leo Tolstoy: "There is no greatness where there is not simplicity, goodness, and truth."

John Bogle invented the index mutual fund, Vanguard's premier product, which tracks the Standard & Poor's (S&P) 500 and thus captures the moves of the broad market. In his eyes, indexes are the superior way to invest in the stock market, bar none. Indexes easily outdo mere humans who are picking stocks with the aid of a spreadsheet, a Bloomberg terminal, and a crafty (they believe) strategy. For Bogle, many non-index funds—run by managers who dodge in and out of stocks chasing glory—tend to be too risky, too costly, and too tax prone.

The octogenarian Bogle gave up running Vanguard in the late 1990s. Boundlessly energetic—he had a heart transplant in 1995—he still keeps a heavy schedule proselytizing about the virtues inherent in the index fund.

Others originated the index-fund concept and tossed it around intellectually, but Bogle in the mid-1970s went ahead and put theory into practice. He launched the S&P-tracking Vanguard 500. Nowadays, the fund is among the largest by assets, and is a stalwart for retirement portfolios. Many non-Vanguard funds, put out by the likes of Fidelity, Schwab, and USAA, have aped Vanguard's innovation and mirror the S&P 500, too.

Index funds are called "passive" investments because they work on autopilot. They don't require expensive legions of analysts and managers to buy and sell the stocks in their portfolios. All an index manager needs to do is make periodic adjustments to ensure that the fund's holdings are as close as possible to the S&P 500. The S&P is a capitalization-weighted collection, meaning that each of the 500 stocks is represented in the index by its market value, the number of shares outstanding times the share price. If Microsoft's market cap was 2.1 percent of the index, and its share price slips so it now makes up only 1.9 percent, then the index fund's manager must sell enough Microsoft stock to bring the software maker in line, and add whatever has gained to match the proper current proportions.

The S&P 500, which covers roughly three quarters of the United States' market value, has long been the key benchmark for investors. In other words, when people ask, "How is the market doing?," they usually mean, "How is the S&P doing?" The much smaller (30 stocks) and older (launched in 1896 versus the S&P's 1957) Dow Jones Industrial Average also is a market proxy, devoted solely to blue chips, and usually correlates well with the S&P. But the S&P 500 has far more index funds that follow it.

To Bogle's way of thinking, the index's very breadth is its greatest strength—it's better to invest in all the stocks, or most of them, in the market, than a few. Bogle believes the smartest course is: "Own the entire stock market. Today, that is as easily said as done."

A rather loose analogy is to place bets on all the horses in a race instead of one, putting the most money on the steeds with the best odds. Over time, race after race, you likely will do better than the guy who bet everything on the probable first-place finisher, which often disappoints. Coupled with diversification is a willingness to, in Bogle's words and continuing the racing conceit, "stay the course." That is, don't panic and pull out whenever the market takes one of its occasional, and very scary, plunges.

The vexing truth about stocks is that they don't rise, or fall, in straight lines. The biggest gains in any given year often occur on just a few days. A study by the University of Michigan's H. Nejat Seyhun shows that, if you had been in the market between 1963 and 2004, your yearly return would be 11 percent. However, if you missed 90 of the best trading days during those four decades, your annual return would drop to 3 percent. And Bogle argues that, since one never knows which stocks will do what, a marketwide bet is the only sensible means of capturing the rises. Active funds can't cover all those bases.

Statistically, Bogle has a point. For decades, index funds have outperformed actively managed funds, where managers shift in and out of stocks in hopes of making a big score. Active managers are forever searching for some advantage that will let them "beat the market." Unfortunately for them, and for their investors, few managers achieve this feat. Over time, an average of 70 percent of active funds fails to beat the S&P per year. (While the amount of active-fund lagging varies by the measure employed and the time studied, it always lies within hailing distance of 70 percent.) Only occasionally do active funds hold their own. In 2009, a spring-back year from the vicious bear market, half the actives did better than the S&P.

With no little zeal, Bogle writes: "Vanguard's corporate structure, focus on cost and service to clients, and pioneering index and index-like funds have combined to [link] idealism and economics: Enlightened idealism is sound economics." Vanguard is owned by its fund holders, and not money-grubbing profiteers like the rest of the mutual fund industry. While Vanguard does offer active funds, they aim for the low-cost, low-tax ideal of an index fund.

Bogle's relentless criticism of the rest of the industry grates on competitors, to say the least. In a 2003 meeting of the Investment Company Institute (ICI), the mutual fund trade group's then-chairman, Paul Haaga, lambasted the industry's detractors, particularly "a saint with his own statue." Saint John Bogle had the last laugh because, a few months later, a messy scandal erupted. Some fund managers were caught favoring big investors over smaller ones and gaming the system.

Regardless, proponents of active management counter that the trick is to find funds that consistently beat the S&P 500, those that number among the magical 30 percent that are the outperformers. This can be done with just a little study, they say. To Adam Bold, founder of the Mutual Fund Store, an investment advisory service, "If you do your homework, you can find" the funds that best the S&P. "I don't like index funds because you know you'll never do better than the index," he says.

But consistently staying ahead of the S&P benchmark is difficult. Until the Great Recession's bear market, Legg Mason Capital Management Value Trust was a constant market beater, bettering the S&P for 15 straight years. Star manager Bill Miller had stoked his portfolio with hot sectors like financial and homebuilder stocks. When they crashed, the fund did, too: losing 55 percent in 2008 versus the S&P's 37 percent loss.

The bulk of the investing public, though, hasn't signed on to Bogle's index crusade. A mere 6 percent of mutual fund assets are in index portfolios, according to ICI figures. Bogle's explanation is much like Barack Obama's on why voters rejected Democrats in the 2010 election: they were beguiled by hucksterism. The fund industry has devilishly clever marketing efforts, Bogle says. If the investing public knew the truth, he proclaims, they would flock to indexes.

Bogle unsparingly dismisses the quest for a market-beating active fund as a fool's errand: "It is the haystack we ought to have been looking for all along rather than seeking out the few needles hidden deep within it." Bogle sprinkles his writings and speeches with scriptural references, as befits a missionary. Spreading what he calls his "gospel,"

Bogle quotes Ecclesiastes: "Wisdom excelleth ignorance as far as light excelleth darkness."

★   ★   ★

Bogle saw the light early, in college. As a junior at Princeton in December 1949, he was scratching around for a thesis subject and only knew that he wanted to write about a topic no student had ever taken on before. He chanced to pick up a copy of *Fortune* magazine and read a story on these curious entities called mutual funds. He had never heard of them. The magazine article described the budding fund industry as "tiny but contentious."

Data at the time were scarce on funds, which then had just $2.5 billion under management ($22 billion in current dollars), compared to around $10 trillion nowadays. Bogle ended up using a predecessor of the S&P 500, the S&P 90, as a gauge to measure the performance of the handful of funds in his study. Although he didn't see any big disparity between how the funds and the index performed, he concluded that these active funds had no inherent capacity to beat the market. He wrote that "funds can make no claim to superiority over market averages."

In what he later called a burst of youthful idealism, he found that some of the funds cost too much and should be more affordable since they were in business to serve their investors. While the fund industry at the time held a mere 1 percent of the shares of U.S. corporations, overshadowed by massive stockholders like life insurers, he hoped for the day when funds would command a much larger amount. Lately, funds have around a quarter of the market's shares.

His college thesis, "The Economic Role of the Investment Company," won Bogle academic honors, but more importantly, it landed him a job offer. A Princeton alumnus, Walter L. Morgan, read the student's paper and liked it. Morgan had started a company called Wellington Management in Philadelphia in 1928. The firm had mutual funds, and seemed a perfect fit for young Bogle when he got the job offer upon his 1951 graduation.

Bogle almost didn't take the offer. "I agonized about the risks of going into what was then a tiny business," he writes in his book, *John*

Bogle on Investing, The First 50 Years. "But, my courage strengthened by the conclusion in my thesis that the industry's future would be bright, I finally accepted the offer. And a good thing, too!"

In the bull market of the 1960s, Wellington was trailing behind competitors. Morgan, telling Bogle he was the heir apparent at Wellington, instructed the protégé to do whatever was needed to speed the firm ahead. The ever-brash Bogle, then 36, chose to merge with another outfit whose four hotshot managers had racked up impressive numbers. "Together," Bogle recalls, "we five whiz kids whizzed high for a few years, then whizzed low." The speculation-fired market of the 1960s gave way to the oil embargo–burdened, inflation-ridden mess of the 1970s. The market dropped by 50 percent. In January 1974, Wellington's board fired Bogle from "what I had considered 'my' company."

Then as now, Bogle wasn't the type to sulk away. Wellington Management Company's directors, who had dismissed him, weren't the sole decision makers at the firm. Another board oversaw the actual Wellington funds. Bogle approached the funds board and offered to run the portfolios from a new company he would start. The funds board argued over that notion for seven months before, by a narrow margin, finally siding with Bogle.

Old Morgan had named the original company Wellington after the Iron Duke who had defeated Napoleon. By chance, a dealer in antique prints came to Bogle's office to show him engravings of Wellington's exploits. The dealer also had some prints and a book about Napoleonic era naval battles. Browsing through the book, Bogle came across a section on the 1798 Battle of the Nile, where Britain's Lord Horatio Nelson destroyed the French fleet, which turned the tide of war against Napoleon. Nelson's flagship was the HMS *Vanguard*. Bogle had an apropos name for his new company.

Nautical motifs are omnipresent around Vanguard, whose employees are called "crew members." The company seldom dwells on its anti-Napoleon roots. Bonaparte was either a warmongering despot or the ruler who brought modern governance to Europe. Either way, defeating him restored, at least for a time, the old royalist system that the French Revolution had thrown out. That's surely not the association Bogle wants. For Bogle, a better take is that the anti-Napoleon imagery demonstrates heroic opposition to a mighty juggernaut—in this case, the rest of the fund industry.

Vanguard became the second-largest fund company, after Fidelity Investments, by superior tactics that would have done Lord Nelson proud. Nelson won his epic battle off the coast of Egypt by splitting his fleet in two and flanking the French ships to catch them in a deadly crossfire. Bogle's method was equally effective: he would charge less.

Starting in 1975 with 28 employees and $1.8 billion in 11 funds, Vanguard has grown to 12,500 people overseeing $1.8 trillion and 160 funds. It takes a tiny 0.23 percent of assets yearly in average fees, a fraction of what the rest of the industry creams off. The average fund charges around 1.4 percent, money that comes out of the investors' pockets to fatten fund managers' paychecks. Bogle is dismayed that so many actively managed funds trade a lot, a practice that rings up expenses in transaction costs, the tariff the funds must pay to buy and sell stocks. Add in the common practice of many managers who keep around 8 percent of their assets in cash, he continues, and investors get even less. The cash stash is kept to buy new stocks, but earns very little for investors while it sits fallow. Vanguard 500 keeps next to no cash on hand.

Bogle is fond of quoting one of his heroes, the Nobel laureate economist Paul Samuelson, on the iniquity of active fund managers: "There was only one place to make money in the mutual fund business— as there is only one place for a temperate man to be in a saloon—behind the bar and not in front of it."

★   ★   ★

Mutual funds, active or passive, are a useful invention, benefiting individual investors by pooling their money so a professional manager can channel it into productive investments that will build wealth. The pro manager spreads it around, and if one group of stocks falters, well, there are other, healthier ones in the pool to offset these slides. At least that's the theory. It works unless an active manager goes big in a favored sector, maybe tech in 2000, and watches it crumble.

Pooled investments have been around for a long time. A 2004 paper by Yale's K. Geert Rouwenhorst shows how the Dutch created a trust in 1774 to combine the resources of investors with modest grubstakes. The trust funded ventures in Latin American plantations, as well as bought securities from central and eastern Europe. The Eendragt Maakt Magt trust, which means "unity creates strength," spawned imitators. Various other European trusts sprang up in the late 1700s to sink money into the promising new United States of America.

Later on in America, ordinary investors could buy into pools designed to profit from the industrial revolution. These creatures, such as Boston Personal Property Trust, which was formed in 1893, are what we now call closed-end funds. Capital is raised from an offering of a fixed number of shares, but investors can't later withdraw their money; their only alternative is to sell the shares on the market like any other stock. This equity capital, plus debt taken out on the side, is used to buy a collection of securities that seldom changes.

The first modern mutual fund was Massachusetts Investors Trust, which debuted in 1924. Under what we now call an open-end structure, investors could put money into the fund and withdraw it, as they can do with their bank accounts. At the end of a trading day, the value of the fund's shares is calculated by toting up how much the portfolio's underlying stocks or bonds are worth. Trouble was, back in the Roaring 20s, the banks that sold these funds had a bad habit of lending way too much to customers so they could buy the products, much like subprime mortgage lenders did in the 2000s housing boom. Guess what happened next? Disaster. During the 1930s and the 1940s, funds and stocks generally were as welcome in American homes as cockroaches.

Smarting from the Depression's horror show, and especially its 1929 market crash opening scene, Washington laid the regulatory groundwork for what would later be a thriving fund sector. To restore confidence in the small if promising industry, Congress passed a law that set standards for funds. The key piece of the Investment Company Act of 1940 was that funds had to disclose their financial condition. By law, the disclosure was required to be accurate. Prior to that, people had to take the word of the sharpie at the teller's window that the fund he peddled was solid and not filled with sawdust.

In the 1950s, the New York Stock Exchange, just then getting off its back, started a program through employers allowing workers to invest automatically. A set amount was deducted from paychecks and used to buy individual stocks. This plan's motto was "Own Your Share of American Business." At the time, not many mutual funds existed— just 150 by 1960. The payroll deduction would later aid the growth of 401(k) retirement plans. The deduction arrangement had another crowd-pleasing virtue: regular investments, in fair seasons and foul, take advantage of "dollar-cost averaging." The constant accumulation of stocks—in bear markets, your dollar buys more of them—is designed to bring you ahead over time. Unless the market dissolves completely, but that's another story.

Funds also got a hand from the Federal Reserve. The inflationary 1970s posed a big problem for the stock market, whose sinking value shunted investors to the safety of Treasury bills. The Fed, bent on defeating the inflation scourge, wasn't wild about the climbing demand for short-term Treasury securities; the onslaught of new buyers jacked up the bills' prices, which in turn held down yields. The Fed wanted the highest yields possible to choke off evil inflation. The big demand for Treasuries tended to mute the Fed's inflation-fighting efforts.

To squelch the problem, the Fed expanded the minimum purchase price for T-bills tenfold to $10,000. It worked. Wall Street responded by creating the money market mutual fund—a pool that allowed investors to own newly lush-yielding T-bills and other instruments that produced lofty interest income. The success of the money funds gave a big popularity push to the old warhorse, pooled investments.

Also aiding funds was a democratization of the investing world— resulting from a sudden drop in income for the gang who sold stocks to the public. In 1975, fixed commissions for stockbrokers ended, and good old-fashioned price competition took hold. With competition shrinking their fees, full-service brokerages weren't as interested in the little guy's penny-ante purchase of 100 shares. But while the large brokers chased the country clubbers' outsized trades, others leapt in to fill the vacuum for small-time investors. Discount brokers like Charles Schwab and the fund houses like Fidelity and Vanguard gathered ordinary folks' investment dollars by the bushel. The discounters started out peddling mostly individual stocks, and later moved into funds, viewing them as a great product for the masses.

Then, in 1978, Congress ginned up a new retirement scheme that saved cost-conscious employers a few bucks, relied on the efficient investment-collection method of payroll deductions, and incidentally introduced their workers to the wild world of investment risk. Lawmakers created 401(k) retirement plans to allow employees to salt away part of their income, tax-deferred until it's withdrawn. Much of the money has gone into mutual funds rather than individual securities, since funds are easy to invest in. Employers offer their workers a menu of fund choices.

Companies loved the idea of the 401(k), as it was less costly than contributing to old-style pension plans and running them. Under the old-style plans, called defined benefit, employers had to maintain a highly regulated kitty of money that paid retirees according to past salaries and years of service. You were assured of getting a set amount. The corporate line to employees was that 401(k)s empowered them to run their own retirement plans, and even to amass decent wealth. The market gods permitting, naturally.

Traditional defined-benefit plans offer employees more certainty, especially since the federal government backs them. Defined contribution plans, as 401(k)s are known, offer employees the opportunity to experience the thrill of market forces. Enron workers saw their retirement money go poof because much of it was in the dastardly company's stock—with no remedy for them except a *c'est la guerre* shrug from the feds. In the wake of the Enron mess and the tech crash, George W. Bush tried—and failed—to change Social Security so its trust money could be invested in the market. Had he succeeded, the 2007–2009 market implosion would have stoked anti–Wall Street ire to a Jacobin-like level.

As it is, funds remain the 401(k) vehicle of choice. One reason that 401(k)s, named after a section of the tax code, caught on is that they are a readily understandable concept to grasp: you can see your nest egg's performance in monthly statements. In the mid-1980s, 401(k)s had only 8 million participants and $100 billion in assets; two decades later, 70 million people were in them, with $3 trillion in assets.

An even bigger reason for the ascent of 401(k)s is that markets, particularly the stock market, go up more than they go down. Mutual funds got a lot of help from the bull market of the 1980s, which spurred excitement about the perceived safety and promise of these newly attractive asset pools. The 1990s tech boom and the 2000s housing mania spurred stocks on to newer heights. Yes, the market experienced a few, ahem, spills along the road. Bogle and his followers have a muscular argument why, in bear markets and bull markets, index funds are the proper place for investment dollars, not the sordid active funds.

★   ★   ★

Bogle's brief against the sins of active fund managers and other unworthy types is evocatively literate and skillfully phrased. In an introduction to the book *The Battle for the Soul of Capitalism*, a Bogle jeremiad against the many sins he sees, hedge fund luminary Pete Peterson quotes Bogle quoting Descartes: "A man is incapable of comprehending any argument that interferes with his revenue." Bad fund managers, in Bogle's view, zip in and out of stocks with no regard for the long term—which means funds have gone from an "own-a-stock" to a "rent-a-stock industry." Bad behavior among managers, as seen by the fund scandal, prompts Bogle to quip: "Bad apples or bad barrel?"

The fund industry's problems, Bogle believes, extend to Corporate America as a whole. Time was, he writes, when *owners' capitalism* was the rule: the people who put up the money and took the risks got the rewards. Now, he laments, we have *managers' capitalism*, whereby the guys who run funds or corporations are paid enormous sums even if they fail; their investors lose, but these panjandrums keep hauling in lovely salaries and bonuses. Only occasionally does the public at large notice. Witness the uproar over bloated pay packages for Wall Street biggies after the credit crunch had laid waste to the economy, the market, and retirement plans.

Institutions, particularly funds, play a curious role in Corporate America, Bogle observes. The top 25 holders of public stocks—and the biggest of them are fund houses like Fidelity, T. Rowe Price, and Bogle's own Vanguard—own a plurality of the shares. But despite the heft they have on paper, the institutions take pains not to wield it. Seldom will a fund manager side with dissidents in a proxy fight against entrenched management.

As Bogle assesses the situation, "our giant institutions have behaved less like King Kong than Mighty Joe Young, the fierce gorilla who was the protagonist in the eponymous 1949 movie." Instead of raging

and rampaging, Mighty Joe Young was lulled into serenity and com-
pliance when he heard the song "Beautiful Dreamer." Sorrowfully,
after various corporate depredations hit the headlines, Bogle notes that
"the only sound we've heard from our investment institutions is the
sound of silence."

Instead, active fund managers are busy trying to make a quick buck.
Bogle does have a case here. Rather than using their muscle to reform
the worst of Corporate America, all too many managers ride market
gyrations and trade like rats in heat, jumping in and out of stocks,
questing for a sudden share-price pop they can exploit. Bogle charts
how fund portfolio turnovers used to be around 15 percent yearly for
decades, even in the go-go 1960s. Since the late 1990s, though, this
figure has zoomed to over 100 percent. In other words, the typical fund
manager turns over the fund's holdings completely every year.

And every time that manic turnover occurs, active managers'
expenses go up. They have to pay transaction fees to make the trades.
Hefty trading costs help push expenses well north of 1 percent of assets
yearly for the bulk of actively managed funds. And 1 percent is what
most financial planners think is the top of what a fund investor should
be paying.

What's more, when funds sell stocks at higher than the original
purchase price, investors get slammed with capital gains tax. Say your
fund bought Cisco Systems stock at $15 per share in March 2009, then
a year later sold it at $25. That $10 gain will shift to you, the investor.
Overall, imagine the fund lost money in 2010, as a welter of bum holdings overwhelmed the Cisco-type scores. No matter. In classic insult-
to-injury fashion, you still are on the IRS hook for that Cisco gain.

Active funds have been very clever at siphoning off money that
otherwise would go to their investors. "Low costs are better than high
costs," Bogle declares, and despairs that the fund industry only cares
about fattening its coffers. In 1980, the industry foisted a misbegotten
gimmick on investors called the 12b-1 fee, named after the Securities
and Exchange Commission rule authorizing the practice. With this
charge, fund providers pass along marketing expenses to investors—to
pay for ads in the media touting the funds, to give financial advisers
commissions to push the funds, and even to mail prospectuses to investors. The 12b-1 fee is larded on top of the regular management fee that

funds take from investors' assets to pay manager salaries and keep the lights on.

Back in 1980, the SEC figured 12b-1 fees were a dandy concept because they would help reverse the investor exodus from funds during the era's stagflation-hobbled market. The idea was that more investor dollars would be enticed into funds, which in turn would be able to service the assets and the customers more cheaply, through economies of scale, and thus lower fees overall.

Well, that didn't happen. Management fees stayed high for active funds, and the 12b-1 part of the fee spectrum has become entrenched, with some 70 percent of funds using it to juice their profit margins. The SEC periodically wrings its hands about 12b-1, and has twice produced reports (in 1990 and 2004) questioning whether investors have benefited from this drain on their assets. The *Wall Street Journal*'s Jason Zweig characterized the 12b-1 process as "somewhat like paying a $100 surcharge on a Chevy so General Motors can keep selling Chevys to other drivers."

As you'd expect, the ICI, the fund industry's trade group, doesn't share the dour take of Bogle and his fellow fund critics on the cost issue. By the ICI's count, fees have actually gone down. Using some clever math, the organization takes the total amount of money spent on fees divided by total fund assets, which have burgeoned over time far faster than fees. Bogle and other critics dismiss that calculation as self-serving and misleading. "When measured against aggregate fund assets, the largest possible denominator, almost any numerator looks small," he observes. Some investors have actually moved to cheaper active funds, but Bogle does not see much price competition in the industry. The sad truth is that most investors don't understand fee structures, and the industry seldom chooses to enlighten them. Bogle adds rather acidly: "Major fee cuts ... have been conspicuous by their absence."

At the heart of the brief against active funds is the performance issue. Or more properly, the drag-ass performance issue. Take Nuveen (formerly First American) Mid Cap Select. During the 2000s, this active fund managed to lose almost 13 percent yearly, far worse than the S&P 500s one-point loss. It churns its holdings energetically, scoring a 154 percent turnover. It charges investors 1.4 percent per year for the privilege, plus 5.75 percent when they buy into the portfolio, an onerous fee called a "load." Certainly, superb active funds also can be found, such as CGM Focus, whose 19 percent annual rise during the decade scorched past almost everybody else. Manager Ken Heebner accomplished this by favoring oil stocks in 2007 and 2008, when they were climbing, then moving to financials for their postcrunch takeoff.

Can you bank on a first-rate active fund to keep up the good work? Unclear. Academics and other market experts have long studied how much manager skill goes into good performance of an active fund, and how much luck is the controlling factor. A Morgan Stanley Smith Barney study, covering the 1994–2007 period, finds that the top 10 percent of managers repeated their leading performance throughout that time. Vexingly, though, many in the bottom 20 percent of performers ended up doing very well, too. The likely reason is that the bottom dwellers' stocks were out of favor; then the cycle turned and they were beloved again. In other words, they got lucky, after enduring a bad stretch.

However, *Advisor Perspectives*, a newsletter for financial advisers, paired low-performing funds with high-performing ones using random selection from 2006 to 2009. Often, the lower-rated fund (using a classification system from research firm Morningstar) outdid the stellar one. Even Morningstar, whose rating system awards from one to five stars based on past showings, admits that its historical performance cannot be used to predict future results.

Another study, from the University of Chicago's Eugene Fama and Dartmouth's Kenneth French in 2009, says that outside of the top 3 percent, it's hard to say whether luck or skill is what drives how well funds do. Fama, credited as the father of the efficient market hypothesis (EMH), has a vested interest in pushing the belief that randomness accounts for much of what happens to stocks, yet his analysis is convincing. As Legg Mason's vaunted Bill Miller showed in 2008, even the brightest investing stars fall prey to human vulnerability and rotten timing—recall that he placed too much faith in financial stocks' innate strengths as bank after bank succumbed to the credit-crisis plague.

But the marketing arms of fund companies are not shy about advertising their active portfolios' track records with frothing enthusiasm, aided by those helpful 12b-1 fees. Vast stands of timber have given their lives to be pulped into newsprint where fund houses have blared their fantabulous results, adorned with a galaxy of Morningstar ratings. Full-page ads routinely contain such self-congratulatory blather as: "Results Speak Louder than Words" and "Global Stocks Fund Ranked #1 Performer." At the bottom of these ads, in much smaller type, are disclaimers saying that past outcomes don't guarantee future results.

Those warnings aren't sufficiently powerful to stop investors from being misled, according to a study by three professors at Wake Forest and Arizona State universities. In the 500-person study, some people were shown ads with the disclaimer, some without. Each group, the warned and the unwarned, was equally likely to believe that past performance was an important factor in deciding whether to put money into a fund—meaning the disclaimer is pretty ineffectual.

To financial consultant Laszlo Birinyi, the preening of active fund managers is too much to bear. These funds, he rails, "are marketing machines first and investing ones second. They typically preach the virtues of buying and holding to their customers. What that means is it's okay for the fund manager to have a trigger finger, but the fund investor should stay put, generating a steady stream of assets and fees, year in, year out."

★   ★   ★

Bogle's fervent belief that few can outsmart the market stems from the scholarly noodlings of Fama and others, but especially those of a fellow Princetonian named Burton Malkiel (PhD, 1964), who is a professor at that Ivy League university and the chief popularizer of EMH. Malkiel's book, *A Random Walk Down Wall Street*, first appeared in 1973 and soon became established as one of the core must-reads of investing, with the tenth edition published in 2011. Malkiel, Bogle says, "sharpened my thinking," and the academic served for a while on Vanguard's board.

Many scholarly treatises have been penned to show how randomly chosen stocks regularly outrace actively managed funds. For many years, the *Wall Street Journal* had a feature where four professional money managers were pitted against stocks chosen by chance—darts were thrown at stock tables on a wall. Each pro independently selected a stock, and the darts method picked four others at random. Results were tallied after six months, with no dividends included. After 100 contests, the darts had triumphed by winning 61. Some question the methodology here, for instance, complaining that six months is too short a period to judge a stock. Still, over time a number of investors came to accept that beating the market is a foolish goal, and concentrated their money in index funds.

The public-relations steam that made indexing possible took a few years to build. In the first edition of his book, Malkiel called for the creation of an index fund: "What we need is a no-load, minimum-management-fee mutual fund that simply buys the hundreds of stocks making up the broad stock-market averages and does no trading from security to security in an attempt to catch the winners." Malkiel, a facile writer with a gift for translating dense technical prose into readable English, was better able to bring EMH into the mainstream than was Fama. The vaunted economist Paul Samuelson, in a 1974 essay in the *Journal of Portfolio Management*, seconded Malkiel's proposal. He slammed the wisdom of most money managers and added that what was needed was an index fund to benefit the frequently gypped small investors.

Bogle secured SEC approval in 1976 to open his index fund. But he initially had trouble getting investors to back his brainchild. Then, to the rescue, came *Fortune* magazine, which had inspired him years before to embark on his Princeton mutual fund thesis. He was delighted to see the magazine run an article entitled "Index Funds—An Idea Whose Time Has Come." The venerated business organ's endorsement was powerfully effective. Bogle suddenly had no trouble raising money and hatching Vanguard 500. "You can now," Malkiel proclaimed in a later edition of his book after Vanguard 500 was a success, "buy the market conveniently and inexpensively."

How true. Vanguard 500, with $106 billion in assets, charges a mere 0.18 percent per year in fees. It turns over its holdings, to adjust to the changes in the S&P 500, only 12 percent annually. Lately, Bogle has come to prefer the even more comprehensive Wilshire 5000, which ropes in the smaller stocks that the S&P 500 excludes. The Wilshire index is composed of 5,000 stocks, almost every one in existence outside of the unregistered penny stocks. Vanguard happens to now offer an index fund that tracks that index, also. A batch of different indexes has appeared since the mid-1970s, to cover small stocks, foreign stocks, and bonds. In each case, during the 2000s, these easily did better than the rest of the fund world in their categories, according to Standard & Poor's.

One index fund innovation has arisen, however, that makes Bogle uneasy, the exchange-traded fund, or ETF. Far more flexible than traditional mutual funds, ETFs are essentially index funds (only a handful are actively managed portfolios) that trade on exchanges during the day. You don't have to wait until the end of trading to see what your fund is worth. Many ETFs are as low cost as regular index funds, and some even cheaper. First appearing in the early 1990s, ETFs have surged in popularity, particularly among professional traders, who use them as hedges. After Bogle stepped down as the head of Vanguard, his successor, Jack Brennan, in 2001 brought out a line of Vanguard ETFs, based on indexes.

This move made Bogle very upset. The new Vanguard ETFs went by the brand name of VIPERs, an acronym for Vanguard Index Participation Equity Receipts. The serpent association seemed apt to Bogle. For Bogle, ETFs run counter to what indexes are about. The stocks inside them, of course, don't change much. But it troubled him that pro traders bat around ETFs more times than a tennis ball at the U.S. Open. Like stocks, ETFs can be sold short—that is, the trader employs them to bet that the index will drop in price. Bogle laments that the average stock is held for 456 days, while the ETF that tracks the biggest tech stocks in an index called the Nasdaq 100 turns over in four days. "There is a crucial difference," he writes, "between designing a product that sells and creating an investment that serves."

This hyperactivity means that some ETFs are too volatile for ordinary investors. Their prices flit around far more than the underlying stocks in the index justify.

★   ★   ★

Now for some more caveats—about regular index funds, not ETFs. Not every index fund sings in the angelic choir. Some don't hew very closely to the benchmark indexes they are following, a failing known as "tracking error," which blunts the advantage of owning an index fund in the first place. One reason for this is that some index funds charge high fees, an un–Bogle-like practice that eats into investor returns, and makes them fall short of the benchmark.

Other index funds aren't big enough and lack the resources to smooth over rebalancing periods, when a manager needs to sell old stocks and buy new ones to properly match changes in the underlying index. This switch–over period can be a hairy time for index funds as the market anticipates their rejiggering requirements, so the stocks they must buy get bid up in advance and become costlier to obtain. Big index funds like Vanguard's use futures contracts to bridge this treacherous gap. Not every index fund has the wherewithal to buy these instruments.

Tracking error also creeps in for those index funds that don't include every stock in their index. Through mathematical juju, they try to replicate the index's movements on the cheap, with perhaps half its stocks, seeking to do more with less. Sometime this works, sometimes it doesn't.

One example of an index fund that perennially falls short of its benchmark is the DWS S&P 500. High fees don't help. The fund's sizable (for a passively managed portfolio) 0.62 percent annual fee is a likely culprit for the tracking error. The fund also slams people with a 4.5 percent load, carved off their investments at the outset, leaving less to work with. As of year-end 2010, the DWS fund over 3, 5, and 10 years had trailed behind the S&P by around half a percentage point annually. A half-point may not sound like much, but compounded over time, which is how investments build wealth for you, the effect is hardly wonderful.

More broadly, the degree that index funds surpass active funds depends on how an index itself is faring. The best-performing index funds, quite obviously, belong to indexes that are doing the best. William Thatcher, a financial adviser at Hammond Associates in St. Louis, crunched the numbers for different stripes of indexes for a 10-year stretch from 1998 through 2007. Middle-sized companies, known as mid–caps, did the best during that time, which was marked by the tech wreck and the beginning of the housing crunch.

The S&P MidCap 400, a benchmark for these stocks, had an annualized return of 11.2 percent, and beat 78 percent of active funds. But the index marking large growth stocks, the S&P 500 Growth, came in with only a 4.8 percent return. And 65 percent of the active funds did better than this growth index, suggesting that the right phase of the moon can favor active managers and their vaunted freedom to maneuver.

More broadly still, index funds have a structural flaw, a weakness that becomes most evident when boom turns to bust. Index funds overexpose you to the hottest stocks during a bull market, and therefore put you disproportionately into areas that suffer the most in corrections or crashes. At the peak of the Internet bubble in 1999, Vanguard 500 had 30 percent of its asset weighting in tech stocks. They were what was sexiest, and investors bid them up toward the troposphere.

As we know, this set up the fund for a dizzying fall once the air went out of dot-com shares. They fell by half. By the same token, financial stocks composed 23 percent of the Vanguard fund in 2007, with similar nasty results. Their slump was almost as dramatic. After the 2009–2010 rally, these two sectors were back up to around 20 percent for tech and 15 percent for financials.

As we saw in the previous chapter, Jeremy Siegel has tried to remedy this flaw by using a different system than market cap for his new, fundamentally weighted index funds—allocating proportions using earnings or dividends or other measures of financial viability. His sometime nemesis, Robert Arnott, sponsors a slightly different version.

Their funds didn't withstand the gale-force winds of the financial crisis well, although maybe the extremity of the downturn makes it an unfair test. Arnott's and Siegel's funds will need a few years before it is clear whether they are the remedy to the weakness of skewing an index fund in favor of the most popular stocks.

Despite the euphoria of a bull market, the old adage remains valid: trees don't grow to the sky. When an index's constituent stocks are expensive, subsequent returns disappoint. According to data by Yale's Robert Shiller, the market's P/E hit 44 in late 1999, right before the tech slump, and 27 in 2007, leading up to the most recent death spiral.

Perversely, hot-money managers and investors, whether they work for active mutual funds or anything else, end up influencing the fate of index fund owners. You'd think this crowd, mostly pros, highly schooled in the workings of the market, would be able to tell when things have gotten frothy, and bail out of stocks. The child learns early that touching a hot stove is unpleasant. If more active money managers backed out of an inflated market, instead of continuing to pump it

higher, fewer investors would be harmed in the inevitable plunge. But
it's the rare manager who wants to go against the momentum of a bull
market. To do that is to risk losing your job. Result: since index funds
are chained to how the market does, the impulses of the active-manager
set affects how they fare.

No one knows how high is too high. When Alan Greenspan, then
the Federal Reserve chairman, delivered his famous cautionary speech
to the American Enterprise Institute (AEI) in December 1996, stocks
were on a tear. Since the 1990–1991 market dip, the S&P 500 had
doubled. The P/E for the S&P 500 stood at 25, well above the historic
average of 16. Greenspan fretted about an "irrational exuberance" that
had gripped investors. Following his AEI remarks, stocks sold off for a
brief time. Anyone getting out of the market then and staying out,
though, would go on to look pretty silly. The index doubled again
over the ensuing three-plus years.

The quirks aside, indexing has delivered the goods for too long to
be dismissed. Which is why many financial advisers say index investing
should be at the core of any portfolio strategy. Defending passive funds,
Bogle writes: "Won't 100 *good* stock pickers inevitably make their picks
at the expense of 100 *bad* stock pickers? And won't the total stock
market provide the same returns as the returns (before costs) of the
good stock pickers and the average stock pickers and the bad stock
pickers combined?" Up to a point, Bogle has a point.

Summary

- John Bogle invented the index mutual fund in 1976, launching
  Vanguard 500. This fund, copied by others many times since,
  mirrors the moves of the Standard & Poor's 500 stock index. Index
  funds give investors exposure to the broad market, hence they have
  greater diversification than with actively managed funds, which
  move in and out of stocks according to managers' strategies.
- But index funds are passively managed—their holdings are adjusted
  automatically and periodically to match changes in the underlying
  index, whether it's the S&P 500 or some other benchmark. Index
  funds, says Bogle, follow the market in such a way that they generate lower taxes, lower costs, and lower risk than do active funds.

- The biggest attraction of index funds: they routinely beat active funds; typically 70 percent of active portfolios fail to do better than the S&P. Proponents of active funds say the trick is to find the winners in the 30 percent that do best the market. Otherwise, they say, you never can excel. Consistently landing in that magic 30 percent, though, is very difficult to do, year after year.
- Mutual funds have roots in investment pools created in Europe in the 1700s, many of them to put money into the young and growing United States. Modern funds began in the 1920s, but the Depression wrecked their appeal for many years. With the invention of the 401(k) retirement plan in the 1970s, both actively and passively managed funds attracted torrents of investment dollars.
- Bogle criticizes active funds for trading too much, as they vainly attempt to outpace the market. Heavy trading expands fund costs, which then eat into investors' returns. Big trading also can inflate the taxes investors must pay on their funds' gains. Many active funds soak investors by tapping their assets to pay for marketing expenses, via so-called 12b-1 fees. What does the extra money you pay get you from active funds? Hard to say. For the elite active funds that do surpass the market, it's unclear how much is due to managers' skill and how much to luck.
- The intellectual framework of indexing is the efficient market hypothesis, originated by one professor, Eugene Fama, and popularized by another, Burton Malkiel in his book, *A Random Walk Down Wall Street*. The idea: since few investors can outperform the market, owning the entire market via an index fund makes the most sense.
- Index funds have flaws, however. Some don't match their benchmark index, a failing that is called tracking error. Chronically coming up short of the index is not good for investors, since the shortfall is compounded over time. Another downside of index funds is that, in bull markets, you are overexposed to the hottest stocks, which poses a problem when bearish times arrive since these stocks tend to deflate the most. When stock valuations are high, subsequent returns tend to disappoint. Since active managers drive a lot of market momentum, they perversely influence how index funds do. There are many more active funds than passive ones.

Chapter 4

From Mild to Wild: Bonds Take Wing

Nick Carraway, a proper young Yale man from a wealthy Midwest family, came to New York in the 1920s to work in the bond trade. This was a fitting calling for a well-mannered fellow from a good background, like Nick. He would deal with his peers, the grandees of Park Avenue and Long Island's North Shore, using his pedigree and good manners to sell them bonds.

In those days, bonds were a genteel and boring asset. Benjamin Graham liked bonds for their stability—gilt-edged corporations like railroads or powerful governmental entities like New York City or the U.S. Treasury would offer pieces of paper that, after a term of several years, were redeemable at the amount invested. Along the way, they would dependably pay interest. Nick's well-heeled customers would "clip coupons"—the certificates that they'd exchange for interest payments.

This was an undemanding line of work. Bonds were unexciting, as no one wanted them to be exciting. Bond prices were fairly stable and had no potential to vault to the stars, as stocks were doing in the Jazz Age. Their investors prized reliability, period. Nick, a bland, naive type who fancied himself "one of the most honest people I have ever known," was the perfect bond salesman for his time, an icon of propriety and order amid the Roaring Twenties fast life in the wealthy North Shore towns of West Egg and East Egg. As the fictional narrator of F. Scott Fitzgerald's classic novel, *The Great Gatsby*, he recoiled at the drunken hedonism all about him. His neighbor, the mysteriously wealthy Jay Gatsby, didn't traffic in bonds; he was a bootlegger with a complex history, some nasty associates, and a yen for subterfuge. When things went awry and Gatsby was murdered, Nick left in disgust, returning home to the more staid Midwest, presumably to sell bonds in peace.

Nick Carraway would not be as comfortable in the 21st-century bond world, where life is every bit as exciting as one of Gatsby's parties. Nowadays, bonds are as intricate and sometimes as dangerous as Jay Gatsby himself.

The man who presides over bonds nowadays is no meek Nick Carraway. Known as the King of Bonds, Bill Gross and his periodically chaotic realm are anything but stodgy. He has transformed how bonds are traded, giving them some sizzle. Gross has shown how investors can turn boring pieces of paper into real wealth.

William H. Gross heads the world's largest bond mutual fund (assets: $238 billion), Pimco Total Return. That fund is part of a collection of Pimco funds, totaling more than $1 trillion, and Gross oversees the whole shebang as chief investment officer. Thanks to his frequent appearances on the investment channel CNBC, his every utterance gets huge global attention.

He is an oddball, someone who would not fit in amid the stylish set of Park Avenue, like Nick did. He has little use for idle chitchat and in social settings seems reserved, if not downright awkward. Gross, who drapes an unfastened tie around his neck like a scarf, collar unbuttoned, and sometimes pads about the Pimco trading floor in stocking feet, comes across as a New Age dude from California. He is given to Zenlike meditations and extended, daily regimens of yoga.

Bill Gross has had a long and eventful reign, stretching back almost four decades. Wringing dazzling results from the wacky world of bonds is no mean feat. Even during bad spells in the market and the economy, he has come through most of the time. In the horrible year of 2008, when so many stock and bond funds lost vast sums, Gross's flagship Total Return fund produced a tidy 4.3 percent profit. This was in a time when bonds backed by mortgages were exploding like rotten fruit. Panicked investors were dumping other bonds issued by corporations and local governments. New bonds weren't being floated because people treated them like rusty, leaking barrels of toxic waste.

How has Gross managed, in fair weather and foul, to rack up bond returns every bit as tantalizing as stocks in a bull market? He's a gambler. But not a bet-the-house desperado slumped over a felt table in Las Vegas, one hand away from either riches or ruin. Gross is like a card counter in blackjack, something he actually was in his youth. He's a cool customer who studies the play and calculates the odds, then makes a long series of modest bets that prevail over an evening. His approach has brought new sophistication to the world of bonds, and it will live long after he is gone.

The stock market has an extensive list of dominant personalities that shaped it: Warren Buffett, Bill Miller, John Templeton, John Bogle, and on and on. For bonds, no one comes close to Gross. Gross plays with bonds the way a stock picker manages a portfolio, moving in on the hot thing before it is hot, selling when its price spikes. Taking a page from Buffett, Gross has adapted the stock market tactics of value investing to bonds. He often finds underappreciated gems and gets in cheap. The value model prompts its adherents to follow a rigorous mathematical analysis to locate these underappreciated goodies. And Gross is very good at math.

Stock investing, of course, has a human element: shares are traded in large volumes every day, often swept by emotional tides. The erratic course stocks followed in early 2009, as Washington wrestled with creating a new federal bailout package for the wounded banks, illustrates that powerfully: up one day on a piece of hopeful news, down the following day on word of another fearful development. But bonds, which aren't traded in the lickety-split way stocks are, don't usually change radically in price from one day to the next. They are more closely tied to interest rates and inflation expectations. Gross's insight is that different classes of bonds behave differently over time, and that he could take advantage of this.

Starting in the 1970s, Gross shook up the bond arena by bold moves among different bond types, a tack that the more stately bond managers of the day never would attempt. In Carraway fashion, they preferred to buy a batch of blue-chip bonds and sit on these, content to collect interest. But since the 1970s, a whole host of new bond instruments has come onto the scene, and Gross has never feared to dabble in any of them. Sometimes he veered into junk bonds, which pay high yields because they have low credit ratings and a greater risk of default. Other times, he went into mortgage-backed securities, formed by packaging home loans into bonds. Or he retreated to U.S. Treasuries, viewed as ultra-safe because they had next to no risk of defaulting—failing to pay interest—since Uncle Sam always can print more money. Gross usually displayed the nimbleness and wit to sell these things before they blew up, as junk did in the early 1990s and mortgage-backeds did in 2007 and 2008.

When the U.S. government scrambled to bolster the financial system in 2009, Gross took a calculated risk: he invested in bonds of ailing financial companies that Washington had bailed out using taxpayer funds. His gamble was that the feds wouldn't permit these companies to go under, whether it was ailing insurer American International Group (AIG), mortgage giant Fannie Mae, or banking conglomerate Citigroup. The Citi bonds he bought were cheap, running around 60 cents on the dollar, and paid hefty yields—the interest payment divided by the bond price—of 13 percent per year. Not many investors were willing to take this kind of a risk. Gross was.

Gross saw before many others that Washington was going to take a bigger role in the economy, which was reeling from the excesses of the century's first decade. He had hired Alan Greenspan, the former chairman of the Federal Reserve, even though some later might argue that Greenspan had helped create the housing bubble that caused the economic mess. But Greenspan is a brilliant mind, and Gross kept consulting his expertise in fiscal and monetary matters. Similarly, Gross in late 2009 brought aboard Neel Kashkari, who had headed the federal bailout effort for the Bush administration. The New York Times quoted

Douglas Elliott, a Brookings Institution fellow, saying that Kashkari would aid Pimco because he "understands what the government is likely to do."

As the Greenspan and Kashkari hires show, Gross is far from a one-man show. He routinely enlists some of the brightest minds in finance. Mohammed El-Erian had a stellar career as chief of emerging market investing for Pimco, left to run Harvard's endowment, at which he racked up important returns, then got lured back to Pimco, where he now serves as chief executive. Some 15 years younger than Gross, he is Gross's presumed successor.

The Bond King has retained a mystique from Pimco's performance, but also from his persona. He is not a predictable fellow. He does things for reasons that at first blush seem murky and even strange. For years, he wore a moustache. Then, at the bottom of the economic crisis in March 2009, he shaved it off. Why? He wrote Pimco investors that his mother, who had "watched too many Charlie Chan movies," thought "there was something shady about a man with hair on his lip."

★   ★   ★

Born middle class in 1944 in Middletown, Ohio, Gross always had a mathematical bent. That deepened during the several months he spent convalescing from a horrible car accident. A senior at Duke University, he was driving one cold night when his Nash Rambler hit an icy patch and skidded into oncoming traffic. He went through the windshield. His scalp was almost entirely sheared off, his face was ravaged, and a lung collapsed. Amid hospital stays and multiple skin grafts, Gross spent his recovery absorbed in a book for ambitious blackjack players called *Beat the Dealer*. It taught how to count cards, so a player could keep track of what had been dealt and figure out the odds of winning the next hand.

Gross developed his investing system during six months at the tables in Las Vegas, where he spent 16 hours daily playing cards and watching other gamblers. He noticed that many fellow players tended to lose because they placed big bets, driven more by emotion than reason. Gross never put down more than 2 percent of his chips, and slowly figured out what the dealer had in his card shoe. He transformed his initial $200 stake into $10,000. Following Navy gunboat duty in Vietnam, he used his winnings to put himself through an MBA program at UCLA.

He started out in the early 1970s as a junior bond analyst at an insurer in Newport Beach, California, called Pacific Mutual. Preferring the California lifestyle, he had no desire to brave New York. The job market was tight then, but his mother, out on a visit, spotted a want ad for Pacific Mutual and told him to apply. He reluctantly did, and got hired.

Life insurers have long preferred bonds to back up their policies because the paper is steady paying. The same interest accumulates year in, year out, to fund insurance policies and annuities. That all worked fine until the wicked, double-digit inflation of the 1970s roared in. Suddenly, with inflation running at 14 percent, a policy undergirded by 5 percent in annual bond interest didn't look very good.

The price of Pacific Mutual's bond portfolio went skidding because richer-paying bonds and instruments like certificates of deposit, designed to keep up better with the wild inflation, were more attractive to buyers. Pacific Mutual managers asked themselves if they should dump their holdings at a loss and chase those higher interest rates. The trouble was that rates bounced around. Buy a 13 percent bond, then gnash your teeth the next month when newer bonds came out at 16 percent.

Gross approached his bosses with an idea: give him some start-up funding and the freedom to trade bonds as stocks were traded. His superiors, exasperated at the pounding their bond trove was taking, decided to give the young man a shot—and they set him up with $15 million in seed money. Gross nearly tripled the money in four years. In 1976, for instance, as other bond managers were suffering with their passive approach, Gross logged an 18 percent return, unheard of for bonds.

Gross and two fellow Pacific Mutual employees, Bill Podlich and James Muzzy, made up the initial team they called Pacific Investment Management Company. In a few years, they were making enough money that they were able to wean their business away from the insurer. Since the 1970s, Gross as chief investment officer had found an increasing number of new instruments that he could use to hold down his risk and boost his return. As he successfully entered and exited Treasury

Inflation Protected Securities (TIPS), convertible bonds, currency futures, and South American debt, his buoyant investment returns made him famous, rich, and powerful.

A typical Gross end-run was his deft play with one of his mutual funds, Pimco Emerging Markets, in 2001. Gross and his lieutenants like El-Erian, well schooled in his strategies, saw that Argentina was headed for economic disaster. The country was beset by rampant inflation and a cruel recession after years of government overspending. Argentines were shipping their money out of the country, where it could be converted into safer dollars.

Pimco responded by shorting Argentine bonds. Shorting is a tactic that is mostly used for stocks. Gross was betting that the Argentine bonds would fall in price. He borrowed a swatch of the bonds, sold them quickly, then waited until their prices tanked. At that point, Pimco bought them back at the lower prices, and returned them to their owners. Pimco pocketed the difference between the higher prices it gleaned from selling the borrowed bonds, and the lower prices it paid to get the bonds back. But Gross didn't stop there. The Argentine financial crisis had prompted panic selling of bonds all over Latin America. Pimco took advantage of that by scarfing up cheaply the stable bonds of Mexico and Brazil, unjustly tarnished thanks to guilt by association. Those bonds recovered, to Pimco's benefit.

★　　★　　★

The great nemesis of bonds is inflation, which eats away at their value like potent acid on metal. Buy a 10-year corporate bond with a face value of $1,000, during a time of 5 percent annual inflation. When the bond comes due, that $1,000 has lost almost two thirds of its value. Meantime, odds are that interest rates on new bonds have shot up along the way, which means the price of your bond plummets. (Who wants to buy a bond with a puny interest rate when better-paying stuff is available?) So if you want to sell it in year six, even ignoring inflation, you will get less than even that nominal $1,000.

Aside from wartime, inflation had not been much of a threat in this country for a long while—right up until the 1970s. By then, the dollar had severed its long-standing link to gold, which acted as a brake on inflation. In 1896, William Jennings Bryan won the Democratic presidential nomination by rousing the party convention with his famous "Cross of Gold" speech—essentially a call to loosen the gold standard and boost inflation, thus lightening the debt burden on strapped farmers. Although Bryan lost, the gold standard wasted away in the 20th century.

Trying during the 1930s to fight a killing *deflation,* which was decimating the value of everything, Franklin Roosevelt devalued the currency by ordering the exchange rate of gold for dollars to increase, from around $20 per ounce to $35. In 1971, Richard Nixon removed the last vestiges of the gold standard as he tried to combat rising inflation. With the United States the overwhelmingly dominant postwar power and the dollar in effect the world's currency, Nixon felt that the only way to restore some kind of order was to let the price of the dollar float. He suspended the convertibility of gold into dollars.

Order wasn't restored that decade. The guns-and-butter policy of Nixon's predecessor pushed up prices, then the oligopoly that was the Organization of the Petroleum Exporting Countries (OPEC) chose to jack up oil prices by an obscene amount. Labor joined the pernicious party by demanding ever-higher wages. Interest rates climbed, and bonds suffered. Next, Paul Volcker took over the Federal Reserve and, in 1979, to choke off ruinous inflation, escalated short-term rates to the ionosphere. Bonds really hurt then.

Come 1982, though, the inflationary trend was over. Volcker's shock cure had worked. Inflation did not end, but it became more muted and manageable, inching up in low single digits from then on. What cost $1,000 in 1982 cost slightly more than $2,000 in 2011. In other words, prices doubled, albeit at an understated and orderly pace. Still, Volcker's victory in the early 1980s was sufficient to set off a historic bond rally that lasted until the 2008 economic meltdown. Over the ensuing three decades since Volcker administered his harsh but effective medicine, long-term Treasury and corporate bonds rose just under 10 percent annualized, slightly less than the Standard & Poor's (S&P) 500—an astonishing outcome since stocks almost always trounce bonds. Then bonds did even better. In the century's first decade, marred by two stock market crashes, the S&P lost almost a percentage point, while the Treasuries and corporates were up around 8 percent annualized.

Bonds' second greatest nemesis is poor credit quality. Defaults, where the bond issuer skips making interest payments, always surge during a recession. In 2007, when the economy was still in good shape, around 50 issues defaulted, a pretty standard level. Come the next year, when the financial crisis erupted, defaults quadrupled. Often, the bonds that go wrong are rated junk, or below investment grade, by the ratings agencies Standard & Poor's, Moody's, and Fitch: 87 percent of issuers that defaulted in 2009 were rated junk, which is BB or lower under the S&P system.

Sadly, the ratings agencies have not always been up to the job of accurately gauging bonds' health. Part of that is because companies pay the agencies for a rating, which critics say is a built-in conflict of interest. But an even bigger problem is that capital structures are getting more complex. The day that Lehman Brothers filed for bankruptcy in the fall of 2008, touching off a scary slide in the market, the doomed investment bank's debt was rated A or better. At the same time, AIG, burdened with an enormous load of exotic instruments called credit default swaps, was a very nice AA when it teetered on the brink and had to be bailed out by Washington. After the financial crisis, the ratings agencies revamped their operations and said they were much tougher on issuers.

Much of the credit quality problem during the Great Recession stemmed from the ubiquity of debt. Certainly, America has never been a frugal nation, despite the fables of nostalgia mongers who like to quote Benjamin Franklin's proverb, taken from Shakespeare: "Neither a borrower nor a lender be." London financial types lent to the Pilgrims for their New World foray. Andrew Carnegie, working as a clerk, borrowed from his boss to make his first investment. General Motors powered to the forefront of American industry in the 1920s by financing the car purchases of consumers who could not otherwise afford such four-wheeled extravagances.

The widespread prosperity of the post–World War II era accelerated the urge to lend and borrow. In September 1958, Bank of America mailed 60,000 envelopes to citizens of Fresno, California. They contained pieces of plastic called credit cards. That, as Joseph Nocera notes in his *A Piece of the Action: How the Middle Class Joined the Money Class*, marked the beginning of the democratization of credit. Debt became even more ingrained in American life. A nation of renters became a nation of homeowners, thanks to an explosion in the availability of mortgages. In the housing boom that marked the run-up to the Great Recession, a whole raft of easy-to-get home loans became available. People could buy a home with little down and pay little interest—until later, when the interest tab soared.

Wall Street, with the aid of fancy new computers, figured out ways to slice and dice all this new debt. Credit cards? Money managers cooked up creatures called asset-backed securities, which were bonds backed by the money due from cardholders' interest payments. That all worked fine until the downturn. Then cardholders finked out on their debt in droves. At one point, 10 percent of card balances were judged uncollectible. The asset-backed paper fell into the basement as a result.

The same thing happened with mortgages. It all started out so well, with home loans the centerpiece of brilliant financial engineering. Since there were so many new low-grade mortgages, known as subprime, banks were happy to sell their loans to Wall Street packagers, who turned these into bonds. The banks got paid to push a bunch of dubious loans off their books, after creaming off tasty fees, and the Street had new bonds to peddle. Buyers were eager for mortgage-backed securities full of subprime loans because they offered very nice interest payments. These bonds were fueled by the homeowners, who were forking over princely sums in interest for the privilege of owning their little slices of real estate heaven.

Meanwhile, companies that had lousy credit ratings were pumping out junk bonds to an eager market. A lot of these were dropped into mutual funds, where investors happily swooped in to enjoy the very pleasant yields.

While all this came crashing down, it's notable that most bond mutual funds didn't suffer as much as stocks did in 2008. Of course, junk funds got slammed the hardest, losing 26 percent. Yet that is 10 percentage points better than the slide of the S&P 500, measuring the broad stock market. Long-term Treasury funds, meanwhile, enjoyed a 9.3 percent increase, as people piled in looking for safety. Funds specializing in investment-grade corporate bonds fell only in the single digits.

That's not to say all bond fund investors were better off than stock fund investors. A number of bond funds delivered returns that stank every bit as pungently as their equity counterparts. A case in point is the ill-fated Schwab YieldPlus, a short-term bond fund that in 2008 succeeded in almost matching the S&P 500s decline—minus 35.4 percent. YieldPlus, an offering by discount broker Charles Schwab, continued to struggle even after the credit markets recovered their balance. YieldPlus had devoted too much of its portfolio to those yummy-seeming mortgage bonds, discovering too late that these things had the nutritional value of the wicked stepmother's apple that Snow White munched on. Alarmed investors fled the fund, making matters worse.

Miriam Sjoblom, an analyst with fund research firm Morningstar, cast aside Schwab's explanation that YieldPlus was merely a victim of broad economic forces. YieldPlus, she wrote, "and its category peers . . . were billed as mellow short-term savings vehicles. As disappointed shareholders rushed for the exit, management had to sell bonds at severely distressed prices." That is, to cash out investors who were leaving, Schwab had no choice other than taking losses by selling chunks of its portfolio for cheap—a sorry situation, and one that could have been avoided.

Another instance of financial engineering that was too clever by half were auction-rate securities, essentially a means of investing in long-term bonds using short-term money. Interest rates would be reset at weekly or monthly auctions. Plenty of individual investors loaded up on these, attracted by Wall Street promises that auction-rates would pay out well and be as easy to cash in as money market funds. When the credit crunch came, though, that promise turned out to be empty. Hordes of investors were left with their money stuck in limbo for years on end.

★　　★　　★

Bonds are supposed to provide ballast to a portfolio. Bonds have nowhere near the appreciation potential of stocks, which can triple or quadruple within weeks, as happened with Google shares after their 2004 launch. What bonds do have is the ability to pay you interest. At the worst, junk defaults run in the teens, which means these low-end bonds have a four in five chance of keeping up payments even in the worst of times. Municipal bonds, from states and localities, have around a 1 percent default rate historically, since their governmental issuers can raise taxes to cover themselves. Amid state budget crunches in 2011, running from California to New Jersey, muni traders kept pointing to the bond category's encouraging history of minimal defaults.

One difficulty with bonds is they often can be tough to buy. Aside from Treasuries and bonds of big corporations, they simply are not that liquid—financial-ese that means they are not available in such abundance that they can readily be bought or sold. It seldom makes sense to buy batches of bonds for anything less than $10,000 a crack. Brokers don't want to exert themselves to bother with much less.

And even at the $10,000 level, investors can get diddled by the bid-ask spread, which tends to be wide for smaller buyers. That is the gap between what you want to pay and the (higher) amount the seller wants. Often, the seller is a brokerage, so you are playing against the pros. Thus, you can end up paying 1 to 2 percent extra on the bond price from the spread. On top of that is a broker's commission. Long-term bonds are riskier than short-term ones, as rising rates skewer the long stuff much worse.

Treasury debt can be bought straight from the government with none of this extra outlay, via a web site called TreasuryDirect. The downside to owning Treasury bonds in 2011 was that so many of them have been issued to fight the Great Recession and fund expanded federal activities that their long-term viability became open to question. In the early part of the year, long-term yields crept upward.

The good news is that large online brokers like Fidelity and Charles Schwab have enacted special deals for individual customers to keep bond trading costs down, charging 50 cents to $1 per trade. Plus, more information is available these days online, using systems like TRACE, which track prices of recent transactions.

In the end, for individuals who want bond exposure, the best alternative is a fund with a good track record and a flexible approach, along the lines of Bill's Gross's Pimco Total Return. The reason is that a professional manager like Gross constructs portfolios with diversity and, one hopes, an eye on macro trends and specific opportunities that nonprofessionals seldom can match without a lot of effort. You pay for the privilege, though. Gross's flagship fund costs 0.9 percent in annual fees, on the steep side. There are other quality bond funds that charge less, such as RidgeWorth Intermediate Bond, which costs just 0.31 percent.

How to tell a good bond fund from a bum one? Bond maven Marilyn Cohen, in her book, *Bonds Now!*, advises: "Always track your bond fund's portfolio of holdings against what its charter says it will buy. Do this quarterly." If the fund deviates from what it says it will do, she goes on, dump it.

A revealing inside peek into how the pros can mistreat individual bond investors is in Michael Lewis's hilarious book about Salomon Brothers during the 1980s, *Liar's Poker*. In those days, before Pimco fully came into its own, Salomon was a rollicking place that controlled many corners of the emerging bond market, such as mortgage-backeds.

So great was the power of Solly (as it was called) over bonds that its bond pros could treat customers with incredible arrogance. Solly's "bond people," writes author Michael Lewis, a Salomon bond salesman then ". . . could also, if they wanted, kick and beat their customers because Salomon was nearly a monopolist in certain bond markets." Lewis explains that Salomon trainees who chose the bond division knew they had a license to misbehave." The ultimate message was lost on no one: "join equities and kiss ass like Willy Loman; join bonds and kick ass like Rambo."

Salomon since has vanished from the scene, weakened by scandal and then swallowed by Citigroup. In this harsher economic time, bond sale folks are nicer. Yet they still can screw over unsuspecting customers who don't know what a spread is until they have been impaled.

★   ★   ★

Gross is not alone anymore. There now is a coterie of brilliant, chart-busting bond managers, who have delivered regardless of the investing weather and have gathered devoted followings. In late 2009, star manager Jeffrey Gundlach, head of the TCW Total Return, left TCW Group after a disagreement with management. Investors pulled billions from the fund and followed him to the new operation he started.

Under Gundlach, named Morningstar's fixed-income manager of the year in 2006, the TCW fund had gained a percentage point in wild and woolly 2008 and over three years had bested its benchmark, the Barclays Capital Aggregate index, by 2.2 points. But TCW Total Return did not fall apart after his departure. The new managers had a big advantage. They had apprenticed at Pimco under the celebrated Bill Gross, receiving a golden training. In 2010, they beat the index by eight points.

Technically, Bill Gross has bosses. But the Bond King's superiors are only nominal. In 2000, Germany's Allianz AG acquired Pimco, impressed by the bond firm's record. But Allianz wanted to ensure that Gross was part of the package. It paid him $200 million to stay. Since then, Gross has continued to run an independent operation, where his strategies are seldom if ever second-guessed by his European owners.

Some market savants worry that Pimco Total Return's immense size will hinder its performance. Many stock mutual funds close to new investors when they get very big, out of concern that any move they make to buy or sell would affect the security's price. If traders hear that a giant fund is buying, they get in on the security ahead of time, aiming to ride the price on the way up. But this trading tactic tends to push the price higher than the fund had planned. By the time the fund starts accumulating, it is chasing a spiraling price.

This phenomenon is a bigger concern for stock funds, however. Gross feels he doesn't have to close Total Return, since bond buying is a gradual process and bond prices are nowhere near as volatile as stock prices. Besides, he says, with global debt totaling $53 trillion, there is plenty of room to play without roiling the waters. Total Return, he told the *Wall Street Journal*, "is a relatively small peanut."

Gross's day begins very early, since he is three hours behind New York, the world's financial hub. He drives a short distance to work every day, arriving at 5:30. Pimco's headquarters is in Newport Beach, near a country club and overlooking the ocean. Known colloquially as The Beach, Pimco has an enormous trading floor. Untied tie draped around his neck, Gross sits in this cavernous space at his horseshoe-shaped desk, studying computer screens, alert for changes and patterns. He may say nothing for hours, as he seems to spiritually commune with the data.

Come midmorning, he takes a break for his exercise regimen, which includes intense yoga. From time to time, he knots his tie and ducks into the TV studio Pimco maintains in the office—to save him time, so he won't have to travel to a TV station—where he opines about the issues of the day on CNBC. Since CNBC is carried on monitors at The Beach and the firm's offices around the world, Pimco employees stop and listen to the great man's musings. It is much like an Islamic call to prayer. Gross is never on the lookout for individual bonds. He leaves that to subordinates. Instead, he looks for broad themes that he sketches out for the troops, who then do his bidding.

Gross is not a gregarious sort. At day's end, he heads home to his oceanfront house and may busy himself with his beloved stamp collection. He has compiled an impressive collection of 1800s U.S. postage stamps and sometimes trades them. In 2006, he swapped a 1918 airmail stamp for an 1868 one-center featuring Benjamin Franklin. Weekends are given over to golf with his wife, Sue. He shuns the party circuit if at all possible. Socializing with Pimco customers is far from his strong suit.

Gross reacts to mistakes seriously. After a bad call on junk bonds, he took a sabbatical of several months to clear his head. His wife told the *New York Times* that he once recommended a Pimco fund to the owner of his local doughnut shop and, when it lagged for a while, "he could hardly go in the shop for his favorite coconut cake doughnut."

For the most part, Gross's calls have been on the money. This big-picture thinker predicted the dot-com bust, the housing crash, and the need for a massive government bailout effort.

His Pimco *Investment Outlook*, which he pens monthly, is a must-read in the bond world. At times, the *Outlook* and other Pimco missives signal a shift in his strategy. In fall 2009, he announced that Pimco was exiting its positions in mortgage-backeds, specifically debt issued by government-sponsored outfits, Freddie Mac, and Fannie Mae. His essays are invariably well written and insightful. In one late-2009 *Outlook*, entitled "Doo-Doo Economics," Gross analyzed the fiscal woes of his home state, California, which suffered from a $26 billion deficit. Hobbled by voter referendums that limited its options and lawmakers too timid to make big changes, the Golden State, he wrote, had turned to "accounting tricks that couldn't fool a grade-schooler." The entire situation, he went on, reminded him of the complex new rules requiring Californians to pick up their dog's droppings, an elaborate procedure that was even more messy than it should be.

Gross likes to be flexible, believing that faithful consistency will hamstring him. During and after the Great Recession, Gross railed against what he saw as the overissuance of Treasury paper, arguing that the government was flooding the market. He proclaimed that the Federal Reserve's low interest rates had pushed investors into risky assets that they would regret. And he quoted from Shakespeare's *Macbeth* in saying that, like life itself, this too would end in grief: "Out, out, brief candle." Later, in 2010 during the European debt crisis, the world raced into the safety of Treasuries, so he reversed himself and surfed that trend.

Many other prominent bond managers echoed Gross's jeremiads about a Treasury surplus. One of the most celebrated was Robert Rodriguez, whose FPA New Income is one of the best-known fixed-income funds. Rodriguez, who races Porsches as a hobby, nevertheless has a risk-averse orientation and kept an enormous amount of his portfolio in cash before the 2008 credit crunch appeared. He continued to warn of Treasury oversupply as capital markets improved in 2009. His paternal grandparents lost everything in the Mexican Civil War of 1910, and he learned to view bonds as potentially dangerous if used recklessly.

That, in some years, kept his performance on the low end, when others like Gross were dazzling. In an interview with public television's Consuelo Mack in November 2009, Rodriguez said, "We protect capital in the negative side, and if we're wrong, we just don't earn as much as our competition. I think that's a better combination than destroying your clients."

★ ★ ★

Treasury bonds are often touted as the concrete foundation of the financial establishment. But a pervasive sense of unease emerged around Treasuries as the nation began, ever so slowly, to pull out of the Great Recession. Bill Gross and Bob Rodriguez weren't alone in worrying. Warren Buffett, many Republicans, and pundits all over began to worry that a Treasury bubble was forming, whose inevitable popping would lead to a mess as bad as or worse than the bursting of the tech and the housing bubbles.

To fight the recession and the credit crunch, the Obama administration committed the government to running trillions of dollars in red ink. The Federal Reserve tried to sop up some of the extra bonds and stimulate the anemic economy by buying billions' worth of them, a scheme called quantitative easing. Circling around the edge of the massive federal debt expansion was a series of ominous *what ifs*. What if the Chinese, who buy bushels of Treasury bonds, chose to dump them or to quit buying new ones? What if all the excess U.S. government spending stokes inflation? What if interest rates, which fell to negligible levels, took the only logical course, and rose, choking off a recovery? What if all the debt made Treasuries lose their vital AAA credit rating? Where would Washington get the money to service this monster debt, and also to pay for Medicare and Social Security once the Baby Boomers have pushed en masse into their retirement years? Then the Treasury market, the cornerstone of the fixed-income world, could collapse. The outcome would be catastrophic.

James Carville, political adviser to Bill Clinton, had it right in the 1990s: "I used to think that if there was reincarnation, I wanted to come back as the president or the pope or as a .400 baseball hitter. But now I would like to come back as the bond market. You can intimidate everybody." That is even more true today.

Time was when Washington needed to borrow only a tenth to a fifth of its yearly spending. The escalation of recession-fighting expenditures has pushed the borrowing up almost to half. Not since World War II has the federal government needed to borrow that much money. Well, the nation survived the vast debt expansion of the early 1940s, didn't it? Some take comfort in this, reasoning that the economy and the bond market will be able to swallow the enormous new glut of Treasuries and come out fine.

Perhaps. But after the war, the United States embarked on a rapid economic expansion that allowed the Treasury debt to be paid for easily and without dire consequences. That was because much of the rest of the globe was in ashes, and postwar America prospered mightily by rebuilding other countries. It had no real competition.

Skeptics may well be right to doubt the wisdom of trusting Treasuries. Maybe other nations' bonds will come to the fore, although most other major economies followed Washington's debt proliferation lead. For a bond investor, what makes sense is to look over the entire fixed-income landscape for the safety and income that bonds classically provide.

★   ★   ★

Following the scary days of early 2009, when the stock market touched its nadir, encouraging signs popped up. Heartened, corporate executives began to float new debt. A relieved Wall Street was happy to help them do it. Companies had been hoarding cash during the downturn as a safety measure, and with interest rates at very low levels, bonds became immensely attractive. Issuance hit record levels. Bonds from industrial companies topped $300 billion in 2009, double the level of 2007, before the recession had fully collided with company balance sheets. Most other kinds of bonds sprang back to life, too.

Outside of U.S. Treasuries and government-supported mortgage-backed securities, every kind of bond had been a loser in 2008, according to Barclays Capital statistics. Among corporate bonds, investment grades lost 5 percent and junk 26 percent. Come 2009, these roared back, up 18 percent and 52 percent, respectively. Much of this was a relief rally. The world was not coming to an end, after all. Emerging market bonds, 15 percent down during 2008, rose 32 percent up the next year. Even municipal bonds, issued by state and local governments, did much better than in horror-stricken 2008, moving from a 2 percent loss to a 12 percent gain.

Nowhere is the story of how fixed income has changed been better told than through junk bonds, a.k.a. high-yield or below-investment-grade bonds, which have made a transformation from unwanted dreck to a key piece of the world's capital structure.

In the late 1970s, according to NYU Stern School's Professor Edward Altman, less than $10 million worth of junk bonds was outstanding in the United States. In those days, companies with less-than-sterling credit could borrow money short term through banks and long term (if they were lucky) directly from insurance companies, in what are known as private placements. These debt arrangements were not good deals for the borrowing companies. The loan agreements often were loaded down with restrictive covenants, meaning if the companies didn't meet certain targets for revenue or earnings or whatever, the lenders could demand immediate repayment. The time-honored route of raising capital from stock was problematical for low-grade businesses. In the stagflation-ridden 1970s, the stock market was so depressed that these companies faced a rough road trying to sell newly minted shares.

Since then, junk volume has grown to more than $1 trillion. New issuance of high-yield paper has for years been between 10 and 20 percent of all bonds, with the number of companies floating new junk between 250 and 325. That new issuance shrank during the queasy days of 2008, and then sprang back to the normal range. Numerous mutual funds have sprung up to cater to junk lovers.

And the allure is palpable: junk historically pays far better than 10-year Treasuries or corporate investment-grade bonds. In late 2008, the fear factor drove junk yields almost 20 percentage points higher than Treasuries. Once the crisis abated, the gap narrowed to about 8 points, a more normal spread, but that was a sweet payout provided that the junk doesn't default. In fact, junk became so popular that by early 2011, average prices had risen to 103 cents on the dollar, and yields were just 3 points higher than Treasuries. High-yield bonds, interestingly, have a closer affinity to stock than to other bonds. Bad economic times hit stock and junk pretty much the same—right in the gut. Rising interest rates, seen in good economic climes, are less bad for this twosome than for investment-grade corporates and Treasuries. Junk's attractive yields tend to cushion its prices better from rising rates.

What has changed for junk since the 1970s, to make it a quasi-respectable asset class? A fellow named Michael Milken.

Milken, who worked for investment firm Drexel Burnham Lambert, got the high-yield religion by reading a study of low-grade bonds between 1900 and 1943 authored by academic W. Bradford Hickman. The Hickman study found that a portfolio of junk, large and well diversified and held for a long time, outperformed a collection of high-grade bonds. Connie Bruck described Hickman's influence in her thorough book on Milken and his era, *The Predators' Ball*. As Milken interpreted Hickman, she wrote, "It was empirical fact: the reward outweighed the risk."

While not everyone agrees with Hickman's methodology or conclusions, it was enough for Milken. A brilliant and driven man with a curly toupee that disguised his bald pate, Milken changed what had been a stodgy, second-tier firm recently cobbled together from several other outfits into a powerhouse. One year in the 1970s, his junk operation had 100 percent return on investment.

Milken had such clout that he moved his junk division back to his native California from Drexel's New York base. There, in swanky Beverly Hills, Milken ruled over his X-shaped trading desks and was a major force in the 1980s' swirl of corporate takeovers. As equities indeed came back to life with inflation tamed, pent-up demand for corporate acquisitions flowered. But now the takeover-minded had a new weapon—a weapon that could be used by both hungry corporations and also by solo financiers bent on gobbling up businesses.

This was the heyday of the corporate raiders, independent financiers who spied underperforming companies and launched bids for them using tender offers, soliciting shares from investors at prices higher than market value. Junk bonds furnished the money for these bids. Raiders like T. Boone Pickens and Saul Steinberg signed up with Drexel, and Milken would produce a "highly confident" letter for them. The letter said that Drexel was "highly confident" that it could raise the amount needed to stage a raid. With junk bonds on the rise and Drexel in the premier position in the high-yield field, such a letter was gilt-edged.

The ascendancy of Drexel had much to do with how Wall Street had loosened up. Securities firms used to be divided between the genteel investment bankers, who arranged underwritings and mergers based on long-standing relationships with companies, and the traders, who bought and sold stocks and bonds. The bankers, writes Bruck, saw the traders as "brutish types with microsecond attention spans." The traders saw the bankers as "masters of little but the long lunch."

Then the end of fixed commission in the 1970s brought these two spheres closer together. Bankers couldn't depend on old links to corporate clients; the clients would seek the best prices and services available. Traders rose in stature because they increasingly were profit centers, reaping the capital ultimately needed for takeover deals. Drexel, which hadn't been around long enough to establish these opposing spheres, was primed to move into a new area that had its own currency and its own goals—junk bonds and takeovers.

Drexel employed the trader mentality in doing deals, the traditional province of investment bankers. Bankers customarily used other people's money in deals and took a fee. Traders put the firm's own capital into play. So Drexel invested alongside the raiders it raised money for. Often, it would get warrants or some other tag-along interest on a deal to acquire a company. At the same time, Milken provided a philosophical cover for his operations, which found form in popular culture from Michael Douglas's speech in the movie *Wall Street*: "Greed is good." Milken set about arguing publicly that takeovers were healthy for capitalism: they made companies more efficient and cleaned out the stodgy old ways and the cobweb-shrouded managers.

Unfortunately for Milken, he overreached. Federal prosecutors accused him of insider trading related to Drexel deals, and he spent time in prison. Unfortunately for Drexel, the trouble helped plunge it into bankruptcy, and the firm disbanded. And unfortunately for the junk market, too much debt had been piled on from these deals. Many savings-and-loan (S&L) institutions, for instance, loaded up on junk to fund real estate and other ventures. When everything collapsed in the early 1990s, junk seemed imperiled as a viable asset class.

The fallout was horrible. Loads of S&Ls went bust, and needed an enormous federal rescue. Other financial institutions were rocked. One noxious example is an insurer called First Executive, a Drexel client. First Executive had sold junk-backed policies called guaranteed investment contracts, or GICs, which were supposed to deliver towering interest rates to their customers. When junk tanked, so did the GICs and First Executive. Customers were left bereft.

But junk rapidly sprang back as the 1990s progressed. Milken and Drexel, while besmirched themselves, had shown America what a flexible and appealing investment junk could be, if only it were handled right.

Bill Gross learned to ride junk the hard way. And he had the nimbleness to realize that he was wrong. In 2005, he thought the economy was going to sag, so he scrambled out of junk into safe Treasuries. He was dead wrong. His flagship Pimco Total Return fund began returning in the mid–single digits, when rivals were blowing out the lights. He lagged behind the Lehman Brothers Aggregate index, then the bond market's benchmark (Barclays runs it now). This was unheard of for Pimco Total Return.

Gross was so distraught from his missteps that he took nine days off and tried to collect his thoughts at home. "People were saying, 'Hey, Gross lost it,'" he later told *Forbes*. Then he came back and bought some junk. And life got a lot better for him and his investors.

To a disillusioned Nick Carraway, optimism seems pointless since the problems of the past make progress impossible. Gatsby's futile stab at joining the moneyed elite proved that. Nick concludes *The Great Gatsby* with this sour assessment: "And so we beat on, boats against the current, borne back ceaselessly into the past." Coddled Nick Carraway, cushioned by his family's wealth, would not have amassed his own fortune in today's turbulent bond market.

Bill Gross, who didn't spring from a wealthy family, has a different take. Skill and hard work do pay off, he feels, especially in the protean universe that now is bond investing. Investing prowess had made many rich, people who were from economic backgrounds worse than Gatsby's. Many of them are members at his golf club, Gross observes. After emerging triumphant from the carnage of a massive economic wreck, Gross wrote in summer 2009: "I remember as a child my parents telling me, perhaps resentfully, that only a doctor, airline pilot, or car dealer could afford to join a country club. My, how things have changed."

Summary

- Pimco's Bill Gross revolutionized bonds with his insight that different classes of them behave differently. So, to great success, he has dodged in and out of the different types. Since he started in the 1970s, a whole new host of bond instruments came onto the scene.
- Still, inflation is the great enemy of bonds and has hurt them badly. Once, aside from wartime, inflation was negligible. Then, in the 1970s, this changed. Inflation today persists, albeit in muted form, and periodically threatens to run wild again.
- Poor credit quality is bonds' second greatest enemy. Given the failings of ratings agencies, credit weaknesses aren't always apparent. The postwar explosion of credit has made discerning quality a tougher job. The world saw that, to its dismay, in the 2008 crisis.

- Bonds are not easy, or cheap, to buy, especially for an individual investor. But new tools now exist to evaluate and purchase them.
- The vast issuance of Treasury bonds to combat the great recession has made Gross uneasy—for fear that an oversupply would harm their prices eventually.
- The increasing complexity of bonds has made them both better opportunities and more dangerous. Junk bonds, for instance, are a promising, if nettlesome instrument. Popularized by Michael Milken, they fueled the 1980s corporate raiders, then went south in the early 1990s. Gross later misjudged them, and got burned. But he learned to adjust.

Chapter 5

The Fast Lane:
Growth Investing

If Ben Graham is the father of value investing, his opposite number is Thomas Rowe Price, who begat the first well-known growth stock strategy. Let's be clear: there is no Graham of growth, no deep-thinking scholar who constructed an intellectual monument that will last through the ages. Price pioneered a practical growth investing technique more in the spirit of a wealth manager looking to compile a good record than of a financial theorist questing for immortality.

Unlike the scintillatingly brainy Graham, Price did not leave behind thick, iconic books filled with ruminations on share valuations. He eked out a few pamphlets and articles, and once said, "I'm not very bright." Unlike Graham, Price did not produce quotable nuggets of wisdom that are repeated to this day by adoring acolytes as if they were utterances from on high. His name is mostly forgotten. Price's most lasting legacy is the firm he built, T. Rowe Price, a prominent Baltimore investment manager that is no longer regarded as a growth shop; many of its mutual funds now have a value tilt.

His contribution to the financial world is that he figured out how to find a good growth stock, distinguishing it from a faddish issue that will fade. His insights offer a clever alternative to the ever-present animal urge to buy hot stocks quickly. In nature, predators instinctively pounce on what is racing away. But what if the fleeing prey is a skunk? Price taught how to tell the difference and how to deal with the quarry, once it is in hand. Not every growth investor has followed his discipline, or any discipline, to their ultimate sorrow.

Price, who died in 1983 (seven years after Graham), surely would have cringed at the late 1990s dot-com darlings that went on to prove yet again the adage about a fool and his money. When Price started out in the red-hot 1920s, the standard Wall Street procedure was: If a stock is going up, buy it and ride it ever higher. Today, we call this approach "momentum investing." Price himself yearned to buy rising stocks; he simply wanted to be sure that they stood a decent chance of continuing to rise. So he laid down some rules, more for himself and his underlings than for the investing world at large, a la Graham.

In searching for potential buys, he wanted them to display at least a 10 percent return on capital, with track records of increasing sales volumes and net earnings. The notion of buying into unprofitable companies, a practice that was popular during the tech boom, was anathema to him. He zeroed in on industries that were undeniably ascending—in his day, aviation, air conditioning, plastics, television—and went for their leaders.

Price's approach sounds similar to what contemporary financial practitioners call "growth at a reasonable price," or GARP, where buying outlandishly expensive rising stocks is avoided. He had a system that he stuck to, and quite successfully. By Train's measure, $1,000 given to Price in 1934, when he opened an investing pool to others, had ballooned into $271,201, with dividends reinvested, by 1972.

If Price bought a stock at $20, he was likely to sell once it had doubled, according to John Train's *Money Masters of Our Time*. But not always. Echoing value god Warren Buffett, Graham's protégé, Price kept some of his especially prized stocks for years, letting them sail skyward. Black & Decker, Honeywell, and Merck were among his long-time holdings.

Price believed that industries and companies have life cycles. As Train writes, Price knew that "the most profitable and least risky time to own a stock was during the early stages of growth." He early on got into Coca-Cola, later one of Buffett's favorites. After World War II, with America's power at its zenith, Coke exploded in sales, spreading to every part of the globe. In the 1961 film comedy, *One, Two, Three*, Jimmy Cagney plays an arrogant Coke executive in postwar Germany, who symbolized the U.S. hegemony and his company's. Cagney's character was an ardent advocate of American consumer goods' superiority, saying, "Any world that can produce the Taj Mahal, William Shakespeare, and striped toothpaste can't be all bad." His big coup was opening up the Soviet Union to Coke sales, which he viewed as a subversive, anticommunist act. From then until the end of the 1990s, the soda maker's stock increased almost 20-fold. But as the 20th century waned, beverage consumers turned to bottled water, juices, coffee, and energy drinks. While today Coke's cash flow remains healthy, Wall Street regards it as mature, that is, no longer a growth stock. During the 2000s, the share price slipped by a third.

In Price's own heyday, the financial world often talked about "the T. Rowe Price approach." That phrase has fallen out of fashion, after too many vicious bear markets shellacked growth shares, and his firm moved away from a pure growth style. As we saw in the value chapter, statistical studies show that growth has done less well over time than value.

Arguments surrounding these findings are endless. Some quibble over exactly when a value stock becomes a growth stock. The value crowd wants to keep classifying one of their newly popular issues, which has finally taken off, as a value stock. They want to demonstrate how their credo has produced a winner—and to pump up value indexes' scores. The other side counters that the stock has passed into growth land and should now be regarded as a naturalized citizen there. Value followers also prefer to include dividends in calculating returns, which gives their stocks an unfair advantage since growth shares often don't make such payouts.

Still, the broader truth is that there have been stretches when growth stocks outperformed value, particularly the 1960s and the 1990s, eras of rapid U.S. economic expansion. Staying out of growth issues during these periods was absurd. With his decades-long holdings in Merck and the like, Price demonstrated that some extraordinary growth stocks can grow for a sustained time. Had he been alive to invest in Microsoft, he likely would have loved the software maker. As lore has it, the tech giant's secretaries became multimillionaires by purchasing their employer's stock. Its shares benefited from a powerful increase, starting at the software company's initial public offering in 1986 and lasting until the 2000 tech wreck, when Wall Street decided that Microsoft belonged in the mature category.

The son of a Maryland doctor, Price trained to be a chemist. Somehow, he became obsessed with investing. A chubby fellow with a dark moustache, he was very harsh with subordinates and did zero succession planning. No one else, in his view, was worthy to replace him. He wanted to be the unchallenged top dog, and insisted that everyone call him "Mr. Price." He started his company in 1937, taking the then-radical step of charging a fee as a percent of client assets, instead of a per-trade commission, the standard arrangement; asset-based fees later became the norm for mutual fund houses. He put a premium on meticulous research and iron discipline. Even in his 80s, Train recounts, Price rose before 5 AM and scrupulously held to his written daily list of tasks.

Like Graham, Price understood that no one style was going to prevail always. He was smart enough to be flexible. After he retired and reluctantly sold his firm to underlings, whose talent he regarded as suspect, the stagflation 1970s decimated growth stocks. He railed against his former company for staying too much in growth, when he had moved part of his personal nest egg into commodities and real estate, sectors buoyed by inflation. But at core, he wanted to invest in companies with shining futures before them. Price always kept a good chunk of money in his sacred growth stocks.

★   ★   ★

Pulling out of a recession, value stocks typically take the lead. One big reason is that they are even cheaper than usual. Investors deserted them during the bear market out of doubt that they were sustainable: they appeared more likely than growth companies to descend into the depths of bankruptcy court, especially the smaller value names. As a recovery gathers force and they start to put up encouraging numbers, investor interest returns to value stocks.

Patterns, though, are made to be broken. The recovery from the 2007–2009 downturn was different, since banks are a component of value indexes. Banks were so fragile that a number of them needed federal bailout money, and their stocks acted as deadweight on overall value index returns. These financial stocks did bounce back, yet they started from such a low point that many reached nowhere near prerecession levels. Bank of America stock had spurted up to over $50 right before the crisis, then tumbled to low single digits by March 2009; it increased almost sixfold as of early 2011, albeit only to around $14, far below the high.

Meanwhile, tech, the heart of the growth realm, dusted itself off after a less serious tumble, amid demand from healthy Asian economies and systems upgrades by American corporate buyers, who felt they could risk spending on enhancements they had been postponing. Stock in Cisco, the networking gear colossus, changed hands for just over $30, precrisis; lost half of that during the bear market; and sold for around $22 by 2011.

Growth stocks owned the 1990s, and ceded the popularity title to value after the 2000 tech debacle. Then the cycle turned once more. From booming 2006 through the scary beginning of 2009, growth again prevailed, meaning it lost less. For a short period after the 2009 market nadir, value nosed into the lead, but recurring doubts about banks' vulnerability to rotten mortgages pulled it back again. For the first three quarters of 2010, the Russell 3000 Growth Index had climbed 9.8 percent, while its value counterpart lagged behind almost two percentage points. Over the trailing three years from fall 2010, a span that encompassed the recession, the growth benchmark was down 3.9 percent annually, and the value metric had fallen twice as much.

Certainly, not all growth stocks (or value stocks) move together. A really strong growth company will power forward with ever-better revenue and earnings, and it won't be hurt too badly in a bear market. The premier example is Google, the search engine business whose comet-like advance has lit up the Wall Street firmament. It went public in 2004 at $85 per share and hasn't looked back.

For the 2007 prerecession year, Google reported revenue of $16.6 billion and earnings of $4.2 billion. Many tech outfits, such as Cisco, saw their financial performance shrink as the economy grew harsh. Not Google, which remained a lodestone for new users and advertising. The up years kept coming. In 2009, revenue had increased 42 percent, compared with 2007, and earnings 54 percent. While the stock was not immune to the overall market rout, it did have recuperative powers few could match, once the madness had passed. Google peaked at around $675 in late 2007, then a year later fell to $300. But by the end of 2010, it had almost been restored to its zenith.

As Price would say, Google is obviously in the early stage of its evolution, showing the same vigor Microsoft did in the 1980s and 1990s. So rapid is its growth that Google in autumn 2010 sported a price-to-earnings ratio (P/E) of 24, higher than the broad market's, although hardly at a nosebleed altitude. Someday, Google's financial results will increase at a much more leisurely pace, and the market will treat it as it treats "mature" Microsoft.

At least Microsoft has kept its status as a backbone of global technology, with its almost ubiquitous software and enviable cash flow. It now is in a comfortable middle age, much like founder Bill Gates, who has diverted his attention to charity. Microsoft doesn't *lose* money for investors; its stock simply is no longer the Topsy-like growth machine of yore. Scads of other high fliers have done an Icarus imitation, their wings melting, careening to earth.

The sad fate of Krispy Kreme comes to mind. The doughnut chain, founded in North Carolina in the 1930s, spread across the nation in the 1990s. Its signature product—deep-fried, glazed doughnuts prepared on-premises and served hot—was a true sensation, with lines forming outside its outlets' doors. The company went public in 2000 at $12 and investors were hit with a sugar high. By mid-decade, the price had vaulted to $50.

Alas, the trend came to an end, ignominious and sad. Profits faltered, franchisees revolted, the stock collapsed. Many rationales were trotted out to explain this humbling turn of events: Krispy Kreme had oversaturated the country with too many stores, the company squelched the magic by selling cold doughnuts in supermarkets, rival Dunkin' Donuts overpowered it (offering coffee, breakfast foods beyond doughnuts, and pretty good doughnuts, to boot), and low-carb diets frightened away consumers who otherwise would he giddily wolfing down fried dough. Red ink became common at Krispy Kreme. The plain fact is that, despite many restructurings, Krispy Kreme's moment had passed. This fad, like those sleeve-blanket Snuggies, unraveled. The one-time growth stock now limps along at under $10.

★   ★   ★

Many mutual funds specializing in growth arose in the wake of Price's success. The prize for the ultimate growth group goes to Janus Capital, the wonder of the tech boom, the despair of the era that ensued. After its 1990s go-go days, Janus illustrated how adherence to growth at any cost proved disastrous. Thomas Price had the wit to diversify out of growth when ill winds blew. Janus took a while to learn that hard lesson.

But oh, its glory days were sweet. As investors fell in love with anything sporting a "com" at the end of its name, Janus and its mutual funds defined the moment. Its portfolios were chock-a-block with tech and telecom names. During that Web-happy time, the company's assets under management expanded at a dizzying rate, from $3 billion to $300 billion. In early 2000, a third of all U.S. investment inflows went to Janus. President Bill Clinton loaded a bunch of his retirement money into the house's flagship, Janus Fund. In 1999, 11 of the firm's 14 stock funds had returns above 50 percent, and four scored triple-digit performances.

In Roman mythology, Janus is the god of change and time, and thus has two faces, one looking forward, one looking back. January, the first month of the year, is named after him. In American investing reality, Janus the fund house didn't change soon enough: in denial, it stayed with those ruinous tech bets well into 2001, long after everyone outside of pond-dwelling protozoa understood that its portfolios were dysfunctional. Although the company appears to have since climbed out of the pit, with a much more sober-minded orientation, it suffered a lot of damage along the way. If Janus's chiefs back in its heady years had asked their namesake god, he would have told them that the past is instructive—namely, that it is folly to focus in one area in the misplaced hope that what is growing now will keep obligingly reaching higher and higher.

Janus didn't start out as a hot-stock fever swamp. Founder Tom Bailey, who had been working in a Denver brokerage, opened Janus in 1970. This was a bad year for the market, amid a recession and mounting inflation. Bailey waited out that rough passage, as well as the far worse 1973–1974 downturn, parked mainly in cash. He then proved to be an adroit market timer and put a premium on researching companies, preferring smaller ones because they were easier to dissect. By the 1980s, he was scoring double-digit results and attracting attention. In 1984, he sold the company to Kansas City Southern Industries, a railroad, realizing a nice payday and also the leeway to run his business with unhindered freedom. *Fortune* magazine wrote that Janus executives jokingly called their parent "the 80 percent minority owner."

Bailey hired numerous talented and ambitious fund managers, such as Tom Marsico from Fred Alger Management. Managers were paid very handsomely and had enormous independence. As the 1990s progressed, Janus racked up those superhuman returns from tech. Marsico performed fabulously at his Janus Twenty, which took the risky tack of investing in only a handful of stocks, and was anointed one of the fund industry's superstars.

But dissension flared in the ranks. Some managers, Marsico in particular, resented that the bon vivant Bailey had grown more disengaged from day-to-day management, opting to spend time skiing, fishing, and enjoying his wealth, seldom showing up at the Denver headquarters. Marsico, after a failed attempt to depose Bailey in 1997, noisily left to form his own funds. Things soured also with Kansas City Southern, which after a prolonged battle spun off the arrogant investment arm.

Janus headed giddily into 2000, laden to the gills with tech stocks, unaware that the whole craze was about to end. It was a slow-motion collapse, not a sharp break. Growth fans told themselves that the March 2000 sell-off, which triggered the slide, was merely a temporary correction. Janus Fund lost 15 percent that year, six points worse than the S&P 500, according to Morningstar, yet close to what other growth funds had dropped. Optimism prevailed that the banshee had passed over the roof and was gone for good.

The portfolio stayed pretty much intact, waiting for the upturn. Then came 2001, down 27 percent. Surely that was the worst, right? Nope: In 2002, it fell even more, 27.5 percent. The double-whammy for the flagship and its kin was that they also had large stakes in Enron, a fraud-riddled company that imploded, and Tyco, hurt by its own scandal. Many Janus investors, who initially had stayed loyal, finally headed for the exit.

Bailey himself fared well as the company was crawling through the mire. In 2001 he unloaded his shares in the now-independent, publicly traded firm at preslump 2000 prices, due to a pact he had struck earlier. A billionaire, he soon retired from Janus and spent his time on his Colorado ranch breeding and training horses. When a *Rocky Mountain News* reporter later asked him about his creation, Bailey responded, "Let's not talk about Janus. Let's talk about life." Back at Janus, more bigshot managers headed for the door. Next came an investigation by New York's attorney general, Eliot Spitzer, into improper trading at Janus and other fund houses. Janus agreed in 2004 to settle the charges by paying $226 million.

The company finally moved away from its willy-nilly pursuit of tech. It canned half the staff and imported new management to impose some order. A week before the Spitzer settlement, it brought on Steven Scheid, a former Charles Schwab executive, as CEO. Goldman Sachs's Gary Black became the new chief investment officer, and in 2006 succeeded Scheid. They dialed back the sovereignty of fund managers, elevated the status of research analysts, and insisted that managers' pay be tied more tightly to performance. They expanded Janus's research scope by tripling the number of stocks it followed to 1,400.

Overall, Janus seems to have survived as a business, with a few blemishes remaining.

Echoing its bad old days, federal investigators in fall 2010 subpoenaed the company, as well as several other investment providers, in a probe of possible insider trading. A Janus spokeswoman defended the "integrity of its processes and people."

Janus Capital may have found stability, yet it is not what it was. By 2009, the 10 biggest Janus funds were all in the top half of their Morningstar categories. That's respectable, just not impressive. Flagship Janus Fund beat the S&P 500 a mere three times from 2000 through decade's end (in 2003, 2007, and 2009). Like the dot-com stocks it once worshipped, Janus—in Thomas Price's parlance—had passed its prime.

★   ★   ★

Momentum is a seemingly mindless stratagem, and to many financial graybeards, a foolish one. Thomas Price disliked momentum investing: He wanted to first inspect a stock before buying, and refused to be dazzled by its recent record of levitation. For momentum players, there's no time to scrutinize company fundamentals. But some very smart people have made killings with momentum, using judicious measures based not on balance-sheet dissection, but on the latest stock price trends.

One is hedge fund operator Clifford Asness, a scholarly, bearded Goldman Sachs alumnus, who studied under Eugene Fama, the father of the efficient market hypothesis (EMH), in the 1980s at the University of Chicago. EMH, as we've noted, holds that beating the market is very difficult, and is the academic bedrock for index funds. Fama's work shows that small stocks and value stocks tend to do best over time. Asness, though, found that a large, diversified group of momentum stocks could indeed outpace the market. With the famed professor as his PhD thesis adviser, Asness told the *New York Times* that he "was nervous telling Fama that I wanted to investigate momentum investing." The older man, no slave to anyone's doctrine, even his own, encouraged Asness to go where the data led. Asness came to believe that the market was not always efficient, that it was pulled by the gravity of human emotions, and that this could be exploited. After his tour of duty at Goldman, Asness opened his hedge fund firm, AQR Capital, and with the help of a computer model, did very well hitching investments to what was trendy.

AQR concocted its own momentum index, taking the top third (based on price gains) of the 1,000 largest-valued U.S. stocks over the preceding 12 months, and rebalancing the list quarterly. The thinking here is that a stock's momentum tends to crap out 6 to 12 months from when it begins climbing. The rebalancing culls out those whose fire has subsided. In a study the firm did, called "The Case for Momentum Investing," the AQR Momentum Index's annual returns are back-tested against the more static Russell value and growth indexes for 30 years ending in April 2009. The rotating roster of AQR stocks increased 13.7 percent annually, beating the value bogey by two percentage points and the growth index by three.

In summer 2009, AQR launched three mutual funds that embodied this method, for large, small, and international stocks. Over the following 18 months, which, except for second quarter 2010, were good for equities, the trio did better than the market by wide margins, although such a short stint is no way to judge their staying power. The funds did turn over their holdings completely during that time, a practice that runs up trading costs and eats into investor returns. Expenses are relatively low at these funds because they don't require a lot of costly research. As indexes, their holdings are automatically reallocated.

★   ★   ★

How different that is from the bathrobe-clad day traders who merrily clacked away at the PCs in their rec rooms during tech's wonder years. Few individual day traders are around anymore since the tech disaster proved it is so very easy to wipe out. Any lapse of alertness, as your positions flicker on the screen, can be deadly. Oops, you missed the negative analyst note on that stock you bought 15 minutes ago? A real shame you were getting a snack when its price went gurgling down the toilet. That is why today this style of trading is found mainly at hedge funds and other perches for professional traders.

Pros often seek to be in and out of a stock in a matter of seconds. Some professional traders do all their business right after the market opens and just before it closes, as those periods are when the most volume occurs. In the morning, overnight orders and new institutional plans appear. In the late afternoon, funds that track indexes rejigger their holdings. At Briargate Trading in New York between 11 AM and 2 PM, the partners take long lunches, visit their kids' schools, or play tennis. Once, they walked five miles to Brooklyn to sample a celebrated pizzeria. Then they returned to their terminals to trade energetically.

Longer-term growth players occupy safer and less fraught terrain than the lightning traders. A spiritual descendant of Thomas Rowe Price is Joe Milano, who manages the New America Growth fund, which happens to be an offering from a company called T. Rowe Price. He doesn't churn his portfolio anywhere near what Cliff Asness does.

Milano's fund was ahead 2 percent yearly during the Lost Decade, when the S&P 500 was down 1 percent. New America Growth consistently ranks near the top of Morningstar's growth category. Milano has big concentrations in tech and health, which have done well for him.

And like a value manager, he can be patient. Monsanto, the world's largest seed maker, has luxuriated in robust growth for years, and got knocked back like many others in the Great Recession. Headwinds remained even as the economy came back to life: European and Japanese officials are suspicious of its genetically altered seeds, designed to yield more and better crops even in unhelpful weather, and U.S. farmers resist higher costs for Monsanto products. With a P/E of 29, this is not a cheap stock. Still, Milano reasons that a growing world economy means that more food will be needed—and that Monsanto stock will get its mojo back. "China and India want to eat more meat," he says. "Livestock need more grain. That's where Monsanto comes in."

Old Mr. Price had a good point that companies have life cycles. But there are second acts for growth stocks. If Milano is right, Monsanto will be one, burnishing the growth manager's holdings anew. The best showcase for such rejuvenation is Apple, which had once been the quintessential growth stock. Forrest Gump, the lucky idiot played in the movie by Tom Hanks, got rich owning its shares. By the 1990s, Apple teetered on the edge of oblivion. Microsoft owned the tech world.

Then this ill-shaven chap named Steve Jobs, who had been thrown out of the company he had founded, returned to Apple. He generated an amazing stream of hit gadgets, like the iPhone. In May 2010, Apple's transformation allowed it to overtake Microsoft as the most valuable tech company. An Apple share gained 50 percent in 2010, rising to over $300.

That is a wonderful growth story. And that is exactly why people invest in growth stocks.

Laszlo Birinyi: Follow the Money

Temperamentally and philosophically, Laszlo Birinyi has a lot in common with Mr. Price. A forthright member of the growth camp, money manager and financial consultant Birinyi is as alert as a hovering hawk for what is moving. But he is skeptical

Laszlo Birinyi: Follow the Money *(Continued)*

about the wisdom of the market as a whole, knowing that public enthusiasms can be misplaced. He and his crew of smart young associates, working out of a small office in Westport, Connecticut, track investment dollar flows to see what stocks are attractive. And not just any dollars. Birinyi homes in on institutional and other smart-money professional buyers, and ignores what clueless retail investors are doing.

Growth investors tend to be bullish: A downbeat market is poison for stocks that aim for the sky. Birinyi loses patience with market commentators who always discern gloom ahead, a mind-set he calls the Cyrano Principle, after the fictional French character Cyrano de Bergerac, who believes that his huge nose prevents his adored Roxane from ever loving him—a self-fulfilling prophecy. "The negative case," Birinyi says, "is always more reasonable." Yet, like Price, Birinyi knows that sunny seasons don't last forever. He warned of trouble ahead in 2007. In 2008, he called a bottom, a tad prematurely, and began buying, mainly the well-known large-cap stocks he prefers.

Birinyi was born in Hungary during World War II. Once Germany was defeated and the Soviets took over, his parents escaped with the small child to the United States, where his father worked as a stonemason. With his MBA in hand from New York University, Birinyi became a trader and joined Salomon Brothers, where he rose to be head of equity research. He left to form his own firm, Birinyi Associates, in 1989.

He has a curmudgeonly side to rival that of Price. Birinyi is disdainful of the lickety-split trading mentality. This is asking for trouble, he says, dubbing the high-frequency approach "Murphy's Law by mouse click." It came as no surprise to him that the May 2010 flash crash occurred, when the Dow Jones Industrial Average dropped 600 points in five minutes, its biggest one-day decline ever, only to quickly retrace its losses.

Summary

- Thomas Rowe Price comes the closest to being the Ben Graham of growth. The founder of investment firm T. Rowe Price, he laid down rules for discovering which growth issues were worthwhile. He wanted stocks with a 10 percent return on capital, plus widening sales and earnings. He believed stocks have life cycles, and the best time to invest is early.

- Value stocks usually do best coming out of an economic downturn, but growth prevailed following the Great Recession due to the prevalence of devastated financial shares in the value category. Many studies have shown value beating growth over time, yet some eras belong to growth, such as the 1960s and 1990s, and avoiding it then would be ridiculous.

- Stellar individual growth names like Google can do relatively well when a recession hits. Krispy Kreme is a sad example of a faddish growth stock that has faded.

- The ultimate growth shop was Janus Capital, highly popular in the 1990s, as it scored soaring returns from the tech craze. Thomas Price thought it wise to diversify out of growth, although Janus didn't heed that wisdom and stayed in tech too long. Janus suffered when tech crashed. It now is more conservative, not the hotshot it had been.

- Momentum investing—simply buying what is going up—is derided as a mindless exercise. Not always, however. Cliff Asness's AQR formed a growth index that, according to its back-testing, beat the Russell growth and value indexes over three decades. The Asness formula is to take the top third of U.S. stocks, by price performance, and rebalance quarterly.

- Traders these days are in and out of stocks in seconds. The 1990s' day traders discovered that this is no place for amateurs. But some longer-term growth funds have done well through active management that avoids lightning trading. Joe Milano, a fund manager at T. Rowe Price and the old man's spiritual descendant, displays value-like patience waiting for a good growth stock to recover.

- Despite Price's admonition about company life cycles, there are second acts in growth. Apple, formerly a surging stock that had lost its way, has been rejuvenated and in 2010 overtook Microsoft as the most valuable tech company.

Chapter 6

Over There:
International Investing

John Templeton saw it before just about anyone else in the United States: the investing allure of faraway places with strange-sounding names. In the mid-20th century, this genial and optimistic soul from small-town Tennessee took his cosmopolitan insight, that international investing was a ripe orchard to pick, and convinced U.S.-centric folks that opportunities lay beyond native shores. More than anyone, Templeton introduced regular American investors to the tantalizingly strange mosaic of foreign stocks.

His timing was exquisite, coming amid the first major cracks in American insularity. Separated from much of the world by immense oceans, imbued with a sense that Europeans were twits and other foreigners were simply bizarre, Americans have traditionally felt themselves special and apart. While the United States is a nation of immigrants, the ideal has been to assimilate foreign-born newcomers. Critics of bilingual education say that English is the nation's official language, so to them, teaching Latino kids in Spanish is wrongheaded and even anti-American. General public knowledge or concern about the rest of the globe has seldom been strong in the United States. For many Americans, everybody else's soccer mania is weird. Ask a European what the country code is for his phone, and odds are he will know; ask an American, and he won't.

Yet over the past 100 years, and particularly since World War II, a growing subset of Americans became interested in what was going on beyond their borders, first by following the news, then by buying foreign stock. Today, U.S. investors still overwhelmingly favor securities from their homeland: a mere 26 percent of equity mutual fund assets in America are foreign, says the Investment Company Institute, even though non-U.S. stocks make up more than half of global capitalization. That said, international investing is way up from practically nothing four decades ago.

The emergence of the United States as the dominant economy, the involvement of its citizens in wars overseas since the early 20th century, and the surge of tourism increased American awareness of life in other lands. Politicians starting with George Washington once warned that entanglement with the corrupt Old World was a very bad idea. Nice try. As America grew economically, it had no choice about becoming a major actor in world affairs, if only to protect its swelling overseas interests.

International trade has been very important to the nation's economy since colonial times. America began as an exporting country, with tobacco, cotton, and fur the initial main products, amid minimal competition. Later, the United States dominated in manufactured and agricultural goods, with big exports to those needing its machinery and food. World War II's massive destruction gave mighty American corporations a vacuum to fill. They readily expanded into devastated foreign markets.

Then, gradually, as other countries caught up, America became a net importer, and thus more beholden to providers elsewhere. Try finding consumer electronic devices made totally in the United States today. Only 6 percent of the parts in an Apple iPhone are from

America; the device is assembled in China, with components provided by Japan, Germany, and South Korea.

This shift from overweening U.S. dominance was inevitable. Economist David Ricardo's (1772–1823) theory of comparative advantage holds that countries predominate in what they are best at producing—and that this is a protean condition. Once, the United States was the leading steel maker, a distinction that corroded as other places learned how to turn out the metal more cheaply. America was self-sufficient in oil, then the fields started playing out. The 1970s' Arab oil embargo, sparked by American support for Israel in the Yom Kippur War, was a bracing tonic showing that what happened in previously obscure regions could affect the United States economically. As gas lines formed, a nasty recession ensued.

There is no stopping the power of rising competitors. Some view their ascent as a sign of American decline. Official U.S. policy since the 1940s, no matter what party was in control, has been to foster free trade, on the theory that economic growth is not a zero-sum game, where one nation's gain is another's loss. While electronic gizmos are mainly made in Asia, multitudes of jobs have been created in America to market and distribute them. Tellingly, trade is less and less of a weapon in an interdependent world. During the oil embargo, suggestions that the U.S. retaliate against Saudi Arabia and its pals didn't go very far.

A general push to remove tariff barriers across the map after World War II accelerated trade among nations. No one wanted to revisit the high tariff walls erected amid the Depression, constructed in an attempt to help local economies—a misguided step that actually ended up deepening the mess. As what once were called Third World nations became thriving export machines, the West, which had erased many of its tariffs, was eager to buy their stuff. Thomas Friedman, in his book *The World Is Flat: A Brief History of the 21st Century*, chronicles the transformation of previously stunted economies like those of China and India into export titans. The end of the Cold War and the spread of information technology, he writes, were major catalysts.

The successful influx of foreign products into the United States since the 1960s, from Japanese electronics to European cars to Saudi oil, showed Americans that powerful economic engines were revving up across the water. As Wharton's Jeremy Siegel points out, U.S. stocks made up 90 percent of global equity capitalization in 1945, two thirds in 1970, and less than half now. Embracing international investments became a stupendously obvious way for Americans to get in on rapid-fire growth.

The bunch that summered at Newport and took coming-of-age Grand Tours through the world's glittering capitals had long been invested overseas. The mass affluence that followed World War II meant that less exalted Americans now owned their own homes, visited Europe, had access to credit, and wanted a taste of the investment opportunities that the toffs took for granted.

John Templeton founded mutual funds made up of foreign stocks, back when it was a rare and exotic notion. In the postwar years, when his fellow Americans viewed Japan as little more than a defeated enemy, he was an early investor in obscure companies with funny-sounding names, like Hitachi and Fuji. With an eye for bargains, he believed not just in value stocks but in value nations. His Templeton Growth Fund, launched in 1954, went on to record some of the best returns ever. Each $10,000 placed in his fund since its inception, with dividends reinvested, grew to $2 million by 1992, when he sold the fund and others he'd founded to Franklin Resources. In 1999, *Money* magazine dubbed him "arguably the greatest global stock picker of the century."

With his deep value leanings, Templeton was always on the lookout for how foreign developments might generate opportunities. In 1939, as war ignited in Europe, he borrowed $10,000 and bought 100 shares in 104 companies with stocks selling below $1; 34 of them were in bankruptcy. Several years later, the overall return proved to be gigantic.

He was alert for what he called "points of maximum pessimism," when the best bargains abounded. Asia's 1997 economic near-collapse was a wonderful buying opportunity for him. Templeton had an eye for these bad spells. He predicted the tech bust, and made a bundle shorting Nasdaq stocks before the March 2000 tumble. In 2004, he prognosticated the end of that bull market due to too much debt, mainly for overpriced housing. "When I was young in the three years after 1929, a high proportion of people lost their homes in foreclosure," he told *Forbes*, four years before the housing-fired financial crisis shook civilization. "It's likely to happen again. It's not abnormal. It's cyclical, and it will put pressure on all prices."

At annual meetings of his fund group, Templeton, who was knighted by Queen Elizabeth, commanded the type of adoration Warren Buffett inspires. At the conclusion of one Templeton funds gathering, a well-dressed elderly lady clasped his hand with both of hers. "Thank you, Sir John," she said, her voice breaking. "Thank, you, thank you for all you have done for me."

"It wasn't much," he told her in his courtly Southern fashion. "What it took was peeking over the horizon."

★   ★   ★

From parochial beginnings, John Templeton became a true citizen of the world, transforming himself from the son of a small-town businessman into a sophisticated investment strategist with an intricate knowledge of even the smallest countries. Deeply religious (he was a Presbyterian elder and served on the board of the American Bible Society), Templeton had an optimistic view of humanity and believed that things eventually turn out for the best, although at the outset they may look lousy.

To Templeton, a grand purpose animated the universe, in the form of a benign creator who guided mankind toward a better tomorrow. He contended that faith and finance were entwined, and started company annual meetings with a prayer. He was unfailingly genial, and had a Norman Vincent Peale view of the utility of positive thinking. "Dwelling on the good things leads to power, peace, and success," he once said, "whereas a focus on the negative leads to weakness, pain, and failure."

While his family had deep roots in the South, which he treasured, and he himself harbored staunch conservative views, Templeton never seemed much of a flag waver. When other young men marched off to war in the 1940s, he stayed on Wall Street. He incorporated his first fund in Canada, which at the time had no capital gains tax, meaning Uncle Sam took one on his furry chops. The Canadian maneuver proved to be a boon for Templeton's investors, surely, and an early example of American asset offshoring. In the late 1960s, he renounced his U.S. citizenship and moved to the Bahamas, which had—guess what?—much lighter taxes. He explained his move as getting away from the Street's herd mind-set.

Templeton had a much broader picture than his contemporary money managers in America, due to his extensive early travels abroad. A top scholar at Yale, he won a Rhodes scholarship to Oxford, where he studied law and acquired the tastes of an English gentleman—useful when he later became a British subject and received his knighthood, awarded for his philanthropic endeavors. After his stay amid the dreaming towers of Oxford, he and a friend embarked on a seven-month trip covering 35 countries. They traveled on the cheap, as money was tight in the mid-1930s.

Templeton learned a lot about the myriad cultures he encountered, although he refrained, at least outwardly, from judging them for good or ill, which, from the cold-blooded viewpoint of an investor, may be a plus. For six days, he attended the 1936 Berlin Games, presided over by Adolf Hitler. His biographer, Robert Herrmann, writes that Templeton took in the opening ceremony each morning, 15-minute displays by Nazi loyalists shouting, "Seig heil." Ever polite and upbeat, Templeton years later had no comment on the Third Reich to his biographer beyond that tepid, matter-of-fact observation.

Templeton had an unflappable nature, and nothing on his journey seemed to faze him, no matter how uncomfortable or scary. He and his pal were arrested for vagrancy in Bulgaria because they were sleeping in a public park. Unable to explain themselves to the non-English-speaking cops, they spent the night in a flea-infested jail. By the Sea of Galilee, tracking the ministries of the disciples James and John and living in desert-dwellers' tents, they were almost stabbed to death. A mob of knife-wielding Arabs thought they were British, who then were in charge of Palestine, or Jewish. Templeton's hosts convinced the throng that the Westerners belonged to neither much-hated group, and no blood was spilled. The young men traveled to China, India, and Japan, at times sleeping on wood-plank beds. Templeton told his biographer that the no-frills expedition let him understand distant peoples and cultures in a way that a luxury tour could never do. The trip, Herrmann writes, led to Templeton's "pioneering decision to search the world for investing opportunities."

Search, he did. Even after he sold his company and retired to his lovely mansion in Lyford Cay, the Bahamas, overlooking a golf course and the ocean, he kept busy managing his own money. For almost two decades until his death at 95 in 2008, he maintained an active investing regimen. In 2004, he bought lots of stock in Kia, the South Korean carmaker, terming it a bargain, and saw it almost triple within a year. He went after bonds issued by Singapore and Hong Kong, as their governments had little debt. Always, Templeton wanted to know all he could about a country and its businesses before he invested. He rummaged through financial statements and also quizzed executives and company observers.

This billionaire, who never flew first class and lived without ostentation, spent his pile on philanthropy, largely in pursuit of religious matters. He established his Templeton Foundation, to encourage scientific research and explore science's relationship to the Almighty, a concept now known as religious science. He set up the Templeton Prize to reward living innovators in spiritual thought. The first winner was Mother Theresa of Calcutta. The fortune that made this giving possible started in one of the countries that he visited as a young vagabond tourist—Japan.

★   ★   ★

The ever-prescient Templeton was heavily into Japanese securities from the 1950s until the mid-1980s, when he sensed something amiss and bailed, a few years before the Land of the Rising Sun headed into dusk. During the first two decades that Templeton invested in Japan, the island nation had the fastest growth of any economy in history. Japan's highly educated, disciplined, and thrifty population consecrated itself to the goal of joining the great nations, an objective that had proved elusive in the 1930s and 1940s, when Tokyo sought Asian supremacy through military conquest. Luckily for postwar Japan, the U.S. nuclear umbrella shielded it from diverting resources into its military, leaving it to concentrate on expanding industry and exports.

In the 1980s, Japan became the world's second-largest economy. Japanese businesses, with their much-vaunted attention to the long term (as opposed to American companies' obsession with next quarter's numbers), inspired universal envy. Much of the growth was owing to the giant oligopolies called *keiretsu*, alliances among companies to achieve scale. Books appeared extolling Japanese genius and denigrating American benightedness, such as Eamonn Fingleton's 1995 jeremiad, *Blindside: Why Japan Is Still on Track to Overtake the U.S. by the Year 2000.*

You may have noticed that didn't quite happen, not in 2000, not in 2010, when Japan's gross domestic product (GDP) totaled a little less than a third of America's. Insane Japanese real estate speculation in the 1980s led to a spectacular bubble bursting. Deflation, a phenomenon America wrestled with in the Depression, paralyzed Asia's one-time miracle spinner. While Japan began inching out of its stagnant funk around 2005, right before the Great Recession, the old swagger was gone. Now analysts were diagnosing structural weaknesses in the erstwhile Japanese juggernaut.

A common assessment: Japan was terrific at marshalling its advantages to advance itself from wartime rubble to prominence, but could only do so using large-scale businesses, namely the *keiretsu*. The next stage needed entrepreneurial talent—the Mark Zuckerbergs who create empires in their college dorm rooms. The Japanese prefer to enlist in a huge and benevolent corporation, rather than braving the risk of failure that starting your own business entails.

John Templeton knew with dauntless clarity that Japan's growth story was over before it had peaked, that the country was overvalued, and thus he exited with his typical good timing. He cut the Japanese holdings in his portfolio from 60 percent to 2 percent. But toward the end of his life, this eagle-eyed investor espied the promising profile of another Asian nation that threatened to overtake the United States. As he told the *Financial Intelligence Report*, "within a short period of 20 years, the gross national product of China will be larger than America's. With four times the U.S. population, that is definitely achievable."

* * *

In the economic size sweepstakes, China overtook Japan for second place at the end of 2010. That left China just shy of $5 trillion and the United States at three times that. Could the prognostication of

Templeton and other China lovers come true? China has been running, by its reports, at an annual growth rate of 9 percent. Let's say America can only eke out a 3 percent rate, which is in keeping with the perennial chorus of gloom and doom that has been foretelling U.S. decrepitude forever.

Then, by 2021, China would be at half of the U.S. GDP of $20 trillion. By 2031, though, China would have nosed past America ($28 trillion to $27 trillion). A possible precursor is that, in 2010, China supplanted the United States as the largest consumer of energy, according to the International Energy Agency. All that was the consequence of Beijing's pell-mell campaign to power the factories and other new infrastructure sprouting across its landscape, burning oil, coal, natural gas, and whatever else it needs.

A latter-day John Templeton, starting out now, would have to ask how sustainable this latest miracle is. The great man himself was hardly infallible: in the 1990s, he largely stayed out of health care, thinking it overpriced—and missed out on one of the best sectors for sustained growth (the world's aging population and medical advances are its drivers). On the surface, China appears to be an improved version of the Japan model. It has sunk lots of capital into education, infrastructure, and technology. With $2 trillion in foreign currency reserves, it is buying assets all over the earth, from an Australian mining company to a Kazakh oil producer. These gargantuan financial reserves permit China to manipulate its currency, which is an estimated 40 percent undervalued versus the dollar, a brawny advantage for its exporting efforts.

The handoff from Japan to China as the favored up-and-comer has occurred within a generation, a blink in the vast span of history. Japan's Nikkei 225 index topped out at 38,916 in December 1989; the key Japanese benchmark stood at one quarter of that in 2010 (it was somewhat higher before the 2008 financial crisis). The Shanghai Stock Exchange, closed in 1949 after the Maoist takeover of the country, was reopened in 1990 and, aside from a downdraft in 2008, climbed steadily. Since 2005, it has tripled.

Yet there is ample reason to be skeptical that China can avoid the Japan snare. Centralized planning is even more pronounced in China, where the communist government owns many of the major companies, making Japan's *keiretsu* look like something out of Ayn Rand.

Chinese executive ranks tend to be occupied by politicos who serve at the behest of the regime, not business types answering to shareholders. As Shaun Rein, managing director of the China Market Research Group, explains it: "Imagine if President Obama directed Lloyd Blankfein to leave Goldman Sachs for Morgan Stanley for a few years before moving to Bank of America and then replacing Ben Bernanke at the Fed." Will state-run corporations, where politics is paramount, be able to out innovate the West once the early growth stage is over?

Moreover, away from the industrial coast, China has a vast poverty-stricken population that is restive. Political ferment stirs beneath the surface of this authoritarian state. The Chinese military is vital to the Beijing regime less for its ability to defend against neighbors like Taiwan than for its use as a force to control it own citizens. Witness the military might massed in Tiananmen Square in 1989, when hundreds of protesters were killed.

Civil liberties and the rule of law are sometime occasions in China. Won't that choke off its much-lauded dynamism eventually? Dissident Liu Xiaobo was thrown into prison, and when he won the Nobel Peace Prize in 2010, his relatives weren't allowed to leave the country to receive it. Free use of the Web is curbed, thwarting the exchange of ideas, the lifeblood of a dynamic economy. Economist Andy Xie, formerly of Morgan Stanley, warns that China has it own real estate bubble, waiting to pop. James Chanos, the famed short seller who predicted Enron's demise, thinks China is another Enron and "on an economic treadmill to hell." He and other skeptics don't buy the rosy economic statistics the Chinese government keeps issuing, and they suspect that its banks hold more putrid loans than Beijing admits.

The counterarguments are that, while housing may be in oversupply on the coast, that isn't true in the rest of the nation. And Chinese real estate purchases are usually done for cash, not the dangerous debt that poisoned the market in the United States. Personal income and productivity, the bulls say, are still rising smartly, and will blow away any social problems.

Regardless, the immediate question for investors is how to invest in China, whether taking a long position or a short one, like Chanos does. For non-Chinese, investments on the Shanghai and other exchanges are hard to arrange due to many government restrictions. Increasing numbers of China's stocks are now listed on U.S. exchanges, however.

Some of these get run up rapidly, although their volatility can be harrowing. Knowing that Chinese stocks have cachet that guarantees demand, hedge funds swoop in and play games with them. In the space of a few days in December 2010, Youku.com, known as the Chinese YouTube, hit the American market at just under $13 per share, then soared to $50, and reversed to $30. Quite a trip. Someone took some tasty profits, and it wasn't the poor investors who bought at the peak. Those who do manage to buy Chinese stocks in Shanghai and the other Mainland bourses have another problem: a flimflam approach to corporate disclosure that should make a diligent investor queasy. In the West, companies that cook their books, if discovered, face harsh penalties.

Accounting transparency of Chinese companies that aren't listed on U.S. exchanges, where disclosure standards are relatively high, can be questionable. China Market Research Group's Rein recalls a client who wanted to invest important money in one and asked his firm to first delve into its bona fides. Turned out, Rein found, that the Chinese company had booked deals as revenue that had not been signed but verbally promised years before. "Many Chinese companies keep three sets of books," Rein reports, "one for the tax bureau, one for investors, and one for senior executives."

China is counted as one of the emerging market countries, though its economic prominence sure makes it look like it already has emerged. It commonly is grouped with three other fast-growing nations, known as the BRIC countries. The others are Brazil, Russia, and India. The latter two share a past mired in leftist governments that hobbled economic growth. Brazil and Russia are resource rich; hence, the prices of commodities, especially oil, are central to their well-being.

Emerging nations have a harrowing history of booms and busts. One of the worst meltdowns was the 1997 "Asian contagion," when the Thai baht collapsed after the government devalued the currency in hopes of papering over the spine-bending debt the nation had incurred. The crisis spread to Indonesia and South Korea, and threatened to suck in more victims until the International Monetary Fund intervened with a rescue package. Templeton, naturally, was attracted to this time of "maximum pessimism," and he invested heavily in Korea, picking up terrific stocks for very little. Some of his money went into Matthews Korea Fund, which had lost 95 percent in 1997. He made a bundle when the financial tsunami subsided.

In light of the upsy-downsy nature of emerging markets, it is seldom clear when these blessings in disguise will come along. As most emerging economies were hurt less in the Great Recession than were developed nations, their stocks flew higher once the worst was over. The question arises: how long will that last?

Postcrisis, the MSCI Emerging Markets Index handily outdid sadsack established benchmarks like those in the West. In 2009 and 2010, emerging market stock mutual funds were flooded with new money, even as investors withdrew from U.S. equity portfolios.

This struck one sage, Jeremy Grantham, the chairman of money manager GMO, as faddish in the extreme. Emerging stocks no longer were bargains, he wrote in GMO's fall 2010 newsletter: "Everyone and his dog are now overweight emerging equities, and most stated intentions are to go higher and higher."

★　　★　　★

In 2010, the region where nothing was looking up was Europe, a place through which old Templeton had trekked three quarters of a century before. To him, the Old World held little investing appeal because of its high taxes on income and strangling regulations on companies. Opening a new business or trimming a workforce there involves lots of red tape, provoking the suspicion that the authorities want to ban new competition and layoffs. Europe typically grows in the low single digits. You may ask how Templeton could be enthused about an autocracy like China and leery about democratic Europe, where dissidents aren't shoved into the hoosegow for their beliefs. The difference is that China is hell-bent on growth, while Europe is indifferent to it, says Scott Phillips, coauthor of *Investing the Templeton Way*, with his wife Lauren Templeton, the legendary investor's great-niece.

Nevertheless, after old Templeton's death, Europe's distress meant that it had met his "maximum pessimism" standard and then some. Europeans, who in 2008 peered down their noses at the stupid, childish

America that had steered itself into a financial bog, woke up two years later to discover that several members of the eurozone, the 17-nation monetary union, were stuck up to their armpits in muck of their own devising. The troubles of Greece and Ireland—crippled sovereign bonds, bare treasuries, street rioting—scared everyone on the planet with an eerie sense of 2008 déjà vu. Suddenly, the euro began dropping against the U.S. dollar.

Europe's common currency, shared by nations ranging from Ireland to Germany, proved to be a trap. Usually, a nation in extremis economically will devalue its money, thus making its industry competitive again as its goods get drastically cheaper. But Greece and Ireland, along with fellow losers Spain and Portugal and suspected loser Italy, were tethered to Germany, Europe's sturdiest economy. The stolid Germans, remembering the chaos that ripped them in the 1920s when their mark went to hell, were in no mood to let the euro be devalued. Sure enough, many European markets began to sputter, and bourses in the so-called PIIGS (that would be Portugal, Ireland, Italy, Greece, Spain) dropped the most, in some cases by double digits. The worst was the Athens exchange, down 31 percent for 2010.

To the Templeton mind-set, however, that fearful situation betokens an opportunity. European stocks had the cheapest valuations going, with an estimated price-to-earnings ratio (P/E) of 10.7 for 2011, compared with 14.7 for China.

Banco Santander, the large Spanish bank, saw its stock fall 35 percent in 2010 to where it had a lowly P/E of eight. But here was a solid bank with ample capital and a nice dividend yield north of 5 percent. The negative karma of the European crisis scared investors away, making the likes of Santander catnip for value players like Templeton. Had he been alive, he surely would have bought European shares.

The vehicles to do so now are legion. Since Templeton paved the path, legions of mutual funds and later exchange-traded funds (ETFs) were hatched, allowing Americans easy access to foreign securities. Country-specific funds are available, although financial advisers tend to discourage buying them, preferring greater diversity.

Since its 2004 launch, the iShares FTSE China 25 Index Fund has had a scorching run, more than doubling by decade's end and showing a low correlation to U.S. stocks. This ETF is overly reliant on the financial sector, with one half its assets in banks, so a lot is riding on a narrow-shouldered horse. Broader stock funds usually tilt toward Europe, which claims 60 percent of the asset values in U.S. international funds.

Meanwhile, a fair number of individual American stocks have wide foreign exposure, such as Aflac, based in Columbus, Georgia, the leading insurer in Japan. A stuffed replica of Aflac's signature duck is ubiquitous in Japanese households. U.S. multinationals from medical supplies maker Baxter International to Coca-Cola derive more than half their revenue from non-U.S. consumers. They represent an easy alternative for internationally minded American investors.

Also, many overseas stocks won listing rights on U.S. exchanges, where they trade as something called an American Depositary Receipt (ADR), which is a cloned version of shares in their home countries. Ancestors to ADRs were introduced in 1927, and the Securities and Exchange Commission (SEC) codified the system in 1985, leading to a surge in issuance. The Chinese are the latest to get in on ADRs and tap what remains the globe's largest storehouse of capital. If you want to buy foreign stock that is not listed as an ADR, like Germany's BMW, then any broker can open an account in its host nation.

As much as he believed in the Lord above, Templeton believed that international stocks, and lots of them, were vital to American investors' financial well-being. One interviewer asked his opinion about fellow value buff Warren Buffett, who incidentally was far richer than Templeton ever could hope to be. Determined to invest only in what he understands well, Buffett's exposure to non-U.S. stocks has been very small.

"I think he's short-sighted," Templeton replied. "If he had spent more time in foreign nations, he would be better off."

Summary

- John Templeton introduced ordinary Americans to the opportunities of investing in foreign stocks. Debuting his Templeton Growth Fund after World War II, he showed perfect timing. Because of the war and increasing U.S. global influence, the first major cracks appeared in Americans' traditional insularity. A subset of his countrymen was willing to listen to him.

- The United States once dominated world trade, especially after it filled the vacuum World War II had left. But the nations ruined in the war eventually rose up and became humming export machines. Overseas stocks kept pace: The United States claimed 90 percent of global equity capitalization in 1945, two thirds in 1970, and less than half in 2010.

- Riding the overseas expansion, Templeton Growth scored some of the best returns of any fund ever. Templeton did extensive research, looking not just for value stocks but for value countries. He was alert for what he called "points of maximum pessimism," where good bargains abound. He cleaned up in the 1997 Asian economic crisis, for instance.

- Templeton had exquisite timing. He got into Japanese stocks early, in the 1950s, and exited in the 1980s, sensing that they were overpriced and a fall was coming. His next favorite was China, whose speedy growth made it an investor's darling. But there are ample arguments for why China may have weaknesses similar to Japan's.

- Chinese stocks can be bought on U.S. exchanges, although they are volatile. Buying on the Mainland is hard for foreigners; worse, much Chinese corporate accounting is suspect. China is still classified as an emerging market, a group whose stock soared after the financial crisis. But emerging nations have a boom-and-bust history.

- As a result of Templeton's pioneering efforts, the vehicles to invest overseas are now extensive. Many mutual funds and ETFs specialize in international stocks.

Chapter 7

Un-Real Estate: Property's Pull

Donald Trump was going through a very, very dark spell. Out walking near Trump Tower, his signature building on New York's Fifth Avenue, he spotted a homeless guy on the opposite sidewalk, holding out a can. "That man is wealthier than I am," Trump told his then girlfriend, Marla Maples.

"What are you talking about?" asked Maples, a blonde model who later would be his second wife. They were on one of the most posh streets in the world. Trump Tower, a 58-story skyscraper, was a celebrated tourist attraction, renowned for its peach-marble atrium and 80-foot lobby waterfall. Trump was famous—famous for his audacity, famous for his impact on real estate, famous for his wealth. Passersby waved at him. No one waved at the homeless guy.

"That man across the street," Trump said, "is worth $900 million more than I am at the moment."

"I don't understand. He's not worth $900 million."

"No," Trump said, "let's assume he is worth nothing. I'm worth minus $900 million."

It was the depth of the 1990 real estate recession. High-flying developers, who had hocked themselves up to their nasal passages to build massive projects during the roaring 80s, now were on their backs. And Trump was the most prominent casualty, his overwhelming debts falling on him like an avalanche.

Yet two-plus decades later, despite another property crash, Trump was back on the map. His 2010 net worth, according to *Forbes* magazine, was $2.4 billion. True, some of his more recent projects got in trouble thanks to the 2008–2009 economic downturn, and his casino company was enmeshed in bankruptcy for the third time, to the detriment of its public investors. But Trump had learned the hard way to survive in the topsy-turvy world of real estate. That's not true of everyone.

Of all investments, real estate is among the trickiest. It can make people very rich and, if they aren't careful, wipe them out. The reason is that investments in buildings, whether single-family homes or soaring palaces like Trump Tower, require heavy debt. Few people have the means or the willingness to buy or build structures using cash from their own pockets. So they turn to lenders, sometimes borrowing too much. But when things go wrong, it is hard to handle a big debt burden.

The old saying goes that all real estate is local. When oil prices went south in the 1980s, the white-hot Houston housing market cooled faster than a branding iron left out in the rain. Housing in the rest of the country was unaffected. Since then, the property market has gone national. That's because Wall Street has gotten heavily involved in real estate, especially in the debt that makes buying and selling it possible. Real estate is divided into two parts: commercial, which is Trump's part (offices, retail, etc.), and residential, meaning mostly single-family homes. Rental apartments and condominiums are in both camps. Offhand, you wouldn't think that the big-money crowd at Goldman Sachs would care about the average couple's $250,000 split level. Yet in the mid-2000s, Goldman bankers and other Wall Streeters really, really did. They got their hands on the mortgages that average couples use to buy their homes. A lot of them made out well financially, and then mayhem followed.

Further down the economic spectrum from Trump, Nick Illich, disabled due to a stroke, and his wife, incapacitated from a lung problem, fought a foreclosure notice on their Philadelphia home after falling behind on payments. With a mortgage debt of $128,000 and interest of 12.7 percent, he had trouble making his payments in 2009 and received his ouster notice from OneWest Bank. He struggled to get the bank to modify the loan, a Sisyphean process of multiple documentation and calls to the lender. "If I die tomorrow, I hope I go to heaven, because what I've gone through is hell," he told the *Philadelphia Inquirer.*

The housing crisis, which touched off the Great Recession, stemmed from a miasma of home loans gone to hell. Nationally, prices tumbled more than a third from their 2006 peak as the housing crunch ground on, and in overbuilt places like Florida, much more. Almost one in four mortgage holders owed more than their homes were worth, a pernicious situation called being "underwater." Worse, 10 percent of prime mortgages were in arrears or foreclosed, and over 30 percent of subprime ones were in these dire straits. Many of the subprimes were "Ninja" loans—requiring "no income, no job, and no assets."

Outside Atlanta sits a 600-acre site called WaterLace. As 2011 dawned, it was as silent as the aftermath of a nuclear war. A nice lake and winding streets serve as reminders of what the upscale subdivision was intended to be. There were a handful of finished homes, occupied by new owners nervous about their property values, and many neighboring lots that lay vacant and covered by chest-high weeds. The developer went bankrupt in 2008, according to the *Atlanta Journal-Constitution.* The property's lender, Security Bank of Macon, went bust in 2009, owing to a millstone of failed loans. That left WaterLace a ward of the Federal Deposit Insurance Corporation (FDIC), with few prospects that anyone would resume building.

Real estate is a realm of cruel ironies. Halfway around the world, the tallest building ever opened its doors in early 2010. The Burj Khalifa, soaring 2,717 feet, was billed as the crown jewel of Dubai, an emirate on the Arabian peninsula. This heady mix of offices, residences, nightclubs, and mosques made its debut amid a fireworks display and a gala party. It was the climax of the emirate's bid to become a world-class city.

Unfortunately, Dubai, the focus of an oil-fueled building frenzy, had a month earlier run into financial trouble and many of its real estate projects were faced with big problems. Nearby Abu Dhabi had to bail out Dubai to the tune of $10 billion. While Burj Khalifa, once known as Burj Dubai—it was renamed in a postbailout tribute, after Abu Dhabi's president—was 90 percent sold, other Dubai commercial structures stood forlorn. A half-mile away, the 24-story Omniyat Bayswater, an office building, was half vacant. That left the Burj as a massive mockery of the promise that real estate was a gift that kept giving forever.

★　　★　　★

More than any other investment, other than perhaps gold, real estate has a visceral appeal to the human psyche. Shelter is a basic need. The earliest shelters were caves, but here even the brutish savages had a pride of place. Some 40,000 years ago, Australian aborigines decorated the walls of their rocky dwellings with the oldest known examples of art, depicting sticklike figures of hunters. Go forward 20,000 years and the cave-dwellers of Lascaux painted surprisingly sophisticated pictures of animals. Five thousand years later, during the Ice Age, people made elaborate teepees with mammoth tusks and bones, covered by animal skins. After the retreat of the ice sheets 5,000 years ago, in the Neolithic Age, they began building huts of stone, timber, and mud.

Over time, people's homes became special spots in the eyes of the law—as seen by the Castle Doctrine in the United States, derived from English Common Law, as in: "A man's home is his castle." This law says that in your residence, you enjoy protection against illegal trespassing and violent attack. Further, the authorities need a good reason to enter your domicile.

Gradually, the business of real estate became a force in society. Originally, the kings owned all the land, then rented it out to the nobles, who in turn rented it out to the peasants working the fields. Any land transfers were done noble-to-noble, usually as the result of marriages or deaths. Come the Industrial Revolution, a wealthy merchant class and a busy middle class had the financial means to buy and sell property among themselves.

In the 1880s, U.S. real estate sales people founded what's now called the National Association of Realtors, which grew to be one of the strongest lobbies in Washington. They adopted standards of conduct in a bid to dispel a raffish reputation that threatened to hinder sales. In Sinclair Lewis's 1922 novel *Babbitt*, real estate agent George Babbitt laments his social standing: "Makes me tired how these doctors and profs and preachers put on the lugs about being 'professional men.' A good realtor has to have more knowledge and finesse than any of them."

Babbitt had an increasingly receptive clientele as America grew in wealth. Popular culture shows how much. Property pride is central to the Jimmy Stewart Christmas film chestnut, *It's a Wonderful Life*. Stewart's character, George Bailey, a decent-minded head of a savings and loan, cuts immigrants and other humble folks a break on their loans so they can own their own castles. In his hour of need, with the evil banker, Mr. Potter, scheming to ruin George's lending operation and send him to jail, the entire town rallies to their benefactor's side.

After World War II, Abraham Levitt and his sons built an enormous housing development in the onion and potato fields on Long Island, to the east of New York. Hordes of returning GIs, helped by government funding, snapped up the mass-produced houses, built at a rate of 30 per day with precut lumber on concrete slabs. By 1951, Levittown and environs had 17,500 homes. With federal help, the young ex-servicemen and their families got 30-year mortgages with no down payment and monthly costs the same as if they were renting. The great postwar housing boom was under way. And except for some pauses, such as in 2008–2011, it kept on.

But even in the postwar euphoria, a grim side emerged. Another movie that came out in 1948, two years later than Stewart's heart-warmer, showed how tough home ownership could be. In *Mr. Blandings Builds His Dream House*, Cary Grant and Myrna Loy move their family out of a cramped city apartment to the rustic delights of an old farm-house. Everything goes expensively awry, and Blandings must pay to get the old house torn down and replaced. The day they move in, the new home has no windows. Through the years, numerous remakes of this film surfaced, such as 1986's *The Money Pit*, starring Tom Hanks and Shelley Long.

One belief that propelled real estate, aside from the nesting impulse, was the allure of the home as an investment. Real estate, it was said, appreciated handsomely over time. Since 1950, according to U.S. Census data, average, inflation-adjusted home prices have more than tripled. The snag here is that prices never rose in a straight line. The biggest increases came right after World War II and from 1998 to 2006. Along the way were serious busts: in the 1930s, in the early 1990s, and, of course, since 2006. Due to the downdrafts, a housing index created by a Yale professor, Robert Shiller, shows that prices adjusted for inflation advanced a mere 0.4 percent per year from 1890 to 2005. After the post-2006 unpleasantness, which saw prices fall by a third or more, few expected a new price spiral soon.

The latest real estate crash was preceded by a frenzy reminiscent of a gold rush. After the messy collapse in 2000 of another mania surrounding Internet stocks, property seemed like a natural outlet. The tech bust triggered a very mild recession, so enough people had money at the ready for investing—and after the chimera of cyber fortunes vanished, what was more solid than real estate? The Federal Reserve was so frightened by the tech bust that it kept interest rates low.

The speculative profligacy that this produced, thanks to the steroid injection of cheap money, was outrageous. The worst froth was near the coasts, although the craze was almost everywhere. *BusinessWeek* reckoned that, from 2000 to 2005, average home prices zoomed 137 percent in San Diego, 105 percent in Miami, and 94 percent in New York, with inland spurts in the likes of Las Vegas, 103 percent.

By mid-decade, real estate was Topic A across the land, from backyard barbecues to swanky yacht club soirees. Fired by the false assurance that property never goes down—"They're not making any more land," the saying went—the chatter took on a tone of absurd bravado. New terms animated the delight-filled conversations. "Flippers" were those who bought a property, waited a short time for the price to climb, then sold it for a quick profit. A web site called condoflip.com did a brisk business. "Teardowns" were older homes bought (for too much, usually) so the new owners could demolish them and put up spiffy McMansions. Home equity lines of credit (HELOCs) made fancy home remodelings possible. HELOCs were, in essence, second mortgages where the owners borrowed against the ever-burgeoning equity of their houses—that was the difference between the first mortgage amount and the climbing property values.

The ease of borrowing, the spiked punch that drove this entire bacchanal, came in many clever guises. Some borrowers were enticed by low "teaser" rates that ballooned later on. Others had deals where the newly ballooned interest payments could be tacked onto the amount of the mortgage, meaning your debt would grow and grow. Thus your payment was now tied to a larger loan. Even people with lousy or no credit, the so-called subprime borrowers, could land those Ninja loans.

★   ★   ★

What made the 2000s' housing boom possible were imaginative uses of the time-honored mortgage. Under the centuries-old concept, a mortgage allowed a bank to lend you money, secured by the value of your property. You paid off the loan over time, typically 30 years, with every month's payment composed of a chunk of returned principal and a chunk of interest. If you defaulted, meaning skipped payments, then the bank could kick you out of your house and take it over. Your castle and the equity it had accrued would be gone. The term *mortgage* is from the French, meaning "dead pledge," where the owner's obligation to the lender ends with repayment of the debt or the seizing of the home through foreclosure.

Over the generations, that system worked well. And then someone slapped a retro-rocket onto it. As a result, a lot of people made a lot of money. Come 2008, the root word *dead* in *mortgage* suddenly had a new and ominous connotation.

That someone with the retro-rocket was Lewis Ranieri. At first blush, Ranieri didn't seem like a man who would change the world. He grew up in a crowded Brooklyn apartment above his grandfather's bakery. Loud and brash, he was the antithesis of a Wall Street smooth operator. But as a kingpin at the swaggering Salomon Brothers investment house in the 1980s, he was in the vanguard of the movement that transformed the humble mortgage into a super-hot Wall Street product and a magnet for big money worldwide. When he was through, a vast new, trillion-plus market had opened up, bringing wealth to many and eventually the global financial system to its knees.

The innovation he pushed and popularized was called the mortgage-backed security, or MBS. In fairness, Ranieri wasn't responsible for the later excesses that made MBSs so dangerous. Nowadays, he heads a program that tries to help people in danger of losing their homes. To overstate matters just a wee bit, he was like Albert Einstein, whose discovery later morphed into atomic weapons. And also to be fair, the mortgage-backed is a very useful invention. Greed-heads simply took the notion too far.

The old way of holding mortgages was to keep them within the walls of the bank that originated them. When the Great Depression sank many lenders, Washington stepped in to create Fannie Mae, an entity that bought mortgages from the banks. This allowed the banks to free up capital to make more mortgages and thereby restart the housing market. Fannie guaranteed timely payments. Later, the feds launched two other rivals, Freddie Mac and Ginnie Mae, in a bid to foster the miracle of competition.

Ginnie created the first MBS, also known as a pass-through, in the 1970s. The idea was brilliant: package a big swatch of mortgages and use them to back bonds. Investors bought the Ginnie bonds, and received interest passed through from homeowners' mortgage payments. Because Washington backed the securities—explicitly in the case of Ginnie, an actual federal arm of the government, implicitly for Fannie and Freddie, which are technically private companies—no one feared they would go bust. Agency pass-throughs, as they're known, usually pay a percentage point or so more than comparable Treasuries since, among other things, individual home loans can be paid off early, can default, and carry higher rates.

Then Salomon Brothers and Lewie Ranieri discovered pass-throughs and worked this undiscovered miracle with all the alacrity of the prince climbing Rapunzel's golden hair. The head of Solly's mortgage desk, a man named Robert Dall, had been trying to form a market for mortgage-backeds, and to create some of the bonds outside the confines of agencies. The bonds came to be known as "private-label" MBSs. The firm brought in a grudging Ranieri, who was having a successful career trading bonds backed by public utilities. Ranieri initially thought the transfer to this strange and obscure corner of the house was a comedown. But pretty soon, Dall was bumped aside, Ranieri was running the mortgage operation, and MBSs were a big part of the 1980s' investomania.

Ranieri, a college dropout who started in the Salomon mailroom after working in his uncle's Italian restaurant, was never one for subtlety. His mortgage desk resembled a frat house. He liked to hire overweight, blue-collar guys like himself. His department was a temple of gluttony. According to Michael Lewis's *Liar's Poker*, a book about Salomon in the 1980s, every Friday was Food Frenzy day, when they might order $400 worth of Mexican food, complete with guacamole in five-gallon drums. "Mortgage traders were the sort of fat people who grunt from the belly and throw their weight around, like sumo wrestlers," Lewis observes.

Ranieri's crew would mock traders in less profitable departments who ran triathlons. Pranks were ubiquitous. Once, an MBS trader was intently telling Ranieri about a plan to sell bonds overseas when he noticed his boss was holding a Bic lighter flickering under the trader's crotch. Another trader was aghast when Lewie poured a bottle of Bailey's Irish cream into his jacket pockets. "When the man complained it was his favorite suit," Lewis writes, "Ranieri whipped out four soiled hundred-dollar bills and said, 'Don't complain. Buy a new one.'"

The reason money was no object for Ranieri was that he had made the mortgage operation the firm's biggest profit center. The 1980s boom had touched off a hot real estate market. Not as hot as the one in the 2000s, but sufficient to be a strong generator of new home loans, the raw material for Ranieri. He is credited with inventing the term *securitization,* and he rode the concept hard. The private-label MBS, one not put together by Fannie Mae and its government-sponsored ilk, came to the fore under Lewie, and brought a lot of green to Salomon.

At the basis of the MBS was some rather daunting math. The problem with these securities is predicting when the homeowners would pay off their loans, the building blocks of the bonds. People do this, of course, when they sell their dwellings and move—they pocket the purchase price and channel part of it to eliminating the mortgage. And when interest rates go down, a surge of home refinancing results.

That is when owners get a new loan at a lower rate and retire the old high-rate mortgage. Either way, such a return of principal has to be factored into the creation of the bond. Ranieri excelled at figuring this out, aided by the crack research team he assembled.

After a while, Ranieri saw his Wall Street star fade. He got fired after challenging Salomon's chief executive on matters ranging from strategy to pay for his subordinates. He went on to other jobs, such as turning around a woebegone software maker, and he lost a lot of weight. Meanwhile, the giant he had gestated grew and grew and grew.

Today, by the reckoning of the Securities Industry and Financial Markets Association, MBSs are worth over $9 trillion, with the bulk of them agency bonds; private-label securities comprise around a quarter of that total. The mortgage-backed bond indeed has the virtue of cleaning out the arteries of banks and permitting them to make more home loans than they might if they had a mountain of mortgages to maintain. Yet as the world discovered, to its horror, this seemingly benign system could be badly abused.

Let's start with a popular home loan called the ARM, or adjustable-rate mortgage, which floats based on the level of indexes like the London Interbank Offered Rate (LIBOR). Initial interest payments on an ARM tend to be lower than if a homeowner had taken out a conventional mortgage, whose rate stays steady for the life of the loan. But should LIBOR start climbing, so will the ARM's rate.

One pernicious variant of this adjustable loan, popular during the housing frenzy, was the option ARM, where a homeowner could choose whether to make a payment, usually a very low one. A lot of folks couldn't resist this. They took out option ARMs and bought a costlier house than they could otherwise purchase. Skip this month's mortgage payment? Why not? The unpaid portion of the interest due would be tacked onto the amount of the loan. If the amount owed reached a certain level, perhaps 110 percent of the original loan amount, then the poor homeowner's interest tab would balloon, all too often to an unaffordable level.

A vast apparatus had sprung up to peddle option ARMs and their bastard brethren. There was an army of mortgage brokers that generated 80 percent of all home loans by 2006, double the level of 10 years before. The banks fielded these sales reps to grab market share. Why, the banks asked, should we wait around for a home-seeking couple to wander in the front door of a branch? Pay a sales force to lure new borrowers.

The more exotic the mortgage, the sweeter the commission for the brokers. Vetting borrowers' creditworthiness was way down the priority list for brokers and banks. Lenders could book all the earnings from option ARMs up front, even though the borrowers might never pay it all. The wonderful out for the banks was that Wall Street would buy bushels of their loans and package them into MBSs. So if the loans went sour, the banks didn't care. For many of the loans they made, the banks were merely functioning as a conduit. And the market was robust for MBSs. Eager for yield, hedge funds, pension plans, and other institutions gobbled up the mortgage bonds with such gluttonous abandon that Ranieri's Friday Food Frenzy seemed genteel.

After a while, though, the financial community got too clever by half. It took MBSs and other debt and put them into even bigger securities, with names like collateralized mortgage obligations (CMOs) and collateralized debt obligations (CDOs). In a strange paradox, this led to banks, which had shoved individual mortgages off their books to be securitized, seeing home loans boomerang back to them—in securitized form. The banks borrowed money to buy CMOs and CDOs, lured by the securities' high returns and seeming safety. Lying behind these instruments was the misplaced faith that Wall Street wizards could assess all that paper and figure out what the risks were for each. Financiers made weighty bonuses by getting in on this racket. As long as home prices kept going up, as long as the housing craze continued, then everyone made out.

The old investing adage still applied, however: trees don't grow to the sky. Eventually, around late 2006, home prices peaked. The world woke up to find that, due to the extent and intricacy of the housing debt, which reached into every corner of the financial realm, the entire system began to crumble. The feds had to bail out the banks and, in effect, acquired American International Group (AIG), the giant insurer that was up to its armpits in debt-related quicksand. Washington did the same thing for Fannie Mae and Freddie Mac, putatively private entities that had taken on an astronomical amount of funky mortgage debt. While the 2000–2002 tech bust was painful, it wasn't as pervasive as the housing bust, which threatened to destroy the global economy.

★   ★   ★

Well, if zesty home appreciation is no longer a given and mortgage debt almost shoved us into the Great Depression 2.0, then can anyone make money from residential real estate? Yes, they can, up to a point. The answer is to avoid gimmicks. And gimmicks are drawn to real estate like iron filings tempted by a magnet.

In the 1980s, there was a real estate fiasco built around a tax dodge that cloaked real estate limited partnerships. These groups let investors own projects like apartment buildings. The gimmick was that the buildings were money losers, and that permitted investors to claim tax losses to offset gains elsewhere in their portfolios. Then, in 1986, Congress took away the tax break, and its removal had a lot to do with the savings-and-loan bust in the latter part of that decade.

At the moment, a somewhat risky but intriguing play is in mortgage bonds that have emerged from the fire of the Great Recession. The Federal Reserve had been buying Fannie and Freddie MBSs to keep the market from collapsing. Then, in 2010, the Fed gradually eased out of its buying spree. Because of the central bank's support, Fannie and Freddie paper had been selling at a premium, 103 cents on the dollar or more. Post-Fed, the bonds got cheaper. They still carried the virtue of implicit federal backing. The government would not let them fail.

Private-label MBSs, however, became very cheap, postcrisis, since few investors wanted them. The problem was a lingering suspicion that some held loans teetering on default. Lewie Ranieri's babies became pariahs and next to no new ones were produced in 2008 and 2009.

In 2010 came the first glimmerings that fresh private-label bonds were not extinct, as banks packaged "jumbo" mortgages—those that were too big to be acquired by Freddie or Fannie. Meanwhile, it became possible to buy software that delved into the innards of private MBSs. The good aspect of private-labels was their scarcity, which meant any hint of demand would drive up their values. As with any other bonds, certainly, buying mortgage securities only makes sense in lots of $10,000 or larger.

Prior to the crisis, some wise people invented easy ways to invest in mortgages—mutual funds specializing in them. The best ones came through the trials of 2008–2009 valiantly. One of the stars has been TCW Total Return bond fund, which wisely navigated the mortgage market during the nastiest of times. In 2008, it eked out a 1 percent return at a time many other bond funds were tanking. Even though TCW canned star manager Jeffrey Gundlach in December 2009, owing to a political row, the fund kept on navigating these waters well, with double-digit returns the following year.

Why even bother with mortgages at all, in light of their horrible recent history? The value investors' credo. They are neglected and unloved, and that is the perfect time to leap on any investment. It seems highly unlikely that history would repeat itself soon, and mortgages would head into the abyss once more. A world without mortgages would be insane, since no one other than cash buyers could ever purchase a house. So an eventual recovery, at some point, appeared baked in.

Aside from trying to perform alchemy with housing debt, a more prosaic method of residentially oriented investing has long been available—the time-honored task of being a landlord. This is so labor intensive that it almost seems not worth the trouble. The pipes burst in the tenant's basement? That's your problem now. Your best hope is to hang on until rising prices let you sell with a good gain, or rents climb sufficiently high to make up for all the *agita* you'll encounter. Owning a lot of property is another way to make this work, yet that involves a huge commitment of capital—and worrisome levels of debt exposure.

The toughest slog is to own a commercial building. Real estate mavens use a calculation called a cap rate to figure out how much they can make on a rental property. That is the equivalent of a dividend on stock: You divide the rental income by the building's price. Cap rates nationally are around 8 to 9 percent, which is better than you earn from stock dividends (average: 2.4 percent). Certainly, you need to need to pay upkeep, property taxes, and mortgage interest out of the rental income, so your return is whittled down a lot, maybe halved. Another expense is for vacancies; landlords always expect some units will be empty and not generating income. Naturally, a nonmonetary hassle factor is involved, too. Hustling for new tenants and holding existing tenants' hands is part of the job.

The somewhat easier path to landlording is to rent out your home. This works well if you must move away for a new job and the local market is wheezing. Then, postponing a sale, awaiting a recovery, is a smart strategy. Here, the tax code is helpful. After getting a professional appraisal of the property, you can deduct interest costs, insurance, and other expenses. The biggest tax deduction comes from depreciation, where you write off a portion of your home's appraised value every year. That break, a remnant of the old passive loss tax provision axed in 1986, can be used to offset up to $25,000 in other income, perhaps from your salary. The limitation is that your annual adjusted gross income must be below $100,000 to take advantage of this. Above that level, this break is phased out very quickly, and vanishes at $150,000. Meantime, you have to ensure that your tenant pays on time and be on the spot when his toilet overflows at 3 AM. Building real wealth likely does not reside here.

★   ★   ★

A preferable alternative is to turn to Wall Street to act as the landlord on your behalf. Yes, the same guys who almost shredded the economy with their real estate shenanigans. They concocted a vehicle called a real estate investment trust, or REIT (pronounced: "reet"). You can buy stock in these entities, and they usually pay decent dividends. Unlike regular corporate dividends from the likes of Kimberly-Clark or IBM, REIT payouts are taxed at higher, ordinary income rates. The one break you get is that sometimes part of a REIT dividend is called a "return of capital," essentially reflecting depreciation, and isn't taxable.

Property trusts, the ancestors of REITs, date from the 1880s, when they were allowed to escape taxation at the corporate level if they passed their income on to investors. That favorable tax situation ended in the 1930s, but amid a postwar surge in demand for real estate investing, was resurrected in 1960 under a bill signed by President Dwight Eisenhower. Thus was the modern REIT born. The deep-sixing of passive investing tax breaks in 1986 channeled a lot of real estate investors toward REITs. That year, the law also changed to allow the trusts to manage their own properties directly. In 1993, Washington scrapped the ban on pension funds' sinking money into REITs, which amped up the dollar flow into them. REITs had managed, for the most part, to avoid heavy damage from the early 1990s' real estate slump, so they seemed doubly enticing to the big-money crowd, and to small investors, too.

In the 1990s, scores of big real estate companies converted to REITs, which allowed them to raise fresh capital via stock issues, and thus ease their traditional reliance on debt. For the next two decades, with only some minor hiccups, REIT total returns (stock price appreciation plus dividends) were in the double digits. Only with the onset of the credit bust did that go south, with a heart-stopping 38 percent loss in 2008. After this, most REITs had the innate strength to pick up the pieces—not all, but most of them.

REITs allow investors to be commercial property landlords, with a big advantage: their real estate portfolio is professionally managed. Obviously, REIT investors have no direct say over strategy. Don't fancy the tenant occupying 222 Broad Street? Tough. If investors don't like how the trust is working, their only alternative is to sell their stock and get out. Should a REIT want to buy a building, it has the expertise to inspect the structure's physical and financial soundness. Their economies of scale make running the properties cheaper to do than what a single landlord faces. There are around 136 publicly traded REITs, the bulk of them owning buildings; they're known as "equity REITs." The rest, like TCW's, invest in mortgages and MBSs.

Equity REITs own office buildings, hotels, self-storage units, apartments, strip shopping centers, and regional malls. The trusts tend to specialize in one type of property, where they have developed an expertise. Hotels are probably the riskiest kind because they don't have long-term leases. Guests check in for a night or two, then leave. When the economy sours, fewer guests show up. Sunstone Hotel Investors bought the W San Diego Hotel in 2006, and later was forced to surrender it to lenders when the property didn't generate sufficient revenue to meet mortgage payments. The least risky REITs are those that own apartments. People have to live somewhere. This sector is better able to withstand economic turbulence than others. During recessions, sales of single-family houses dip, as many people can't afford down payments or qualify for financing. That means they rent apartments.

As REITs own dozens and sometimes hundreds of properties—one tenth of U.S. commercial property sits in their hands—they are better able to withstand tenant departures than other landlords. While the 2008–2009 bear market was as unkind to the trusts as it was to other investments, REITs did emerge a lot more affordable. According to real estate research firm Green Street, REIT stock fell from 25 times earnings during the boom to 13 times in 2010. (REIT earnings, called adjusted funds from operations, are figured out by taking net income, adding back depreciation and subtracting maintenance costs.)

To get through the tough times, some REITs cut their dividends or paid investors with new stock. Vacancies in some of their holdings were so high that they had to slash rents to attract and keep tenants. When the stock market recovered in 2009, many REITs scrambled to fill holes in their balance sheet with fresh capital. They offered new shares, which diluted the stakes of existing investors but put the trusts back in good shape.

So REITs, often paying around 4 percent dividend yields, have the feel of good long-term investments. Some of the most solid, like office owner Vornado Realty Trust and mall operator Simon Properties, took advantage of the downturn by snapping up cheap, distressed properties. The shakeout from the Great Recession made such vulture investing a very ripe opportunity.

REITs, to be sure, carry lots of mortgage debt. Most stayed sane about it. Even at the very top of the boom, the REIT average was just 43 percent of their properties' market value. Just the same, some REITs could not resist the siren song of debt, and piled it on to buy more holdings. It goes to show that smart operators don't always do the smartest things and that investors should beware of them. Too much debt and too much optimism are a bad combination. Financial wizardry cannot make that right, ever.

★   ★   ★

The biggest horror story involving poisonous debt loads and REITs is that of General Growth Properties. The REIT had transformed itself from a steady landlord concentrated on second-tier shopping emporiums in the heart of the country to a major player on the world scene.

In 2004, General Growth bought a rival, the Rouse Companies, for a hefty $12 billion, adding such treasured retail locales as Boston's Fanueil Hall Marketplace and New York's South Street Seaport. It had an interest in or managed more than 200 malls in 45 states. The REIT's malls boasted high-end occupants like Tiffany, Saks Fifth Avenue, and Neiman Marcus. Its portfolio contained the world's largest open-air mall, Ala Moana Center in Honolulu. To do all that, the debt had expanded to a stifling 83 percent of assets. In 2009, the bloated REIT declared bankruptcy.

The demise of General Growth was a personal tragedy for the Bucksbaum family, who had nurtured a snatch of holdings into an empire. Brothers Martin and Matthew Bucksbaum expanded their grocery business and opened their first shopping mecca, the Town & County Shopping Center in Cedar Rapids, Iowa. To attract families, they installed a trampoline for kids. Martin, the more dynamic of the brothers, was a workaholic who toiled late into the night, crunching numbers. Their shopping centers began popping up all over the postwar landscape. The family, which moved the company's headquarters from Des Moines to more cosmopolitan Chicago in the mid-1990s, became fabulously wealthy. Matthew Buckbaum settled into an art-filled apartment in a luxury Chicago high-rise and threw star-studded New Year's Eve bashes at his Aspen retreat.

Emboldened by success, the family began buying more properties. First, they acquired a stake in CenterMark Properties, which gave them big presences in the Los Angeles and Washington markets. The next year, General Growth and four partners bought Homart, a division of Sears, Roebuck, bringing it 40 more malls. The REIT got a reputation as a very shrewd investor. It sank $182 million into a collection of 19 shopping centers, bought from Prudential Insurance, and sold it all three years later, for a $108 million gain.

Martin Bucksbaum died in 1995 of a heart attack, and his brother took over. Matthew turned over General Growth four years later to his son, John, a competitive fellow who was an avid cyclist—he rode with Lance Armstrong occasionally. Under John and his chief financial officer, Bernie Feinbaum, the firm piled on mortgage debt to expand even more. In 2004, it acquired Rouse at a 30 percent premium. Much of the financing was floating-rate debt, which seemed intelligent at the time, since rates were declining. With that deal came an obligation Rouse had struck with the estate of Howard Hughes to buy large land tracts outside Las Vegas, putting General Growth on the hook for $1 billion.

As long as everything kept going up, there were no worries. But as the subprime mess spread over the rest of the financial world, General Growth found it could no longer roll over its mortgages. The first big sign of weakness came when it couldn't pay loans backed by Las Vegas retail properties. The Hughes obligation was a nightmare. The REIT's stock was in free-fall in late 2008, and the board removed John Bucksbaum as the company's chief, although he stayed on as chairman. It tumbled into Chapter 11, and somehow managed to fend off hungry acquirers lusting for a court-ordered bargain. In late 2010, the REIT emerged from bankruptcy, somewhat smaller, and chastened.

★   ★   ★

At the other end of the spectrum are REITs that survived the debacle and, in classic Darwinian fashion, thrived on the bones of the fallen. They had learned one very clever lesson: don't get too deeply in debt. Add to that one corollary: watch what you buy (like no liabilities to Hughes heirs). Then toss in a second corollary: be prepared for bad times, as these are as sure to arrive as a heavy rainfall. And—why not?—a third: take advantage of those bad times to pick up bargains. Investors eyeing REITs are smart to be on the lookout for these traits.

The embodiment of all this real estate wisdom is a motor-mouthed mass of energy named Steve Roth, who heads Vornado Realty Trust, one of the premiere REITs of all time. Fittingly, Roth benefited from Bernard Madoff's demise. When the super-swindler got sentenced to the clink for near-eternity, much of his holdings had to be liquidated. Roth topped three other bidders for Madoff's beach house in Montauk, at the ass-end of New York's Long Island, where the glamour of the Hamptons begins to fade. Montauk is still a port for fishermen, a rougher-hewn version of tonier Hamptons enclaves like Amagansett and Southampton. Montauk is not brimming with artisanal cheese shops. Roth's winning bid, $9.4 million, was 6 percent more than its asking price.

At first blush, that doesn't sound too shrewd. The 3,000-square-foot house, set on 1.2 acres, is hardly an architectural masterpiece. Sure, it has a pool and a deck, and nice waterfront frontage, some 182 feet. But paying a premium for a disgraced financier's digs in a down market? Roth, who likes to talk about almost anything, has kept mum about the deal. But his reasoning isn't hard to guess. Oceanfront homes are perhaps one of the few sure bets in property investing. A finite supply exists; hence, the prices will gain over the long pull. Plus, the Hamptons are still the Hamptons. Years ago, parts of them were considered dumps, and now are the height of chi-chi. More specifically, living in the one-time home of a famous person—even an infamous person like Madoff—has a certain cachet. When Al Capone's South Side Chicago house went on the market in 2009, according to the *Chicago Tribune*, the asking price of $450,000 was about double that of nearby houses.

Roth always had an eye for a good buy, even if he had to pay dearly for it, but he prefers bargains. His company started out collecting shopping centers. Then he came across a New Jersey discount retail chain, Two Guys, owner of appliance maker Vornado, which produced fans and room air conditioners for the stores. Two Guys changed the name of the entire company to Vornado, which rhymes with "tornado." The swirling winds of stagflation in the 1970s battered the retailer, so Roth and his partners launched a proxy fight and snorked it up in 1980. The fan maker was spun off and still produces appliances under the Vornado name.

In 1995, Roth and his hungry shopping center operation bought the Alexander's department store company out of bankruptcy. They closed the tacky stores, including the dowdy Alexander's flagship in Manhattan's Midtown, as Roth saw more of an opportunity in the locations. The Alexander's flagship was leveled, and a newer, shinier edifice replaced it. Standing on the Alexander's site now is a gleaming, 56-story skyscraper that combines luxury condos with the headquarters for Bloomberg LP, the financial information colossus, commanding primo rents.

The ebullient Roth, a snappy dresser who bestows hugs and kisses on employees and anyone else within reach, has a sharp eye for detail. He is besotted with architectural design. It is "like a narcotic," he told *Forbes*'s Stephane Fitch. On a 2005 inspection with Fitch of the

Bloomberg building, then under construction, Roth chewed out contractors for small flaws in the lobby's herringbone stonework. Vornado staffers and contractors have a love-hate relationship with Roth. So do competitors, such as fellow property magnate Sam Zell, whom Roth jokingly refers to as a "bald-headed chicken-f--ker."

In early 2008, Roth handed the chief executive's post to Michael Fascitelli, a Goldman Sachs executive he had lured with a lucrative offer. But Roth, who stayed on as chairman, continued to play a big role. The company Roth has created is remarkably ambidextrous. Many REITs specialize in one sector, such as offices. Vornado has an enormous portfolio of office buildings and shopping centers, many in the Northeast, particularly around New York and Washington, D.C. It also owns Chicago's Merchandise Mart, a massive art deco structure that houses wholesalers and retailers, and once was the world's largest building (400,000 square feet).

When Vornado bought the Merchandise Mart from the Kennedy family in 1998, Roth wisely kept on Christopher Kennedy—son of Robert F. Kennedy—as its chief. Kennedy had proved himself a deft manager, and his golden name didn't hurt. Vornado is one of the few REITs that also constructs its own buildings; most trusts want to buy ready-made properties with proven track records. Roth has big, and expensive, plans to develop the area around New York's Penn Station.

Along the way, Roth and Vornado have made many smart moves. And they have deftly avoided some pitfalls, aided by luck. In early 2001, Vornado was in the bidding to acquire a long-term lease for the World Trade Center from the Port Authority of New York and New Jersey. Putting up $3.25 billion, it had outbid chief rival Larry Silverstein, but then backed out when Roth and his lieutenants became uneasy over lease terms and tax liabilities. Silverstein ended up winning. Then came the 9/11 terrorist attacks, which destroyed the Twin Towers. The task of rebuilding the site has been a trial for Silverstein ever since.

Vornado has made its share of mistakes, certainly. It invested $66 million to buy debt on four properties owned by New York developer Harry Macklowe and, when that went into the flames, had to write down most of the loan.

Nonetheless, its debt load overall was not onerous—about half of capital. One sign of strength is its ability to raise fresh equity capital.

Vornado in 2009 sold $710 million in new shares of stock. Others such as Simon Property and Boston Properties also raked in torrents of new cash from stock sales. Cohen & Steers, the largest mutual fund manager of REITs, was an eager buyer of the trusts' stock.

All this has enabled Roth to eye vulture investing, using Vornado's financial resources to buy distressed properties for cheap. In 2008, along with partner Syms Corporation, it bagged bankrupt retailer Filene's Basement. The idea was to erect a mixed-use complex on the site of the partly demolished Filene's main store in the Downtown Crossing section of Boston. Getting the financing to keep the project going has been a challenge. But then, Roth has done this before, again and again.

An investment in Vornado stock in 1993, when it became a REIT, had advanced by 2010 almost 16 percent annualized. To be sure, since peaking in 2007, it has been cut in half. However, the Standard & Poor's 500 had gone up a fraction of that. In other words, Vornado has outpaced the stock market, despite one of the biggest real estate crashes in history. Roth's secret was to find that delicate balance between being bold and careful, never easy in the field of dreams that is real estate, where the build-it-and-they-will-come prospect is intoxicating.

★   ★   ★

One real estate player who learned the virtue of caution, on the hard road, is Donald Trump. He started his real estate career with an in—his father, Fred, was a developer. With his father's connections, the young man converted a skanky Midtown Manhattan hotel, near Grand Central Station, into a swanky Hyatt (in partnership with Chicago's wealthy Pritzker family). Donald Trump became a billionaire in the 1980s, owning an East Coast air shuttle, a yacht, helicopters, and a vast real estate empire, which included three Atlantic City casinos and part of New York's fabled Plaza Hotel. Once that collection of assets collapsed during the early 1990s' real estate crash, it was a horrifying mess. That he was able to make it back says a lot about his spunk and smarts.

Businessmen celebrities are rare, but Trump has cultivated his own brand with care. He slaps his name on every property he has an interest in. When an unflattering story appears about him in the media, he often mounts a counterattack. Tim O'Brien, then a *New York Times* editor, riled Trump in a book he wrote about the man, *TrumpNation: The Art of Being the Donald,* which claimed he was not a billionaire at all. An outraged Trump sued O'Brien. The suit went nowhere. But Trump served notice, yet again, that he would not tolerate disparagement, such as being called a mere millionaire. The trappings of wealth and power are very important to Trump. His TV show, *The Apprentice*, was all about burnishing that persona.

More than most, Trump's success rests on that image. When he was drowning in debt in 1990, his lenders balked at pushing his wholly owned Trump Organization into bankruptcy court. One reason was that they viewed it as too big to fail. But another was the very convincing case he made, with his usual bravado: that the magic of the Trump name was worth a great deal. Why sully it by putting his entire company into bankruptcy? "You'll never see me in the corner sucking my thumb," he told me during that time. "The name Trump will be hotter than ever." And after a while, he proved to be right.

When his casino operation went into Chapter 11 in 2009, for the third time, his cachet had increased to such a degree that the filing didn't dent him one bit. Amid court deliberations, he brazenly suggested that he keep a stake in the casinos—and that they retain his name. If anyone else had suggested such a thing, he would have been laughed out of court. Yet everyone knew Trump's name still carried weight.

Personally, Trump is hardly a palsy-walsy guy. His ego is too large for camaraderie. Even with social and economic peers, he tends to talk about himself a lot. To hear him tell it, his holdings are always the biggest, the best, the classiest, the most popular. The Trump brand is so very important to him that he must be flogging it every available moment.

Trump's first success in the 1980s came on the back of billions in debt that he took on, as the phrase goes, with recourse to him. In other words, he personally was liable for it. With the forbearance of his lenders, he managed to mount his comeback and, these days, conducts his property business very differently.

He now runs a franchising operation for other developers. He might have a small equity piece of their projects, yet they take the risk. Trump provides his considerable expertise in figuring out where to place the buildings, guiding construction, and marketing them. Dozens of developments, many condo towers, have the name Trump on the building. At core, he has avoided going deeply into debt again. He thus enjoys a luxury that few others do, using his name as leverage. The lesson remains: in real estate, debt is vital, although beyond a certain level, it is deadly.

Toll Brothers: Making It Through

He practically invented McMansions, those $1 million-plus deluxe domiciles sporting baronial porticos, cathedral ceilings, marble foyers, three-car garages, and stainless steel, side-by-side refrigerators.

Robert Toll, whose real estate investor father got slammed in the Depression, founded Toll Brothers in the late 1960s and made it one of the dominant homebuilders in the land, specializing in high-end houses. Growing up in suburban Philadelphia, Bob Toll quickly realized that housing was an area that, by the laws of demographics, should be a yellow-brick road to prosperity. Starting in the 1970s, the gigantic Baby Boom generation would be needing housing, he reasoned, and the older they got, the more upscale shelter they'd want.

That's pretty much how it worked out. Toll and his brother, Bruce, kept their focus on the upper end of the market, figuring that better-heeled buyers would be harmed less in economically bad stretches, such as what their dad went through. With Bob serving as chairman and chief executive officer, Toll Brothers spread throughout the Northeast and into growing Sunbelt markets like Texas and Florida.

A gruff, hard-charging type with a law degree, Bob Toll is known as someone who likes to drive a hard bargain. He scooped up vacant land when it was cheap during recessions. He fought yearlong legal battles with local governments that were trying to stop suburban sprawl. To get the economies of scale that mass production brings, he also opened factories where components of his homes were built. Customers had a

(Continued)

Toll Brothers: Making It Through *(Continued)*

vast array of choices to customize their homes. Like many true believers during the housing craze, Toll convinced himself that it would spiral upward in perpetuity. In 2005, he told *Fortune* magazine, "Prices will keep going up in double digits for years."

He was spectacularly wrong, as he discovered to his dismay. In 2009, Toll Brothers experienced a rare event: a loss. Sales of its luxury homes collapsed faster than a termite-infested A-frame in a windstorm. But while Bob Toll at one point may have been overly optimistic, he also knew to be prepared for reversals of fortune. Thus, he had a lot of cash on hand to make his way through the gale. He didn't have to slash prices on his houses to move them off his rolls. The company returned to profitability in 2010. Toll, like every real estate investor, knew that, in a market of ups and downs, you have to be ready to simply endure.

Summary

- Real estate is among the diciest investments due to its heavy reliance on debt. Few can pay for property with cash, so they need mortgages. But if not handled properly, debt can be one's undoing.
- Shelter, a primal human need, has become a major asset class for big investors and ordinary people alike. Since World War II it has zoomed in inflation-adjusted value, yet this growth has been in fits and starts. After the 2000 tech bust, the Federal Reserve made borrowing money cheap, and that move touched off a housing craze that went too far.
- Meanwhile, real estate investing, once a local matter, has become nationalized. Wall Street raked in profits by packaging mortgages into bonds, called mortgage-backed securities. Lewis Ranieri of Salomon Brothers invented the market for mortgage-backed securities in the 1980s. But the eagerness to get in on this boodle let many lenders relax standards, and they offered gimmicky loans that

ended up blowing up as the home owners could no longer afford to pay. The collapse of mortgage bonds almost put the world into another Great Depression.

- Despite the real estate pile-up, ways remain to profit from property. You can be a landlord yourself, although this may not be worth the hassle. Or you can invest in real estate investment trusts, entities that pay nice dividends and have a tax advantage. These are professionally managed organizations that own real estate and are publicly traded.

- One key to tell a good REIT from a bad one is its debt load. General Growth, a mall operator, landed in bankruptcy after taking on too much debt. The more clever Vornado avoided that trap by watching its debt exposure.

- Donald Trump is an example of a real estate investor who learned the hard way to stay clear of too much debt. Now he franchises out his name and expertise, letting other developers take on the risk.

Chapter 8

Not Just for the Rich: Alternatives

Mega-rich investors long have dabbled in high-end exotica not meant for the common herd. In the hushed finery of oak-paneled asset management firms, they would sip tea from gold-rimmed Limoges china, and listen to an obsequious, well-dressed adviser speak of currency plays, commodities positions, and hedging maneuvers—stratagems that rove far beyond the everyday realms of stocks and bonds. Many of these niche methods, after taking their licks in 2008, came back into favor with the fabulously wealthy and their cuff-linked coddlers.

But more and more, nonbillionaires are able to avail themselves of alternative investments, a rubric that encompasses all manner of things that fall outside the regular run of assets. Whether they should or not is another question. With a little study, stocks and bonds are readily understandable. Alternatives . . . not always.

The way to make money in alternatives, some smarties say, is to invest in money, specifically, in currencies. Here is an activity that is far, far, far out on the risk curve—big potential rewards or soul-shattering losses await. Much foreign exchange trading (known as forex or simply FX) occurs between large banks handling international payments or among multinational corporations, such as a Finnish electronics company that needs to buy components from a Taiwanese manufacturer. The fluctuations of foreign currencies against the dollar, the world's dominant denomination and thus the chief character in this drama, are vast.

In 2009, with the United States painfully extricating itself from the financial crisis, the price of the euro soared versus the buck. While plainly affected by the crisis, the nations of the European Union that used the common currency felt downright smug, pleased that those boorish Americans had come to such grief. Germany, the leading economy in the 17-nation eurozone, had much less of a debt problem than did the United States. Then along came Greece, one of the smallest economies in the monetary union; its enormous borrowings, held by many big banks from elsewhere in Europe, freaked out everybody. By spring 2010, the euro had tumbled against the dollar. Americans vacationing in Europe were once again feeling good. A lot of currency players were not.

Foreign exchange once was an unpretentious affair. The Medici clan in 1300s Florence began as exchange traders. They sat behind wooden tables in public spaces and excelled at converting the multiple types of Italian coins in circulation, from gold to silver to other metals. The family opened a Rome branch and landed the business of the foremost international organization of the day, the Catholic Church. As Niall Ferguson writes in *The Ascent of Money*, "The papacy was in many ways the ideal client, given the number of different currencies flowing in and out of the Vatican's coffers." This line of work brought the Medicis great riches that allowed them to influence affairs of state, to acquire grand titles (two popes were from the family), to sponsor geniuses like Galileo and Michelangelo, and to own magnificent structures like the Palazzo Vecchio.

With the Industrial Revolution came a rigid international exchange code, designed to facilitate burgeoning cross-border commerce. From the 1800s to the 1930s, the world was on the gold standard, which pegged each currency to an immutable amount of bullion. Carolina tobacco growers knew that, when sending their crops to Britain, the pound was 24 grains of gold and the dollar 12. As paper money was convertible into gold, the metal often got shifted across borders to keep up with international trade.

The Great Depression wrecked that system. Trade imbalances meant some nations faced a gold drain, which played hell with their currencies. The 1944 Bretton Woods agreement replaced gold with the U.S. dollar, and other currencies were tethered to the legal tender of the world's richest nation. That went well for a couple of decades or so. Then, by the early 1970s, amid the postwar economic emergence of Europe and Japan, America's mounting trade deficits made the dollar peg untenable. While some emerging nations today still link their currencies to the dollar, exchange rates float—at times on very turbulent seas. The turmoil has led to the creation of the world's largest market, conducted by contracts to swap currencies. Danger and opportunity lurk there.

The shining goal of every currency investor is to do a George Soros. In 1992, during Britain's Black Wednesday currency crisis, the wily New York financier earned a reported $1 billion and the sobriquet "The Man Who Broke the Bank of England." This saga took place because the United Kingdom's central bank refused to raise interest rates in line with hikes occurring on the continent. Soros saw the United Kingdom's policy as unsustainable folly, and he shorted the pound. When Britain eventually had to devalue the pound to get in line with reality, Soros cleaned up.

Doing a Soros is not easy, much as walking along a high wire in the Big Top while juggling flaming torches is not easy. It requires the ability to make a good forecast, and then to stick to your convictions as you wait in hope that events will cut your way. In 2009, who would have thought that a small economy like that of Greece would bring the mighty euro to its knees? Besides a need for augury and courage, the rules of the currency game are so daunting that nonprofessional investors are seriously cautioned about entering these lists. The same can be said for many professional investors.

Any number of factors can, and often do, render currencies extremely volatile. Interest rate changes, economic reports, cross-border trade, and investment flows rattle this market. In 2007, for instance, the British pound stood at \$2, up from its customary \$1.50 due to higher U.K. interest rates. Canny FX investors indulged in what's known as the "carry trade," borrowing cheaply in the United States and buying better-paying British debt. This tended to buoy the pound, further goosing their returns. Pounds were a good play, for a while.

Also impacting forex is technical analysis, which looks for patterns and trends in price charts. Traders shift their bets radically on the basis of these arcane readings, like "Fibonacci retracements," where rising currency prices reverse and go partway in the other direction. Key scheduled events also play a role. When options expire in New York or Tokyo, the positions must be unwound, which means currencies will be affected as options investors' money changes hands worldwide. Currency futures are traded around the clock, making keeping abreast of developments an exhausting enterprise.

The most challenging method of tapping forex is to use currency contracts. For the uninitiated, the concept of the contracts takes some getting used to. These come in packaged pairs, like euros and dollars, and are in effect wagers that one will rise against the other. If you are bullish on the euro, you are buying it and selling the dollar.

Pairs trading is dominated by matches against the U.S. dollar, whether involving the Japanese yen, the Swiss franc, or the British pound. This make sense because America possesses the richest economy, it has the largest and most liquid markets, its dollars are the primary international reserve currency, and the greenback is the leading medium of exchange. Oil, for example, is priced in dollars, so a French buyer of Saudi crude must convert euros into U.S. currency to get hold of the stuff. Other contracts, not containing dollars, are junior versions called "cross-currency pairs," linking the likes of the pound and the yen.

Currency contracts most often are struck by using a lot of leverage—that is, borrowing. You need to put down a minimum of merely 1 to 3 percent of a contract's value, which means you will make a killing if the market runs where you predict. Let's say you put down \$500 on a euro-dollar contract, with 200:1 leverage, a pretty standard ratio. That results in your controlling a \$100,000 position. But if a mere half-cent move occurs, your capital is wiped out.

Just as with day traders in stocks, individuals in the 1990s started to get into forex. Globally, around \$4 trillion in currencies are traded daily, and of that, a mere $100 billion is by individuals. But that figure has been steadily climbing. Large institutional players in this realm, ranging from Citigroup to Deutsche Bank, have created online trading platforms for the retail bunch. Currency trading used to occur in person on physical exchanges, a process called "open outcry," where traders in a pit would shout out their bids. Starting in the 1980s, the system gradually converted to electronics. The typical lot in an FX trade is 100,000 units of a currency. For the dollar, that would be $100,000.

For individuals, though, trading currencies is like midgets entering extreme fighting bouts, pitted against six-foot-five brutes. Good luck. Banks most often do business in chunks of a million units. Individual investors trade in mini-lots of 10,000 units.

Since currency trends can change in a blink, wiping out small practitioners, a wiser course for many might be to use the forex mutual funds that have appeared. They are unlikely to make you rich, but at least they get you in on the FX game a little more safely.

Many funds are of recent vintage. The PowerShares DB US Dollar Bullish fund, an ETF that launched in 2007, pairs the dollar against a basket of currencies from the other major old-line industrial powers, such as the euro and the yen. As the name implies, you prosper only if the dollar goes up. In the three years since the fund's debut, it started meekly, then romped in 2008 when investors the world over flocked to the perceived safety of U.S. Treasuries. The fund dipped in 2009 when doubts arose about Washington's budget deficit, then took heart in 2010 as the mess in Greece humbled the euro and Treasuries got popular again. This fund has a mirror-image twin, which offers a bearish take on the dollar, and has performed just the opposite.

The two haven't been huge moneymakers for their investors. Over the four years since they began, through early 2011, the bullish fund was down about 7 percent, and the bearish one was up a comparable amount. Still, they had not fallen as much as did the Standard & Poor's (S&P) 500 during the financial crisis, and the bearish fund was ahead of the S&P, which had returned to its level in early 2007. And that supports the argument that alternatives like currencies are good at providing diversification.

Another currency tactic, and one involving less risk, is to buy foreign certificates of deposit. These short-term bank instruments permit you to get in on higher interest rates elsewhere and also to bet on a rise in its host country's currency. EverBank in Jacksonville, Florida, has a robust international CD program for Americans, with the added selling point that the Federal Deposit Insurance Corporation (FDIC) insures the foreign paper.

For a minimum deposit of $10,000 with the bank, you can buy certificates of deposit (CDs) for single currencies or baskets of several. Say in summer 2010 you bought a $10,000 Australian CD due in 12 months. Then, most large economies had CDs offering microscopic rates. But Australia, an important supplier of raw materials to booming Asia, was different: The world's 14th-largest economy, it basked in growth—to such a degree that, in 2009, as a precaution against infla- tion, the country started hiking rates. The Down Under dollar is called a "commodity currency" because of those exports. Thus, in mid-2010, its CD paid 3.75 percent per year, as opposed to about a fraction of a percent for the comparable U.S. product.

At the end of the year's term in mid-2011, you may well get a double benefit from the currency swing (emphasis on the *may*). From June 2009 to June 2010, the Australian dollar gained 7.6 percent against the U.S. dollar. Suppose from June 2010 to June 2011, the Australian currency rose another 5 percent. As a result, the return is magnified. First, you get $10,375 back—your original principal with the 3.75 percent interest added. On top of that comes the currency appreciation. When your CD is converted back into American money, the total take is $10,893, or a 5 percent enlargement of your principal and interest, thanks to forex rates swinging in your favor. Still, there's no assurance that the Australian currency will continue to appreciate. At the end of 2009, it was up 18 percent from midyear 2009, then lost altitude amid the European crisis because scared investors crowded into what they perceived as safer, dollar-denominated holdings.

For currencies and kindred alternatives, steadiness and predictability are simply not on the menu.

★   ★   ★

Just as wacky are commodities. Those who cast their lot with the ups and downs of investing in metals, energy, and food products are sure to find a wild ride. For a select group of the fortunate, however, commodities can be a very lucrative corner of the investing world. Ask Hillary Clinton.

In 1978, when her husband was running for Arkansas governor, the future first lady, U.S. senator, and secretary of state wanted to lay in a nest egg for the future. While she was doing well financially at a Little Rock law firm, Bill's job as a law professor and then as governor did not pay much. With the help of a family friend, James Blair, who was a lawyer for Tyson Foods and also a commodities investor, she parlayed a $1,000 grubstake in cattle futures into $100,000 over 10 months. After this blazing performance, she got out and slid the proceeds into safer harbors like Treasuries.

What an amazing run. Commodity players, amateurs in particular, seldom have that kind of record. When her trading success came to light in 1994, with the Clintons in the White House, there were dark mutterings that she must have cheated somehow. The editor of the *Journal of Futures Markets* was quoted as saying: "This is like buying ice skates one day, and entering the Olympics one day later." But no malfeasance was ever proved. Most likely, Hillary Clinton was preternaturally lucky.

Two decades after Hillary cleaned up, commodities as an asset class went on a tear. They surged starting in the late 1990s, as the voracious appetites of China and other emerging market growth centers bid up their prices. Many commodities took a drubbing in *annus horribilis* 2008, and then began inching fitfully back. To some seers, commodities' ascent is far from over. One such bull is Jim Rogers, the investment guru who once partnered with fellow trend-spotter George Soros. Rogers has bragging rights on this score: back in the mid-1990s, he called the coming commodities uptrend. He continues to believe that they still have a long climb ahead, as new industrial powers gain wealth and population.

Known for his brightly colored bow ties and unorthodox enthusiasms (from 1990 to 1992, he rode his motorcycle around the world), Rogers has a special affinity for commodities. He refers to sugar as "white gold." In 1998, dissatisfied with other commodity benchmarks, he forged his own, the Rogers International Commodity Index, which with 35 components is the most comprehensive. It lists all the usual commodities, like oil and wheat, and throws in some offbeat ones such as adzuki beans. While down from its highs, the Rogers index has more than tripled since its inception. To Rogers, commodities are the fulcrum of investing. Early in his career, he toyed with getting an MBA, until an older Wall Street hand advised him: "Go short some beans and you'll learn more in just one trade than you would in two years at B-school."

One lesson is that, in the shorter term, unless you are as blessed as Hillary Clinton, commodities can be hazardous to your portfolio's health. There are many different commodity markets subject to their own peculiar forces. As always, the quirks of these myriad markets can eviscerate the smartest forecasts, to the distress of investors who took long—meaning optimistic—positions.

Rice, one of the world's premier foodstuffs, provides a cautionary tale. The rice price per hundredweight (100 pounds) peaked at $25 in spring 2008, spurred by fears of a global food shortage. Then farmers began planting madly, and crops moved into that dread condition—oversupply. Hopes for relief were fleeting. For a while in late 2009, a tepid monsoon season in India led savants to predict relief from bad prices. They believed that India's relative dryness would hurt the output of this major rice producer (second largest after China). The prospect of a shortfall nudged up prices worldwide. But the Indian crop came in better than forecast, and once more, rice was not nice. By mid-2010, prices were at around $11, less than half the level two years before.

No doubt, big players have a great influence on commodities. Bart Chilton, who sits on the Commodity Futures Trading Commission, thinks the advent of pension and other institutional investors has led to crazed swings in prices for the likes of oil. In summer 2008, when a barrel of oil commanded $145 and pump prices were $4 per gallon, he blamed the behemoth institutions, which he ironically calls "massive passives." Chilton has proposed that his regulatory body limit large accumulations of commodity positions. Regardless of who was running the market, its gyrations are maddening. On one day in May 2010, a discouraging report on retail sales caused crude prices to slip 2 percent.

Commodity futures contracts were hatched in the boom years following the Civil War. With prices oscillating madly, exasperated farmers needed a tool to lock in returns for crops. The first innovation was a "forward" contract, where buyers would guarantee a price for future delivery. This evolved into a more complex system that permitted buyers to sell their contracts, thus letting capital flow more freely. The new structure of futures contracts established standard rules and a clearinghouse that investors could trust. The first futures bourse, established in 1874, was the Chicago Produce Exchange, later known as the Chicago Mercantile Exchange.

Every futures contract has two parties, the "holder" or buyer, who expects prices to rise, and the "writer" or seller, who anticipates they will fall. If you buy a contract for oil at $70 for delivery several months away in December, and the spot price (what it goes for on the open market at any given moment) ends up at $69 by year-end, then you must send money to the seller. Between 1983 and 1994, the price of oil fell 53 percent, yet someone made money on futures transactions then. One helpful aspect of futures contracts is that you don't have to accept delivery of 10,000 bushels of wheat sitting in a Kansas silo. Investors can deal with actual raw materials as abstractions that will make, or lose, them money.

Futures aren't the only method of investing in commodities. One vehicle is the master limited partnership, or MLP, whose shares trade on public stock exchanges. They benefit from great tax treatment because their profits are taxed just once, unlike those of conventional companies, which must pay a levy at the corporate level—and when the tax-diminished proceeds are sent to investors as dividends, the IRS takes another nick. Much like a real estate investment trust, an MLP passes the bulk of its earnings to shareholders. Dividend yields are tantalizing. One prominent MLP, Kinder Morgan Energy Partners, which owns natural gas pipelines and storage tanks, pays out almost 7 percent of its share price in dividends, versus around 2 percent for the S&P 500.

The mutual fund industry offers a slew of portfolios, some focused on baskets of various commodities. The Pimco Commodity Real Return Strategy fund follows an index and charges a rather lofty sales charge of 5.5 percent to get in on the action. Or you can buy exchange-traded funds (ETFs) to track specific commodities, such as oil or gold. The United States Oil Fund took flight in 2008 as crude prices spurted ever higher, then received a licking as they deflated. To get a good picture of the wonderful world of commodities, let's zero in on a very popular one, whose allure is storied. That would be gold.

★   ★   ★

Famously and wickedly, John Maynard Keynes called gold a "barbarous relic," since, leading up to the Great Depression, it stood behind the world's currencies. To Keynes, the gold standard's sin was that it blocked expansion of the money supply and the government stimulus that his namesake economics called for to combat the economic calamity.

Small wonder that, even with the world off the gold standard, gold retains a special affection among mankind. The metal's shining beauty has drawn the eye and quickened the heart for untold millennia. Gold is the ultimate decoration and in places such as India is an omnipresent status symbol: wedding dresses are trimmed with it. Of the 163,000 metric tons in human hands, according to the World Gold Council, a little more than half is in jewelry. About a fifth of the supply is held by central banks, 12 percent is used in practical applications like electronic circuitry, and 16 percent is in private investments (i.e., the area you might want to get into).

The power of gold has molded history. Christopher Columbus, searching for a sea route to the Far East, was intrigued by Marco Polo's description of Japan as an island of "endless gold." After the Caribbean natives showed him their supplies of gold, the news electrified Columbus's sponsors on the Spanish throne. In the early 1500s, Spanish conquistador Francisco Pizarro decimated the Incan Empire in his quest for the inhabitants' gold. The Incas had no monetary system and appreciated gold solely for its aesthetics. The called it the "sweat of the sun." The conquistadors promptly put the defeated Indians to work mining for silver and gold, thereby providing Spain the financial might to build its own vast empire.

Three centuries later, the Rothschild banking clan smuggled gold into Portugal to pay merchants for furnishing provisions to British troops fighting Napoleon. The British commander, later named the Duke of Wellington, couldn't get the locals to accept a then-common paper IOU for the supplies. They insisted on gold. Using gold as a basis, the Rothschilds went on to fund the overall war effort against the

French, and emerged very wealthy. Without them, more Europeans today would be speaking French as a first language.

Compared to pixels on a computer screen denoting stock prices, gold's eternal tangibility has kept its place as a store of value over the centuries. Most other commodities will corrode (example: iron) or be consumed (soybeans). Gold is all but indestructible. Fire and water won't hurt it. While the yellow metal can be melted down, it retains its weight and chemistry. Values of stocks and bonds may fall to zero, but gold always is worth a decent amount. Yes, it fluctuates, but the stuff is never cheap.

Bad times are gold's friend. Since the 2000 tech bust, the metal has done well. Gold started 2001 at a tad below $300 per ounce, then as the Iraq War flared, gradually rose to double that, hitting $607 in 2007. Along came the Great Recession, and gold really sparkled, topping $1,400 by late 2010. Whether the culprit was fear of economic collapse or the Obama administration's massive federal spending and the attendant risk of inflation, investors flocked to gold as a safe haven.

Gold moves in cycles, and the direction isn't always upward. When inflation or other catastrophes fade away, the gold price does, too. In the 1970s stagflation era, gold vaulted into another galaxy. It reached $850 in January 1980, or just over $2,300 in current dollars. But when inflation ebbed, the economy leapt, and the stock market roared. As fear diminished and investors rushed into the stock market, gold took a painful tumble. After its 1980 peak, it fell 44 percent in two months. The metal didn't return to $850 until January 2008. Over the three decades since 1980, inflation had gradually risen 175 percent. Gold had failed to keep up, to say the very least. A study by Truepoint Capital finds that, over the past four decades, which encompasses the inflation-ridden 1970s when the metal did well, gold had a lower annual return (8.4 percent) than the S&P 500 (9.1 percent), yet had one-third higher volatility.

Sure that economic collapse is coming, diehard "gold bugs" sweep aside this inconvenient history. Survivalist blogs are rife with talk about a coming doomsday, so stocking up on gold—in addition to weapons, freeze-dried food, and bottled water—makes sense to these folks, if to no one else. The practicality of a gold-based economy is questionable: should you need to buy a loaf of bread, do you chip a sliver of bullion from your stash? If the gold standard were to return, calculates Société Générale, then gold would have to be priced at over $7,600 an ounce to back all the dollars now circulating.

But beyond the fringe element, many respectable financial minds believe that holding some gold is a prudent measure, given possible upcoming economic distress. David Einhorn, George Soros, and John Paulson have argued eloquently for gold investing. Einhorn, the hedge fund manager who warned that Lehman Brothers was in trouble, told the *New York Times* in 2010 that his firm's gold position reflected worries that "fiscal and monetary policies are not sufficiently geared toward heading off a possible crisis."

Starting in 2008, gold gained in popularity to rival any electronic gadget that Steve Jobs could produce. New cash-for-gold businesses sprang up. Some dealers sponsored Tupperware-type parties where people gathered at homes to peddle their metal. Various gold investments like mining stocks and dedicated gold funds won acclaim.

Buying bullion (physical gold) enjoyed immense vogue. Bullion is sold either in bars, some the size of bricks, others only as big as cell phones, or it's sold as coins. The American Eagle, Canadian Maple Leaf, and South African Krugerrand are the most numerous coins available. In 2009, in response to robust demand, the U.S. Mint, the federal agency that makes coins, had to step up production after an order backlog developed.

Owning 100 ounces of gold is a lot harder than owning 100 shares of stock. Bullion purchases come with a sizable tariff: markups are around 5 percent. Further, security is an issue. The stuff always can be stolen. Most homeowners' policies don't cover gold; hence, expensive riders must be added. For 0.75 percent annually of the gold's value, special storage sites will safeguard your gold, in vaults with many steel doors, reminiscent of the movie *Ocean's Eleven*.

Commodities futures contracts are available for gold, with their usual ups and downs. Funds like SPDR Gold Shares track the metal's price, without the inconvenience of holding actual bullion. You also can own gold mining stocks, such as Newmont Mining from the United States and Barrick Gold from Canada, which dig for the metal all over the world. The trouble with gold stocks is they sometimes lag gold prices. They reflect the broader stock market, which gold does not. The mining companies are laden with capital costs and run the risk of developing worthless, gold-free mines.

Gold has a dark side. People kill for it. Wars have been fought over it. It can attract a rapacious fiend like the fictional Auric Goldfinger, James Bond's nemesis, or the very real barbarian, Attila the Hun. He extorted thousands of tons of gold from the Eastern Roman Empire, to spare it from attack, then attacked anyway. King Midas, the mythical character most associated with gold, came to grief when his magical touch turned all around him, even his beloved daughter, into his favorite metal.

In commodities, the most intriguing long-term play involves something that grows, but unlike wheat or corn, has a life measured in many decades. In a word, timber. This quintessential rich guys' investment is increasingly available to the rest of us. Plus, few wars have been fought over it.

Paul Bunyan's preferred commodity never brought him sorrow. Wood, the bounty of the forest, evokes not greed, but hearth and home. Wood provides warmth, shelter, and a sense of sturdiness that lasts through the ages.

★　　★　　★

Timber investors love to say that money grows on trees. They are right, although that money grows very slowly. A pine tree takes up to 14 years before it reaches the height where it may profitably be cut down. Depending on the quality of the wood, the tree can be hewn into everything from pulp (to make paper, fetching $10 per ton) to lumber (for home building, $30).

Timber has done extraordinarily well over the fullness of time. An index calculated by the National Council of Real Estate Investment Fiduciaries, dating from 1987, indicates that timberland's value has blown past stocks' performance, an annual 14 percent versus 9.4 percent through 2009. The group measures appreciation of both land and trees, based on appraised property values and timber sales. In 2008, the housing crisis did slow the Timberland Index's advance amid declining construction activity. But the index's growth rate cooled to a frankly still-robust 10 percent growth rate, off from 15 percent in 2007. The

S&P 500 in 2008 was in the red to a scandalous extent, down almost 40 percent. In 2009, as construction continued to limp, the Timberland Index did turn slightly negative. That marked a rare year; the index otherwise never had a downward movement.

Trees grow at around 4 percent a year. Pests, diseases, fires, and droughts can stunt that, to be sure. Yet timber investors avoid such short-term trading problems as bad earnings surprises and new-product misfires, which bedevil stockholders. (There are commodities contracts for lumber, traded daily, but no contracts exist for timber as a whole.) Each time trees are felled and hauled off to the mill, the timber stand's owner garners thousands of dollars in income. Unlike other commodities, wood does not have to be brought to market at the end of a season. Timberland owners can wait out bad periods. For that reason, timber is highly uncorrelated with other asset classes. While waiting for better prices, owners can reap income from leasing out the property for hunting, or by selling water and mineral exploration rights to the land.

No one creates investor income as dramatically as a woodsman. In the deep forests 100 miles west of Boston, where 70-foot trees thrust toward the blue New England sky, a blond, rangy fellow named Dag Rutherford supervises what is known as a harvest, that is, a tree-cutting operation. He has been working on timber his entire life, starting with his family's woodlands in his ancestral Norway. Standing in the underbrush, he watches an enormous machine, resembling a tank with a giant claw, slice through the trunks of dozens of trees. They fall to earth with a world-ending crash that, the first time, sends birds flapping away. Then the machine strips off branches and leaves, and splits the trunks into 16-foot logs. One man pilots the tree-harvesting machine, from a cab mounted on its chassis.

"This is a very efficient process," says Rutherford, a senior vice president at Bank of America's U.S. Trust, which oversees investments of the wealthy. Each tree is felled in a matter of minutes. Before the cutting machine was invented, a lumberjack with a chain saw would take an entire day to duplicate its production. As he observes the machine he has hired for the day, Rutherford explains how the wood will be sold and the proceeds will benefit the wealthy family that owns the tract.

With timberland costing about $2,000 per acre, the price of buying your own stand of trees can be well north of $1 million. To get diversification, wealthy investors and institutions put money into multiproperty pools called timber investment management organizations, or TIMOs. Minimum investments run from $1 million to $5 million, but some TIMOs permit investors to combine their money to reach the entry level. Timberland needs tending, and that can be expensive. TIMOs charge up to 5 percent of asset value yearly to handle property management, taxes, and insurance.

Fortunately for rank-and-file investors, a number of timber real estate investment trusts (REITs) are around, charging a great deal less. The largest timber REIT, Plum Creek Timber, changed hands for around $40 per share in 2010—a lot less than the entry fee for a TIMO. It owns 7 million acres spread over 19 states. While revenue and earnings were down in 2008 and 2009, Plum Creek stayed profitable. The stock fell hard along with the market debacle, then by early 2011 had almost clambered back to its 2008 high. So for plucky investors, doing well is possible, even after enduring an evil bear market.

★   ★   ★

The ultimate alternative is art. This is as much the province of the wealthy as polo ponies. Henry Kravis, the buyout king, is forever collecting pieces by such masters as Monet, Renoir, and Sargent. He has donated so much money to New York's Metropolitan Museum of Art that they named a wing after him. According to the Mei Moses All Art Index, art rose at around 5 percent annually during the 2000s, while the S&P 500 was down slightly. Such numbers argue persuasively that art is a good long-term investment, no?

Art did flag during the Great Recession, as even the rich focused on the small matter of survival. Then the art market gradually returned to life. In May 2010, a collector paid almost $107 million for Pablo Picasso's "Nude, Green Leaves, and Bust," a 1932 portrait of his mistress, Marie Therese Walter. In nominal terms, this set a record. (Adjust for inflation, and the champ still is Vincent Van Gogh's "Portrait of Dr. Gachet," sold in 1990 for what in current dollars is $138 million.)

Aside from having the jack to buy Picasso, the rich must put up with a lot to be art collectors. Auction fees can be sky-high, often a fifth of a piece's value. Also, art is exceedingly illiquid. If you need some quick cash, it is very hard to peddle your Jackson Pollock on the spot. Vexingly, tastes change: sometimes, American paintings before 1950 are hot; sometimes, they are in the dumper. When you buy, sales taxes can be astronomical. When you sell, art, as a collectible, gets socked with a higher capital gains tax than do shares of Google. Always, there's an ongoing need to document every last detail of an art acquisition, which adds to your costs. Nobody wants to put a Picasso up for auction at Christie's and suffer the embarrassment, not to mention the financial misfortune, of a challenge to the masterwork's authenticity.

For those below the financial level of a Henry Kravis, new hedge fund–like vehicles, such as the Fine Art Fund Group, have arisen to buy and sell art. Minimum investments can be as relatively low as $100,000. The first of the Fine Art Fund's portfolios, which began in 2004, claimed a 34 percent annual return on works sold. Much of that period, though, was during an art boom. Right before its debut, the art market was in a flat spell. Meanwhile, fees for art funds are on the high-flying order of hedge funds, with 2 percent taken per year, and 20 percent of the profit above a given level. So, as with mutual funds, art fund managers will do well, even if you don't.

The great Benjamin Graham drew a distinction between investors and speculators. In *The Intelligent Investor*, he wrote that investors perform "thorough analysis" in the hunt for a place to put their money that promises safety of principal and a decent return. Speculators are unrepentantly reckless fools, in Graham's view. Lamentably, the line between wisdom and foolishness is never clear. But the task of investing is to look for it, diligently and ceaselessly. Not easy with alternatives.

Summary

- Alternative investments, like currencies and commodities, have long been the domain of billionaires. But, increasingly, retail investors are getting involved. While alternatives can be very risky and hard to understand, that hasn't stopped investors from looking for a good score.

- Success at currency trading involves a high degree of forecasting, and few are consistently right. With foreign exchange (known as forex or FX), you can take out a contract to bet that one nation's currency will rise against another's. Since the world's currencies were decoupled from their postwar peg to the dollar in the 1970s, FX has become especially risky, and prices fluctuate wildly. All manner of forces influence how currency investments play out, from interest rate changes to economic reports. While forex is mostly practiced by banks, institutions, and corporations, a smaller-sized contract is now available for individuals. New currency mutual funds did not take the hit the S&P 500 did during the financial crisis.

- Commodities—metals, energy, food—are just as risky and volatile. Rice, for instance, fell from a peak of $25 in 2008 to $11 in 2010, after many undulations in between. From the late 1990s until the financial crisis, commodities were soaring. Some predict they will rise for a long time, thanks to demand from China and other emerging economies. A commodities futures contract has two parties on either side of it: one is betting that the commodity will rise, the other the opposite. So someone always makes money on commodities, and vice versa. A safer method of investing in commodities is through mutual funds or ETFs.

- Gold, the classic balm for fearful investors, rose smartly in price since the 2000 tech crash, and even more in the wake of the 2008 financial debacle. However, gold has a sorry history of slumping badly when anxiety departs, as it did in the 1980s and 1990s. Gold can be owned either directly as bars or coins, or indirectly with a futures contract or a fund. Stock in gold mining companies sometimes lags the gold price.

- Timber is the ultimate long-term investment, since a tree takes more than a decade until it can be cut. Since 1987, timber has had only one down year, 2009, due to the housing slump. The financial barriers to entry are large. A stand of trees costs $1 million, but there are REITs that let ordinary investors in.

- Art collecting has been the exclusive realm of a rich-o like Henry
  Kravis. This is a very mercurial and illiquid market, with high fees
  and taxes. Today, new funds make art buying do-able for the less
  well-heeled. Art is no investing slam-dunk. It did well in the 2000s
  except for during the Great Recession. The 1990s, though, was a
  flat spell.

Chapter 9

Spreading It Around:
Asset Allocation

A s a credo for living, it's right up there with looking both ways
before you cross the street and avoiding high places during
lightning storms. One of the standard pieces of financial advice
is that, for safety's sake, your investments should be diversified—some
in stocks, some in bonds, some in cash, maybe some in commodities
or in real estate, and so on. The commonsense thinking here is that, if
one component of your portfolio goes screaming down the chute,
others will be okay, and you will fare fine overall.

What a shame that in 2008 and early 2009, almost everything
except Treasury bonds took the express elevator to the basement. The
gods seemed to be merrily mocking a central belief of investment
planning. They weren't alone. Critics of diversification have long said
that scattering one's assets across the financial landscape is a recipe

for mediocre returns—better to plunk your chips in one place that is poised for greatness and get rich. (Assuming you can find this El Dorado, of course.)

Sometimes, concentration works. One key diversification tenet is that a fund should hold a large number of stocks, hundreds even. But there are almost 300 mutual funds containing only 40 stocks or fewer. A study from research firm Morningstar, covering 1992 to 2006, found these concentrated funds to be no more volatile than other funds, meaning they were no more risky. And a number of them have enviable records, such as Weitz Partners Value. Managed by Wallace Weitz, a Warren Buffett devotee who also lives in Omaha and has a down-home, un–Wall Street penchant for plaid shirts, this 37-stock fund returned an average 3.2 percent annually over the turbulent 10-year span through 2010, a lot better than the S&P 500s piddling showing.

Nonetheless, few are graced with the gifts of a Wally Weitz. As Mark Twain wrote in *Pudd'nhead Wilson*: "Put all your eggs in one basket and—WATCH THAT BASKET." Spreading the goods around is safer. In finance-speak, the diversification ideal is to collect several baskets of assets that don't correlate, meaning move in the same direction. Finding assets that will zig and others that will zag is easier said than done.

Especially when it comes to finding bad-weather offsets for stocks. According to Roger Ibbotson's research shop, Ibbotson Associates (now owned by Morningstar), stock market slumps in recent years feature tighter correlations of stocks with other asset classes. Panic is contagious, as we saw in 2008. A score of 1.0 is perfect correlation to the S&P 500. Commodities move hardly at all in relation to stocks—from 1970 to 2009, their correlation was a mere 0.04, Ibbotson data indicate. Then came the financial crisis to give the lie to this notion.

During 2008–2009, commodities leapt up to 0.54. They moved in the same general direction as stocks. The two didn't match yet were within hailing distance. In 2008, the Dow Jones UBS Commodity Index lost less than a percentage point more than the Standard & Poor's (S&P) 500, and in recovery 2009 it rose along with stocks, although not as much—the S&P outdid the commodities index by six percentage points. Over the full span of time, only gold (a commodity), intermediate Treasuries, and cash generate gains reliably during stock slides. To be truly uncorrelated, commodities would have to gain when stocks lost, and vice versa.

What about diversification within the equities class itself? Since stocks are so very important for portfolio growth, spreading them around among different sectors is a sound idea. Trouble is, while different types of stocks usually do behave differently from each other, they tend to move almost as one when times are tough. Gerstein Fisher Associates, a money management firm, calculates that, from January 2007 through February 2010, three different classes of stocks became almost perfectly correlated: the S&P 500 (large issues), the MSCI World ex U.S. (foreign), and the Russell 2000 (small capitalizations). That phenomenon has been true in previous crises. During the 1997–1998 debt and currency blowup in Asia and Russia, emerging-market stocks, which typically are outliers, began moving almost in tandem with the S&P.

Well, okay. If you can shrug off the occasional turbulence, then putting eggs in different baskets makes sense. It all depends on how you offset your stocks. The S&P 500 took a 37 percent drubbing in 2008. According to a T. Rowe Price study, a portfolio of 80 percent stocks and 20 percent intermediate-term government bonds fell 28.6 percent then. While that was painful, it wasn't as painful as the S&P's torment. Further, a mixture of 60 percent stocks, 30 percent bonds, and 10 percent cash dropped just 20.4 percent.

★   ★   ★

As financial planner Roger Gibson notes in his 1989 book, *Asset Allocation: Balancing Financial Risk*, diversification "is a time-honored investment principle." The Jewish *Talmud*, written thousands of years ago, says: "Let every man divide his money into three parts, and invest a third in land, a third in business, and a third let him keep in reserve."

The unfortunate Irving Fisher, who right before the 1929 crash made the bad market call of more bullishness ahead, did presciently advise that safety lay in spreading assets around. "The more unsafe the investments are, taken individually, the safer they are collectively," he wrote. Ben Graham also supported diversification, except he didn't lay out exactly how to achieve that, instead counseling that bonds should in general be part of a portfolio along with stocks.

Nowadays, an entire industry has sprung up to tell investors how to diversify. It has a sort of guild, which awards the Certified Financial Planner (CFP) designations to those who have passed a grueling series of tests. At last count, 61,000 licensed CFPs were at work in the United States, a dramatic expansion from the 36,000 a decade before. Worldwide, CFP certifications have doubled to 118,000.

While the idea of diversification has been around for a long while, it has become a core philosophy only in recent times. In the 1950s, economist Harry Markowitz provided the intellectual framework for asset allocation by inventing Modern Portfolio Theory, or MPT, which explores how investors must diversify their portfolios to get the best return in light of the risk they're taking. Until then, scholars had examined the role of risk only as it related to individual securities, not how they offset one another, or failed to.

The son of a Chicago grocer, Markowitz had zipped through the University of Chicago's undergrad program in two years and was going for his PhD when, looking for a subject to tackle, he decided to immerse himself in stock market literature. What he read left him unsatisfied. One highly regarded text, John Burr Williams's *The Theory of Investment Value*, struck him as falling spectacularly short. The book described how to value stocks by calculating their projected dividends. Markowitz felt that Williams didn't go far enough: Williams did not explain how one pieced together an entire portfolio, according to its risk exposure, from these bountiful stocks. Sweet dividends are marvelous only as long as the stock doesn't shatter like glass in a hailstorm.

For his doctoral dissertation, Markowitz hit upon a mathematical concept to measure the risk of a collection of assets in terms of "how they moved up and down together." At the time, this was a radical notion. While defending his dissertation, Markowitz recalls the hard time he got over his novel approach from the University of Chicago's reigning eminence, Milton Friedman: "Two minutes into the defense, Friedman says: 'Well, I don't find any mistake in the mathematics, but this isn't a dissertation in economics and we can't give you a PhD in economics." Markowitz did get the degree, although he didn't find much demand in academia for his newly invented discipline, called quantitative finance. So he went to work for the Rand Corporation, a think tank set up to help the U.S. government deal with its Cold War nemesis glowering behind the Iron Curtain. Rand scholars had a purview that ranged far wider than developing new war strategies.

This berth gave Markowitz a good dollop of freedom. In 1952, the 25-year-old economist expanded his doctoral thesis into a paper called "Portfolio Selection," which became the foundation for MPT. For this seminal theory, Markowitz went on to win the Nobel Prize for economics in 1990, an award he shared with two other American economists, Merton Miller and William Sharpe. At core, the idea of avoiding a concentration in matched investments, such as owning both Ford and General Motors stocks, is self-evident. Markowitz's theory goes beyond those obvious pairings into complex statistical formulations that helpfully result in—drum roll and horn fanfare—a portfolio that balances reasonable safety and decent returns. Or tries to.

The mathematical trade-off between risk and return is a tricky business because it depends on historical norms to arrive at a statistical conclusion. A cornerstone of statistically measuring risk is a tool called "standard deviation," which tracks how far an investment varies from its average return. The highest risk investments offer the better chances of handsome returns, provided that they don't crash and burn. Markowitz figured out how to plot investment choices on a graph that uses risk, as represented by standard deviation on a horizontal axis and expected returns on a vertical axis. A curve drawn along the upper end of the plot points is called the "efficient frontier," marking the choices with the lowest risk for the best return levels.

After the near-apocalypse of 2008 and early 2009, many began to question MPT. Normal distributions of risk and return were thrown into disarray after Lehman Brothers collapsed into an ignominious heap. When corporate bonds, real estate, and commodities followed stocks into the pit, chaos had arrived. Everyone crowded into Treasuries in September 2008 like the last train out of Paris in June 1940. In some circles, diversification became a dirty word.

Post-meltdown, Markowitz told the *Wall Street Journal* that solid, actively managed mutual funds and index funds continue to hold excess risk at bay. The problem, he went on, was with the mortgage-linked exotica: that "the layers of financially engineered products of recent years, combined with high levels of leverage, have proved to be too much of a good thing." The toxic investments that nearly immolated the world economy were too tightly correlated, he argued, namely mortgage-backed securities stuffed with rotten home loans.

Fine, up to a point. The fact remains that constructing the perfect portfolio is far from an exact science, whether a global financial collapse is occurring or not. MPT rests on the efficient market hypothesis, which holds that investors behave rationally. It also assumes that investors are all well informed. Often, they are irrational and clueless.

Investors are supposed to figure out how to diversify like a champ? Ben McClure, a director of consulting firm McClure & Co., has a study showing that investors have great difficulty locating stocks whose "performance is independent of other investments in the portfolio." Further, selecting risk-free assets to balance riskier holdings is nigh unto impossible, he says. Treasury bonds, for example, are assumed to be immune to default, yet interest rate hikes and inflation can lay them waste. Asset allocation is a matter of collecting items that may surprise, and in a very unpleasant manner.

★   ★   ★

A daunting thought for anyone trying to figure out where to put those precious eggs: the best of the best have screwed up this task. Consider David Swensen, the investment chief at Yale since 1986, whose scorching record had made him a near-deity among the investing elite. His "Yale Model," based on MPT, regularly produced double-digit advances that put the S&P 500 to shame. Swensen divvies up his portfolio into a half-dozen equal parts, with different asset classes in each. One of those classes took it hard in the 2008–2009 school year, the so-called "real assets" category, focused mainly in real estate and commodities. Their experience then was reminiscent of *Night of the Living Dead*. Swensen suffered the embarrassment of a 24.6 percent investment loss, when other college funds averaged a 17.2 percent dip. Okay, you can say that the financial crisis was an aberration. But isn't the point of asset allocation to stormproof your portfolio, so at least its fall is minimized?

Lots of scholarly ink has been spilled over how much of a portfolio's return is based on asset mix, and how much on skill at making smart individual picks or timing the market. The case for asset allocation's primacy was a blast of a study in 1986 from three financial savants— Gary Brinson, L. Randolph Hood, and Gilbert Beebower, together known as BHB.

After analyzing 91 pension funds' performances from 1974 to 1983, they concluded that asset allocation is responsible for the vast majority of fund returns. A decade later, another financial wise man named William Jahnke attacked BHB with his own study that said asset allocation was responsible for just a small amount. BHB returned fire with updated numbers and others chimed in.

The latest word on the subject comes from Roger Ibbotson, who won renown for establishing the best data bank for security prices anywhere. His number crunching, as set forth in a spring 2010 *Financial Analysts Journal*, leads him to conclude that asset allocation and skillful market maneuvering have equal impact on outcomes.

While pondering how many data points can dance on the head of a pin, it's still logical to surmise that diversifying your portfolio is smarter to do than not. Hey, nobody wants to be stuck with 80 percent of his holdings in Lehman Brothers stock. The question then becomes: *How much should I own of what?* Let's zero in on how different asset classes interact with one another, plus what history tells us about their strengths and weaknesses.

★   ★   ★

Stocks, as Jeremy Siegel attests fervently, are the engine of any portfolio, the most volatile over the short term and the most dependable performers over the long term (excluding the Lost Decade that started in 2000). If the economy does well, stocks generally do, also.

The younger you are, the smarter it is to own a big chunk of stocks, since you have more time to recover from the periodic downturns. Small stocks get slammed the hardest in a recession, since their companies lack the heft and resources to weather economic upheavals. Once a recovery blossoms, small-capitalization stocks sprout higher than large issues. And as Warren Buffett and his adherents know full well, value stocks do the best over time. Foreign stocks were long viewed as a nice offset to U.S. shares, but nowadays the best opportunities seem to lie with a subset of them: emerging market names, with the foremost examples in fast-growing markets like China. Stocks in the developed world, with some exceptions, often stay fairly close to American results.

Bonds typically don't correlate well with stocks, as fixed income tends to do best when interest rates are low, and that's usually when the economy is in a funk. You are rewarded with regular interest payments—many stocks don't pay dividends—and bond prices are less volatile than those of stocks. Rising rates and inflation are the nemeses of bonds, knocking their prices down. Investment-grade corporates, munis, and Treasuries are the safest of the fixed-income bunch.

Zero-coupon bonds, which don't pay interest till they mature, and junk bonds are the most volatile. Zeros don't have that regular interest payout to cushion the shock of any adverse news. You get the interest when the bonds mature. In fact, junk performance usually tracks stocks' results because economic troubles spur fears that financially pressed junk issuers will skip interest payments or not repay principals.

In the bond world, the outliers are Treasury Inflation Protected Securities, or TIPS. As the name implies, they are constructed to insulate you from inflation's ravages. Because of that special power, they have a low correlation to other types of bonds, and correlate even less to stocks than other bonds.

Cash and cash equivalents, like certificates of deposit and money market funds, are the ballast of a portfolio. The equivalents are very liquid, meaning they can be converted into folding green quickly. Downside: since cash pays no interest and its cousins pay low interest, inflation has a nasty habit of chewing away this asset's returns over time. A basic rule of thumb is to keep six months' living expenses in cash for an emergency, or for deployment if you spy an opportunity to buy something good.

Hard or real assets—most notably energy, timber, and gold—have historically low correlations to both stocks and bonds. Generally, energy does well if the economy is expanding, as greater demand exists for gasoline and oil-based products like plastic. Timber benefits from a robust housing industry, although the calculus for it is different due to the decades-long growth required for a stand of trees to be ready for cutting. In early 2009, when housing was in horrible shape, the price of timber held steady. Gold benefits whenever a tear appears in the social fabric, whether inflation or recession or war. It retains its aura as the ultimate store of value. But energy and gold are roller-coaster assets: they sport records of long-running rises, followed by long-running slumps.

Real estate is the most commonly held asset, and it used to be the one sure thing that didn't wobble around like the gyrating stock market. Some 67 percent of the U.S. homes are owner occupied. Until 2006, the conventional wisdom was that housing values almost always go up. They may plateau for a while, during a recession, or even dip a tiny bit, then they resume their ascent.

This is one asset that the U.S. government encourages people to buy, on the theory that homeownership enhances family values, community cohesiveness, and, of course, revenue for local governments through property taxes. Washington provides mortgage deductions for federal taxes and also sponsors organizations, like Fannie Mae and Freddie Mac, that buy mortgages from lenders, who then have more leeway to make more home loans. Odds are that, when the vast, post-bust inventory of unsold and foreclosed houses is finally depleted, home values will continue their usual trek north.

Meanwhile, a separate method of investing in commercial property (office buildings, shopping malls, warehouses) has developed, the real estate investment trust, or REIT. These trusts, sold on exchanges like stocks, are for the most part collections of buildings that throw off rent and pay decent dividends. They resemble bonds after a fashion. The difference is that REITs are fairly volatile, with a standard deviation more than double that of bonds.

Hedge funds and their kin, private-equity (PE) funds, have an increasing place in portfolios. The hedgies employ exotic trades, and the PE crowd buys and sells whole companies. Big controversies exist about their heavy fees. Some of these high-end funds have fared spectacularly, others have disappointed. They are available solely to the wealthy, yet a number are publicly traded and open to ordinary investors via common stocks.

★   ★   ★

Diversification alone is not asset allocation. People need to take into account their time horizons—how long it is until you'll need the money you are salting away. Did you just have a baby and you need to save for her college bills? Is retirement 30 years out or 10? What are the odds your goals will be met? How much risk can you stand?

The mix is crucial when risk is involved. In its simplest form, that translates to how much of the portfolio is in stocks, versus bonds and cash. A conservative strategy has a low stocks portion, perhaps 20 to 40 percent in equities. That gives a large margin of safety, and may be best for those near or in retirement. But it won't provide the growth needed if you have years to go before retiring. A middle-ground approach has stocks making up 50 to 60 percent of the portfolio. Such a proportion fuels growth well, and also offers a reliable buffer from bonds' income and cash's stability. For aggressive types, 65 to 80 percent in stocks gives lots of oomph, with only a partial shield provided by bonds and cash. Here, the cash often is deployed to buy more stocks.

In allocating those eggs to different baskets, dealing with fees and taxes are vital to success. High fees go into someone else's pocket, not yours. A mutual fund that charges a weighty 5.75 percent up-front fee, for the privilege of getting in its door, is doing you no favors. Taxes have a similar eroding effect on your wealth. Wise investors, for instance, place bond funds in tax-sheltered accounts as the interest these funds throw off is taxed at high, ordinary-income rates. Stock dividends have an advantage over interest payments since their payouts are taxed at a lighter rate than interest.

Rebalancing is key to making diversifying schemes work. As you grow older, you likely want to tilt in a more conservative direction. In the near term, changes in portfolio values may skew your preferred mix. You may end up with a collection of assets far from what you want. Maybe you desire a 50–50 split between stocks and bonds, but the stock market has romped and now stocks dominate 60–40. So you need to add bonds and subtract stocks to return to the correct proportion for you. The touchy part is timing. Frequent rebalancing may result in the sale of winning holdings that still have growth ahead, and infrequent rebalancing could load you with assets past their prime and on the downswing. The best advice is to rebalance no more than twice a year, thus avoiding excessive cap gains taxes and trading fees, which harm returns.

★   ★   ★

The financial services industry is no slouch at spotting a demand. The hunger for products that offer decent diversification and rebalancing has spawned mutual funds that become more conservative (i.e., they increase the proportion of bonds) as time goes by. Called "target-date funds," these vehicles focus on age groups and flag these folks' expected retirement dates, such as Fidelity Freedom 2020 and T. Rowe Price Retirement 2030. The funds don't necessarily end on those dates, but the names offer investors easy goals to identify their retirement-planning needs.

Target-date funds have seen spectacular growth as U.S. Baby Boomers noticed they were edging ever closer to 65, the traditional age to hang it up. The funds began small in the early 1990s and really got going with the 2006 pension act, which permitted employers to automatically enroll workers in 401(k) plans, thus countering employee inertia that kept them from investing for the future. Before, workers had to choose whether to join a plan or not; now, management plunks them into one, and they have to bestir themselves to get out.

Target-date funds were an ideal offering to keep employees happy and enrolled in 401(k)s, since the dates in the funds' titles drove home the reason that people invest, to have money when they no longer are working—plus, the funds offer the comfort of automatically shifting into less risky assets as time goes by. From 2005 to 2006, target-date assets expanded from $69 billion to $114 billion. Spooked investors pulled money out of the funds in 2008, but the portfolios resumed their popularity afterward. At the end of 2009, target-dates boasted $259 billion.

These funds, though, are not panaceas. They're not all the same and not all terrific. Some of those puppies are riskier than others; the levels of stock exposure vary. T. Rowe's funds lean more toward stocks, even for folks who are near retirement. Putnam's are more bond heavy. The old saw is that your fixed-income allocation should track your age.

Thus, if you are 55, then you should be 55 percent in bonds with the rest in stocks. This formulation, of course, is simplistic to the max. Many more considerations go into assembling a retirement kitty, such as how long you want to keep working.

Still, the mix of T. Rowe Price Retirement 2020, a fund set up for those who want to retire then, at year-end 2010 was 71 percent stocks, 22 percent bonds, and the rest in cash and other stuff. Compare that to Putnam's 2020 fund, whose stock-bond allocation is 32–46. Target-date funds have been around for only a short while, yet their five-year annual average returns give the edge to the more aggressive T. Rowe fund, which gained 4.4 percent, while the Putnam offering was up just 1.4 percent. Once again, the financial crisis distorted traditional performances since most bonds suffered along with stocks then. In the bad-bad-bad year 2008, the more conservative Putnam fund didn't lose as much as the T. Rowe one, although the difference wasn't much: down 32.9 percent for Putnam and 33.5 for T. Rowe. In the 2009 recovery year, T. Rowe did four points better than Putnam.

Over the next decade, though, assuming that stocks and bonds behave as they normally do, odds are that the Putnam fund will be a more comfortable fit for those retiring in 2020. However, let's say there is another awful bout of inflation. Sitting with a load of bonds like Putnam's might not be the best place to be.

Critics of target-date funds say that you are better off being the captain of your own asset allocation, maybe aided by a good financial planner. A lot of these set-it-and-forget-it portfolios have weaknesses that go way beyond their asset mixes. One is the Procrustean bed approach the target-date funds employ. At a 2009 Securities and Exchange Commission (SEC) hearing, Morningstar's director of asset allocation strategy, Rod Bare, called for target-date funds for each year to offer conservative, moderate, and aggressive versions, allowing investors a choice of risk exposure. If T. Rowe Price is your company's 401(k) provider, then under Bare's proposal, the fund house would offer you a wider array of choices to fit your needs than just its usual stock-laden fare.

In the wake of the late 2000s catastrophe, Washington hearings demonstrated that much was awry with target-date funds. One of the worst 2008 performances came from Oppenheimer Transition 2010, which fell a scary 41 percent. The fund had a large (60 percent) alloca-tion in stocks and also weighed down its bond component with lethal mortgage-backeds. In putting together target-date funds, many invest-ment houses use other funds they sponsor, not all of them heroes. And some funds charge far too much. MassMutual's 2020 fund, for instance, costs investors 1.3 percent yearly, while its Vanguard counterpart wants merely a seventh of that.

Target-date funds can work well for investors who have good savings habits. In promotional materials, the fund industry has con-cocted models to show how these funds should deliver satisfying returns to allow participants a comfortable old age. J. P. Morgan Chase research spoils that dream picture, saying that the funds make rosy assumptions about investors that are crushingly unrealistic. The models assume 35-year-olds will put 10 percent of their salaries into their 401(k)s; statistically, that doesn't happen until they are 55. Also, the industry acts as if no one, preretirement, takes loans or makes withdrawals from 401(k)s, when 20 percent borrow and 15 percent withdraw. Finally, the industry expects retirees will extract just 4 to 5 percent of their sheltered money annually, yet many pull out 20 percent or more. Asset allocation becomes asset immolation.

★   ★   ★

How does one come up, pray tell, with the right asset allocation?

Plenty of tools are available for free or low cost on the Web. One well-regarded tool is MarketRiders, which for around $10 per month, can give you a list of exchange-traded funds (ETFs) that spans the investing spectrum. This program is based on a questionnaire that takes about an hour to fill out, detailing your age, risk tolerance, and the like. You go out and buy the ETFs (mutual funds that are sold throughout the day on exchanges) from brokers like Charles Schwab, and MarketRiders doesn't take a cut. It will alert you when rebalancing is needed.

Other online calculators are free, like ESPlannerBASIC, the brain-child of Boston University economist Laurence Kotlikoff. It asks you a series of questions that takes around 30 minutes, on matters ranging from your income to your spending level to when junior will leave the nest. You will get back answers to matters like how much you can afford to spend in retirement to what an ideal asset allocation is for you, divided into asset classes. It does not make specific recommendations on ETFs or any other particular security.

Many do-it-yourself approaches to asset allocation have limitations, however. A December 2009 report by the Society of Actuaries and Actuarial Foundation knocks planning tools for failing to take into account longevity (how long you likely will live), housing (will you sell your place and rent, or will you take out a reverse mortgage?), what your expected Social Security income is, and the possibility you might buy an annuity, where you fork over a lump sum to an insurance company in return for a lifetime of payments. Distressingly, a survey by the group finds that, while 10 percent used computer tools to plan their investing, 37 percent turned to friends and relatives for advice. While cousin Charlie may be a fine barbecue chef, he likely knows squat about finances. Planner Joel Bruckenstein tells the MarketWatch financial web site that the biggest problem for ordinary people planning investments is that many don't want to devote the time to the task.

Enter financial planners, the living, breathing kind, who figure out what you should put your money into. Lots of full-service brokerages employ these advisers, although they may recommend whatever the house is pushing, even if the touted products belong in a compost heap. While in-house planners take a flat fee, they may get a cut of a broker's commission when clients go down the hall to execute the plan. Increasingly and mercifully, independent advisers are proliferating, some of them refugees from big Wall Street firms. They will charge a flat fee ranging from 0.25 to 1.5 percent of client assets per year. Brokers somewhere else make the recommended trades, and the planners don't get a taste of this action.

Financial advisers are relatively new on the scene. *The History of Financial Planning* by E. Denby Brandon Jr. and H. Oliver Welch recounts how insurance salesmen and stockbrokers used to be the only pros you could consult when figuring out how to save for your old age. In steadily more affluent postwar America, there was a growing need for someone to offer financial advice. A group of sales reps met near Chicago's O'Hare Airport in 1969 to launch a new profession, financial consulting, which would service this need, and along the way, generate additional fees. The CFP exam, a board to evaluate professional standards, educational programs, and other trappings of a real profession emerged. The CFP test is very hard, with a pass rate of a little over half. The group formulated a code of ethics and in 1978 expelled its first member for alleged improprieties. By the end of 2008, 213 colleges and universities offered financial planning education, from a bachelor's degree to a doctorate.

For a long while, CFPs wrestled whether they should have a fiduciary standard, where planners were required to act in the best interests of the clientele, and not in the best interests of their own wallets. One planner, John Blankinship, regularly called for a fiduciary duty to be a part of the CFP ethics canon, a controversial stance because some planners feared it would open them up to lawsuits. When he spoke at one planners' conference, Brandon and Welch write, the audience "threw pennies and cherry tomatoes at the podium in protest." Eventually, Blankinship's side won and fiduciary duty was installed in the ethics code.

★   ★   ★

What investors want to know is: *will I outlive my assets?* Visions of ragged elderly folks huddled in a tiny room with peeling paint and a single lightbulb dangling from the ceiling, as they clasp a rusty tin of cat food in one arthritic hand and with the other spoon it into their near-toothless gobs, a single, bitter tear spilling down their lined cheeks—that's the essence of the nightmare everyone wants to avoid.

When setting up investment programs, many planners use new tools to test for long-term durability. The most prominent such test is the Monte Carlo simulation, which seeks to project the odds your asset allocation will last until you depart the planet. A computer runs myriad projections based on your information, plus assumptions about the economy and the markets in the future. Planning outfit Financial Engines in 2009, says the *Wall Street Journal*, calculated the likely outcomes for retiring at 65 for a 50-year-old male earning $250,000 yearly with a $1 million portfolio, split 50–50 between stocks and bonds: the chances he would have between $161,000 and $193,000 per year in retirement income were 27 percent; between zero and $110,000, 5 percent; over $286,000, 5 percent.

Monte Carlo methods originally were concocted in the 1940s to design nuclear weapons, and named after the hot spot on the French Riviera, known for its beaches and its casinos. Retirement investing, to be sure, resembles gambling only in that you are betting on the future and calculating the odds. A mathematician, David Hertz, adopted the method for finance in 1964, and it has been used for planning corporate projects, stock options valuation, and portfolio analysis.

A weakness of Monte Carlo and other such portfolio-building tools emerged in the late 2000s market debacle: As the Financial Engines example shows, the simulation tends to give the greatest odds to the middle range of possible outcomes. The possibilities are spread along a bell curve. The chances of a huge drop are rated as low, on the narrow left end of the curve. As the *Journal*'s Eleanor Laise reports, a portfolio of 60 percent stocks and 40 percent bonds dropped by one fifth in 2008. The odds of that happening were rated as once in 111 years. Extraordinary market slides, lamentably, have occurred a lot more often than that in recent years: the 1987 crash, the dot-com disaster in the early 2000s, the housing-crunch hell in the last part of the decade. To combat that, various planners are striving to adopt "fat-tailed" distributions, where the seemingly rare market free-falls are treated as more likely to hit. So the narrowing tail on the left of a bell curve grows wider.

In a casino, some games are pure luck, like roulette. Others, such as blackjack, give you a better shot at winning because they involve strategy and math. Asset allocation is a cut above gambling. If you are smart about it, and the gods aren't too harsh, you likely will be fine in old age. No one wants to end up sitting in a shabby room eating cat food.

Summary

- Diversification of assets, combining those that zig with others that zag, has become a standard of financial planning. But this core of asset allocation didn't seem to work in the 2008–2009 market collapse, when almost everything but Treasuries lost.

- Since a key tenet of asset allocation is finding things that don't correlate, investors are always looking for what doesn't track stocks, which are the engine of any portfolio. This is hard to do. During downturns, even outliers like commodities tend to move more like stocks.

- Economist Harry Markowitz provided the framework for diversification in the early 1950s by inventing Modern Portfolio Theory (MPT), a statistical method of assembling a portfolio that balances risks and returns, with a stress on assets that don't move in tandem. But MPT is based on statistical norms, and the theory took a beating from the 2008–2009 madness, which battered pretty much everything.

- Bonds, particularly Treasuries, don't correlate well with stocks. Hard assets like energy, timber, and gold usually don't track either stocks or bonds. Real estate used to be a steady riser until the late 2000s, and may be again.

- Conservative allocations are bond heavy and stock light, but may not build the wealth needed for a good retirement. Aggressive portfolios, tilted toward stocks, may blow up in bad times. An even split might work better over the long pull. Investors should rebalance their portfolios at best twice a year to make sure they haven't strayed from their strategies.

- Target-date funds, which automatically become more conservative as the years roll on, are increasingly popular. Yet some are riskier than others, and some are clunkers. Meanwhile, an entire industry of financial planners has emerged to help people set up their investments.

- Many planners use Monte Carlo simulations, which calculate the odds of your living a financially secure old age. But Monte Carlo and other tools can fall short because they hinge on results that fall on a bell curve. Recent years have shown that extraordinary market slides occur far more often than a bell-curve distribution foresees.

Chapter 10

Looking for the Bad: Short Selling

His face gaunt and mournful, James Chanos is not an upbeat guy. He certainly is not a popular man in Corporate America. If Chanos is poking around a stock, it usually indicates he sees something wrong. And that means he might well short the shares, a bet they will decline in value.

While shorting is a very risky proposition, investors often have made out well siding with Chanos and other short sellers with good track records. Once obscure figures, shorts now are prominently part of the financial landscape, and their views are well displayed in the media and on the Web. They have become a real force.

Chanos is the person who exposed the accounting shenanigans at Enron, once a sterling company, universally admired on Wall Street for its dynamic growth and innovative spirit. After Chanos unmasked the

firm, it tumbled into bankruptcy and some of its executives went
to prison. He burrows deep into the books of a company like Enron
and, if the accounting is suspect, he shorts the stock, expecting that
the weaknesses he found will eventually lead other investors to sell it
and thus lower the price. Chanos is of Grecian descent and the investment outfit that he heads is called Kynikos Associates, which in Greek
means "cynic."

In the 1990s, Enron was so revered that it regularly made magazines'
lists of best corporations. In an interview with *Barron's*, Chanos said
he initially thought Enron stock was "viable," but simply overpriced.
Changing hands for $90 per share in 2000, the stock was astronomically
valued at 60 times earnings. That was on the high end for stocks during
the dot-com boom then ongoing.

Enron was in the business of trading electricity, as well as natural
gas, broadband, and paper. The company's initial name was EnterOn,
apparently a verbal play having to do with progress. Someone noticed
that this word meant "intestines" in Greek (this was before Chanos
came on the scene) and the name was shortened to Enron. The
company operated from opulent offices in Houston, the nation's energy
capital. It had the naming rights for the pro baseball stadium. After the
scandal, Enron Field became Minute Maid Park. Now, on the far wall
of the stadium, where the Houston Astros play, is a large mock loco-
motive that chugs along pulling a coal hopper filled with oranges. The
joke is that, in Enron's time as corporate sponsor, the hopper was filed
with subpoenas.

Chanos's suspicions about Enron started when he read an article by
Jonathan Weil, then with the *Wall Street Journal*, about how the company
was pumping up its profits by reporting as earnings the returns on deals
that it would book in the future, a dodgy maneuver called "gain-on-
sale" accounting. Executives, like those at Enron, realized fatter paychecks if they delivered higher profits, so they had a strong motive to
make things look better than they were. As Chanos told *Barron's*, "It
has been our experience that gain-on-sale accounting creates an irresist-
ible temptation on the part of management heavily incentivized with
options and heavy stock ownership to create earnings out of thin air."

Chanos and other shorts want to publicly circulate their bearish
views on a company, in the hopes of awakening the market to its fail-

ings. At his annual Bears in Hibernation conference in early 2001, he named Enron one of his top short picks. Scores of money managers were on hand. Chanos helped Bethany McLean, then a reporter at *Fortune* magazine, research a story about Enron's questionable accounting. Enron executives tried to squelch her article by telling her bosses that she simply didn't understand the sophisticated techniques that they were using as they boldly marched into the future. At the end of 2001, Enron filed for Chapter 11 bankruptcy.

There are two ways of looking at short sellers. One view, favored by the shorts' targets, is that these bearish types are ghouls who want to damage the reputations of fine companies, harming hardworking employees, good-hearted long-term investors, and sometimes even the capitalist system. In October 2001, Enron's chief, Ken Lay, told employees that shorts were attacking the company "just like America is under attack by terrorism." The other view is that shorts expose what's rotten, and provoke the market and maybe the government into cleaning up the mess before it gets worse.

David Einhorn, a prominent short who spotlighted the dangerous condition of Lehman Brothers before the ill-fated Wall Street house imploded, refers to short sellers as "the de facto enforcement division of the SEC." Allowing malefactors and their "toxic assets" to keep rolling along unimpeded is harmful to investors, he believes. He has a very good point. In a presentation at the University of Virginia in late 2009, Chanos derided what he called the "mark to model fantasy," where companies concoct offbeat math to show that standard accounting does not accurately measure their brilliant approach. He displayed a cartoon where one executive says to another, "Our books are balanced: 50 percent of our numbers are real and 50 percent are made up."

★　　★　　★

Heavy short selling of a stock does not necessarily mean that a company is fudging its books and that its executives are crooks. Often, it means that shorts think investors have pushed the company's value absurdly high.

Sometimes, a heavily shorted stock will stay up because it is worth the price. Netflix, which pioneered sending DVD movies to subscribers in the mail, has been a perennial whipping boy for the shorts. Its price-to-earnings multiple is close to Enron's at the peak. Netflix's stock has had volatile spells, and cratered along with the rest of the market in 2008. Since then, the shares rallied and did well into 2011, for good reason: revenue and earnings have excelled. Once, short interest was half of Netflix's float (the amount of stock outstanding), and then in 2010 it fell to around a quarter. Continuously shorting a rising stock is an occupational hazard for shorts, who need a strong stomach to stick with their negative views.

Shorts are a force nowadays, with people like Chanos devoted to the practice, and in a very public fashion. Before, shorts tended to work behind the curtain. Much of their new prominence is owing to the rise of hedge funds—pools of capital provided by institutions and rich individuals, and (at their best) run by outside-the-box thinkers who strive to beat the market. Shorting is as outside the box as you can get. Chanos's Kynikos is, of course, a hedge fund.

For individual investors without a lot of market savvy, and lacking the riches needed to get into a hedge fund, shorting can be a perilous exercise they may well regret. For those who bone up on company financials and strategy, shorting can be very lucrative, a good tactic to expand and protect existing stock holdings. Investors also can benefit from shorts' views without shorting stocks themselves: They use the shorts as bellwethers. Being alert to what shorts are doing can signal you at the very least to get out of a stock before it goes down the pipe. Several mutual funds exist that short broad stretches of the market, like the Standard & Poor's (S&P) 500, but they tend to charge high fees and mainly work during big market retreats. Other times, these funds don't usually do very well.

In a short sale, your broker borrows shares in a company for you, then sells them. The money you make from the sale goes to your account. You are expecting that the price will go down. Assuming the market cooperates, you buy back the borrowed shares, a move called covering. The difference between what you made on the sale and the lesser amount to cover is your gain. If the stock has the bad fortune (for you) of rising, then you are in a fix. A stock's ability to fall—it can go no lower than zero—is dwarfed by its potential to rise. Netflix jumped from $50 per share in January 2010 to $220 a year later.

Here's an illustration. You suspect that XYZ's stock is up in the clouds at $50 and bound to return to earth. Its multiple is higher than the eye can see, and prospects for earnings growth are limited by new competition and management turmoil. You go to your broker and ask to borrow 1,000 shares of XYZ. The broker locates the shares, and requires you to put up half its value in cash, known as margin. You dutifully fork over $25,000. You sell the borrowed shares, for $50,000. Sure enough, the market then rubs the cinders from its eyes and agrees with your baleful take on XYZ. The stock does a death dive to $10. You waltz in and buy the stock back for a mere $10,000. The bedraggled shares you borrowed slink back to their hapless owner. You have netted $40,000. Not too shabby.

Should fate take a different turn, you will be the one sobbing about the fickleness of life. Maybe XYZ's rivals trip over themselves and the company's management gets its act together. Amid joyous shouts on Wall Street, XYZ vaults to where the air is rare, hitting $100. Your broker will want you to put up more margin, often an extra 30 percent of the value. Worse, you have an unlimited liability. The damn XYZ stock could keep on levitating. The higher it flies, the more you are out of pocket to buy it back. For you, this is a real nightmare on Wall Street, with the broker playing the role of Freddy Krueger.

Professional shorts limit their losses by obeying a few rules. A common one is to cover if a shorted stock rises more than 25 percent over the price where the borrowed shares were sold. The pros tend to stay clear of small stocks, with market values below $1 billion or daily trading volumes below 5 million shares. Small stocks are more vulnerable to what's called a short squeeze, in which shares are hard to find when you're trying to return the infernal things to their owner. With many shorts scrambling to cover, the price jets very high very quickly, making your losses even more excruciating.

Not all shorting involves capitalizing on another investor's bad luck, namely, the poor schnook who owns XYZ stock. You can use short selling to hedge your own portfolio and limit your taxes. Maybe you bought a stock at $20 and now it has spiraled up to $150, making you nervous. You always could sell and realize the $130 return per share. You will owe capital gains tax on that $130, for sure. A better alternative might be to short your position, to shield yourself from a decline. Once you are confident the stock will stay aloft, then you can cover.

Whatever your reason for shorting, know that you must pay close attention to your chosen stock's behavior. File and forget is not an option. And know that you require buckets of pure, unadulterated bravery.

★   ★   ★

Shorting has been around for a long time, and often has been in ill repute. The concept of profiting off someone else's misery is inherently unsympathetic. But when put in perspective, shorts aren't the predators they appear to be, argues Robert Sloan, managing partner of money manager S3 Partners, in his book, *Don't Blame the Shorts*: "The person who shorts oil in this country is a hero because he wants the price to go down. But he who shorts an oil company is a villain because he wants the oil company's fortune to sour." This might not be as paradoxical as it seems. A distinction can certainly be drawn here, naturally. A stockholder in energy shares wishes to pay less at the pump but also desires his wealth, partly in oil stocks, to grow rather than shrink. Sloan's broader point is that the oil stock might deserve to drop, that a decline is healthy for the market, if not for an individual investor's portfolio short term.

The vile image of shorts began when they first appeared in the 1600s with the global expansion of trade, thanks to colonization of the New World and general economic growth. The Dutch East India Company, known as VOC, complained loudly about short sellers. Amsterdam's stock exchange then was a wild place, perfect for schemers. According to historian Niall Ferguson, the bourse was full of shorts who "spread negative rumors to try to drive down VOC." In retaliation, the Dutch ended up taxing short sales. Napoleon outlawed shorting with the justification that shorts were "enemies of the state." In New York, a ban on short selling was in place from 1812 to 1858, although the restriction proved impossible to enforce.

From the earliest days of the United States, there has been a populist disdain for practitioners of high finance, with the shorts painted as the worst of a bad lot. In Sloan's telling, "The notion that it was un-

American to play the financial game is nearly as old as the country itself." Thomas Jefferson and his followers, who championed agrarian simplicity, loathed financiers. To the squire of Monticello, whose own finances often were in shoddy condition, the Wall Street lords were a threat to the new Republic's ideals. All this money grubbing seemed, to him, so very English. The Jeffersonians' arch-foe, Alexander Hamilton, espoused the creation of a large banking establishment to harness the nation's resources. The Jeffersonians said the money arena was rigged in favor of the financial plutocrats. Amid the economic turmoil that boiled up in the early 20th century and again in the early 21st century, that charge arose repeatedly. Among all the money manipulators, none appeared more devious than the shorts, those heartless fiends who want to decimate your portfolio for their own private gain.

The market panic of 1907 evaporated public confidence in the financial system. A congressional probe, headed by a Louisiana Democrat named Arsene Pujo, delved into the crisis. During the House of Representatives inquiry, shorts soon came to the fore as major culprits. Beyond rhetoric, though, no clampdown on shorting resulted from the Pujo Committee. Because the previous shorting ban hadn't worked, no one could see a practical way of curbing the negative wagers. The imperious J. P. Morgan, testifying before the Pujo Committee, claimed he never shorted stocks and disliked the practice. Nevertheless, Sloan recounts, Morgan added that "he would not criticize it because he did not see how it could be avoided."

The one time that short selling seemed to enjoy at least modest public acceptance was amid the booming market of the 1920s. The market as a whole was roaring, everyone was making money, and the occasional bearish bet was tolerated. The *Wall Street Journal* even listed interest rates to borrow stock for shorting.

Then came the 1929 crash and the Great Depression. Jefferson-style disdain for perceived financial manipulation, not seen since Pujo's time, staged a reprise. Joseph Kennedy, who had made a pile as a bootlegger, infamously hauled in another $15 million in 1929 by shorting stocks. As citizens' wealth disintegrated, President Herbert Hoover grew enraged at short selling. He believed that shorting was a Democratic conspiracy to hurt his reelection chances. He was sure that a group of shorts met every Sunday to hatch plots to further weaken the market in the coming week.

New congressional inquiries convened to get to the bottom of the crisis, and shorts once more were the fall guys. Richard Whitney, president of the New York Stock Exchange (NYSE), got summoned to Capitol Hill to defend Wall Street's ways. He shocked his listeners with his defense of shorting. When a senator told Whitney he had "brought this country to the greatest panic in history," the NYSE chief retorted: "We brought this country, sir, to its standing in the world by speculation."

This defiance wasn't what the lawmakers wanted to hear. At a House committee hearing, Fiorello LaGuardia told Whitney that "since 1929, we haven't had any short sellers in the bread lines." Nobody wanted to listen to Whitney's response that shorts had kept the market operating in 1929 by providing liquidity through covering. He remonstrated in vain that it was "the willingness of people who have sold short at higher levels to buy when prices were breaking that helped maintain the market." Besides, he went on, shorting between 1929 and 1932, constituted just 5 percent of NYSE trades, so the idea that such bearish transactions were a monstrous, market-wrecking force was preposterous.

Unfortunately for the shorts' cause, Whitney turned out to be a crook. Hoping to cash in on the end of Prohibition, he bought a big interest in a distiller. The investment turned out to be a loser, and the cash-strapped Whitney declared bankruptcy. To make margin calls, he embezzled money from customers and the New York Yacht Club (he was its treasurer). In 1938, he was thrown into prison.

That same year, the Securities and Exchange Commission (SEC) adopted the uptick rule, which forbids short selling when a stock is dropping. The only time a stock could be sold short was when its price rose, that is, ticked up. The point was to prevent shorts from piling on a "bear raid," where a stock price gets hammered into powder. The uptick regulation lasted until 2007, when the commission repealed it due to a study that showed the rule did little to affect stock prices. Interestingly, the repeal came during a bull run, right before the market seized up. As Wall Street came apart the following year, guess who once again got to play the role of bad guy.

The heads of securities firms were quick to point an accusing finger. Robert Pozen, the chairman of MFS Investment Management, collected their tales of woe in his book, *Too Big to Save?* In 2008, Morgan Stanley chief executive John Mack wrote a memo to employees saying that "we're in the midst of a market controlled by fear and rumors, and short sellers are driving our stock down." In congressional testimony, Lehman Brothers head Dick Fuld lamented that "unsubstantiated rumors in the marketplace caused significant harm to Lehman." Never mind that it carried too much rotten debt. John Thain, Merrill Lynch's top dog, also blamed shorts for Merrill's stock slide, although Pozen finds little correlation between short sales volume and Merrill's price movements.

As Lehman failed and other banking giants teetered, the SEC in September 2008 temporarily outlawed short selling of financial stocks. The commission let the rule expire a month later, since it appeared to do no good. Financial stocks, which got a quick bump up after the ban took effect, had then fallen even lower than their level before the rule. So maybe, just maybe, the shorts weren't to blame for the crisis. Enemies of the shorts weren't pleased. Certainly, they contended, shorts should not be allowed to feast on a stock that was in full retreat. In early 2010, the SEC imposed a new uptick rule covering all types of shares. It forbids short selling if a stock has gone down by 10 percent in a trading session—unless the most recent bid is above the previous one.

Do shorts these days peddle false rumors to batter a stock and profit from its descent? While this ploy is illegal, proving it is difficult. One 2010 academic study, however, suggests that shorts' lying manipulation is rare. The study indicates that shorts seldom make their negative trades ahead of the market. Two University of North Carolina professors, Joseph Engelberg and Adam Reed, show that the average short tends to react to news events, much like the market as a whole. In other words, he is not playing tricks, which would require him to be ahead of the news. Short sale volume and overall market volume track each other three weeks before and after some news breaks that moves the stock price. Yet while shorts may not be ahead of the market, they tend to move in aggressively and confidently. The professors say that shorts have a leg up on many others because they are better at analyzing information, and thus acting on it.

Critics of shorts like to slam them for a maneuver called "naked shorting," which is illegal. With this, shorted stock is sold that never was borrowed in the first place. In other words, a phantom sale occurs. Since trades are digits flickering on a screen and not paper stock certificates, it is highly conceivable that this flimflam could go on. Hedge fund manager David Einhorn, though, suspects that it is minimal. In-and-out traders indeed could pull off such a scam, since the whole process is over very quickly. But, he says, long-term players like himself would be discovered.

★   ★   ★

Exactly how a first-rate short seller works nowadays is fascinating and instructive. A nose for accounting is crucial. So is a relentless ability to track down information that doesn't appear on the books. A sweeping view of broader economics comes in very handy, as well.

Jim Chanos has had a fascination with stocks most of his life. He grew up in Milwaukee, where his father owned a chain of dry cleaners. His dad introduced him to the market when he was in the fifth grade. He started out as a premed student at Yale, then shifted to economics, where his heart lay. His first finance job was with Gilford Securities in Chicago. He grew suspicious about Baldwin-United, an insurance company whose stock was performing very well. Chanos saw a shaky foundation. Records from Arkansas regulators convinced him that its bookkeeping was funky to the extreme. A one-time piano maker, Baldwin had played a blissful tune for Wall Street; it inflated its stock price by pumping up the value of its acquisitions. The company threatened to sue Chanos for disparaging it. Wall Street houses joined in to vilify him. In 1983, Baldwin couldn't keep the rickety structure together and it filed for bankruptcy.

The Baldwin call made Chanos a star. A big-time job offer followed. The young analyst joined Deutsche Bank in New York. But his Baldwin success hardly secured his status. The red-hot 1980s were at full blast, which meant that shorts were having a tough time. All stocks seemed to be going up. Nothing was hotter than Drexel Burnham Lambert and its crown prince, Michael Milken, whose empire of junk bonds propelled that era's takeover boom. Sensing that many of the Drexel deals were as flimsy as balsa wood, Chanos placed them under scrutiny.

Chanos found out personally that dishing out criticism put him in the gunsights of people who had the power to fight back. He told *New York* magazine that private detectives in the mid-1980s were sifting through the trash outside his East Side townhouse. A *Wall Street Journal* article cited him as a shifty type who spread false rumors about companies and even impersonated reporters. He soon found himself out of a job and decided to start Kynikos. Life as a short without a major firm's support in a rising market was scary. It didn't matter that he often was right.

Patience is required to be a short. One of Chanos's targets was Integrated Resources, a financial services company that had grown magnificently, fueled by Milken's junk financing. This business specialized in tax shelters for commercial real estate, where investors handed bundles of cash to Integrated's property partnerships. Integrated used the capital to buy questionable buildings that obligingly lost money. So the investors could write off these passive losses on their tax returns. Then came the 1986 tax reform law, which removed this tasty little ploy from the tax avoiders' playbook. Integrated collapsed in 1990, shortly before Drexel's demise. Chanos had been slamming Integrated for five years before it finally filed for bankruptcy.

Accounting, which few find fun, is Chanos's great skill. He smelled trouble at an industrial conglomerate called Tyco International because of how it kept its books. Tyco was a serial acquirer. Chanos charged that Tyco arranged for companies it coveted to artificially hold down their results as the takeover date approached. After Tyco finally swallowed the companies, they miraculously began reporting bounteous sales gains, he said. Tyco also used conjurer's tricks to minimize charge-offs of goodwill—an intangible asset reflecting such items as a company's brand value, which usually must be subtracted from earnings after a merger. Tyco, Chanos claimed, stretched goodwill charges out for decades and kept them from eating too much into profits.

Chanos's crusade against Tyco started in 1999. Three years elapsed before he was vindicated. Tyco lost $9 billion largely due to its ill-fated fiber-optic network, a victim of the tech bust. By then, the market saw that Tyco had overreached, and the stock descended harshly. The company got another black mark in 2002 when its aggressive CEO, Dennis Kozlowski, was forced to resign as news spread about his personal excesses with Tyco money. Koslowski went to prison for dipping into the corporate till. One of his most notorious escapades was the 40th birthday party he threw for his wife on the Italian isle of Sardinia. Tyco paid for half of the $2 million bash, which was billed as a shareholders' meeting. The Roman orgy-themed shindig featured an ice sculpture of Michelangelo's Statue of David, urinating vodka.

★   ★   ★

John Paulson detected a foul aroma from the 2000s real estate mania when others giddily smelled only the sweet perfumes of their ever-growing fortunes. The bearish positions he daringly took—in effect, shorting the housing market—were for vast sums, far beyond the means of most ordinary investors. But they illustrate both how a broad macroeconomic scope can aid a short seller, and how he risks being painted as a blackguard for implementing it.

The feat Paulson pulled off earned his firm, Paulson & Co., $15 billion in 2007. His personal slice was $4 billion. The *Wall Street Journal*'s Gregory Zuckerman chronicles Paulson's epic short strategy in his aptly named book, *The Greatest Trade Ever*. Paulson's 2007 payout, he writes, "was more than the earnings of J. K. Rowling, Oprah Winfrey, and Tiger Woods put together." Zuckerman quotes an envious rival telling him, in the fall of 2007: "Paulson's not even a housing or mortgage guy. . . . And until this trade, he was run-of-the-mill, nothing special."

Paulson started his hedge fund in 1994, and schlumped along with so-so performances for years. By 2006, he saw younger hedgies eclipsing him in the bull market. A retiring personality, he lacked the salesman's chops needed to raise money and appease impatient investors. His specialty was investing in corporate mergers before they were completed, a safe if boring strategy that wowed no one. Frustrated, and sure that what he called the "casino" market couldn't keep climbing forever, he took a chance on shorting the spiraling stocks of auto suppliers and financial services providers, which he figured must be overvalued by then. He was wrong. Stocks kept chugging ever higher. There must be something to short that is very likely to crash, he told his analysts. Find it.

The answer came from an analyst whom Paulson had hired almost as a favor. As Zuckerman tells it, Paolo Pellegrini, a very sharp man who had done poorly on Wall Street, landed the job with Paulson largely because they were old friends. Pellegrini, working alongside young analysts the ages of his children, crunched the numbers and discovered that housing prices were far out of whack with historical growth patterns—averaging 7 percent yearly since 2001 after inflation, when the norm was 1.4 percent. Home values, he told his boss, would have to drop almost by half to return to their customary trend line. Paulson was convinced.

Next, Paulson and Pellegrini alighted on a method to bet against housing, called credit default swaps (CDSs). This is insurance that is issued to offset the chances that bonds will stop paying interest. Paulson zeroed in on CDSs that insured mortgage bonds. This coverage was cheap at the time, as few thought homeowners would default on paying off their mortgages. These loans were bundled into mortgage-backed securities. Paulson had a rough time convincing investors to sink money into his shorting strategy. But he stayed the course, and his timing proved perfect.

Along the way, Paulson forged an alliance with Goldman Sachs that went on to cause the securities firm enormous headaches. He volunteered to help form an investment vehicle, called Abacus 2007-ACI, to hold mortgage bonds that Paulson thought would decline in value. He identified 123 suspect mortgage bonds that then were stuffed into Abacus. Investors took positions in Abacus in spring 2007, with housing seemingly still rocking, but Paulson wagered against it using swaps. An abacus is an ancient calculating tool that involves beads sliding along a wire. When the beads fell off the wire and scattered on the floor, Paulson made another killing.

In the smoldering aftermath of the housing bust, the SEC smacked Goldman with a civil fraud suit, claiming that it had duped clients who took long positions in Abacus, believing it was a solid investment. The SEC alleged that customers weren't told that Paulson had handpicked the mortgage bonds and that the vehicle was booby-trapped. Goldman protested that it had lost money on Abacus, too, by buying a stake in it, a long position the same as the clients'. While Paulson wasn't charged, he came in for heaps of criticism. In mid-2010, the SEC and Goldman settled, with the Wall Street firm paying $550 million and conceding that it mistakenly failed to disclose Paulson's involvement.

At one point before the settlement, Goldman told the SEC that Paulson was not a central player in Abacus's formation since he was hardly a big name in 2007, and therefore disclosure of his influence on Abacus seemed unimportant. Paulson, the firm told the government, was "no Warren Buffett or E. F. Hutton."

While that was accurate, Paulson did pull off an audaciously profitable deal that those towering figures might well admire. What it took was ample foresight and immense grit.

★   ★   ★

Greenlight Capital is the name that David Einhorn gives his firm. It would more appropriately be called Redlight because Einhorn is a master at detecting danger ahead. One of his early successes was shorting food chain Boston Chicken in the late 1990s. The chicken chain, Einhorn discovered, reported nice returns from fees and loans it made to franchisees opening new outlets. But Einhorn determined that many of the new restaurants were not making the money needed to support payments to the parent. Eventually, the entire enterprise tumbled into Chapter 11. It later was resurrected, under new ownership, as Boston Market.

His finest hour was his call on Lehman Brothers, long a sterling name on Wall Street. The firm harks back to 1844 when a German immigrant named Henry Lehman extended financing to Alabama cotton growers. The firm helped smuggle cotton past Union blockades during the Civil War. With the end of hostilities, it moved to New York and helped finance such brands as Woolworth, Sears Roebuck, and Pan Am. American Express took over Lehman in the 1980s, but after seven years of captivity, it reclaimed its independence under Fuld, a hardnosed former trader known as "the Gorilla." Fuld led Lehman deeper into the exciting world of subprime mortgages and derivatives. In 2007, it reported a nice $4 billion in earnings. Lehman stock headed north.

Einhorn was not impressed. He began shorting the stock in mid-2007. He trumpeted his skepticism at investment conferences and to the media, criticizing how Lehman valued its assets. He vociferously doubted that it had disclosed the shakiness of its positions.

In April 2008, a month after the demise of Bear Stearns, another securities firm with a strong stomach for risky plays, Einhorn wrote his investors that there "was good reason to question Lehman's fair value calculations" of mortgage and kindred hinky holdings. Lehman had a worrisome amount of debt, at one point 37 times its equity. In the heady days of the housing boom, Lehman assured everyone that it possessed the smarts to manage the debt, which afforded it the firepower to make even more money. Too bad for them this boast proved untrue.

Lehman executives described Einhorn's approach as "short and distort." The short seller responded that the company had every reason to present itself in a positive light as management's pay was tied to performance. Later, it came out that Lehman had prettified results by moving $50 billion in debt off the books, using a maneuver called a Repo 105 transaction. In September 2008, Lehman crumbled and touched off the financial crisis. Lehman could evade the U.S. Navy in the 1860s, but not Einhorn in the 2000s.

In ancient Troy, Cassandra, the king's daughter, had the gift of prophecy, but carried the curse that no one would believe her. All she foretold came to pass. She warned of the Greeks' sneaky Trojan horse tactic and met shrugs. Modern-day Cassandras, like Einhorn and Chanos, may not have her 100 percent accuracy. Still, they should be paid heed.

Frank Parish: The Blame Deflector

Frank Parish, a Depression-era businessman, mounted the classic corporate defense against the shorts. An entrepreneur whose machinery company went bust after World War I, Parish figured he could score in the energy industry. He started a natural gas pipeline concern, but it encountered troubles in the straitened 1930s. He built the nation's second-largest pipeline, which began in the Texas gas fields and stretched toward the Midwest. Parish's project stopped short at Indiana, however, when the company couldn't raise the capital to complete the mammoth job. The pipeline's stock price disintegrated.

(Continued)

Frank Parish: The Blame Deflector *(Continued)*

What to do? Parish saw an opportunity in President Hoover's campaign against the shorts. As author Robert Sloan describes it, "The president's conspiracy accusations gave corporate chiefs the political cover to . . . blame the shorts for their own failings and fabrications."

In a 1932 statement sent to a congressional panel probing the shorts, Parish explained away the financial hardships and the stock drop of his Missouri-Kansas Pipeline Company as the iniquitous result of a bear raid. Since many examples of 1920s financial foulness had come to light by then, he got a sympathetic hearing.

The shorts had linked arms with his rivals to undermine the company, he told the committee. Competitors threatened to sink the stock even more if he didn't sell them his gas reserves, he testified. Parish recounted a meeting with a Standard Oil of New Jersey executive who warned he'd be ruined if he didn't capitulate. "How do you like it?" the Standard Oil man purportedly told Parish, referring to his stock's fall up to that point. Parish's nemeses denied that such a meeting had occurred. His complaint to lawmakers apparently bought him some time with Wall Street, yet eventually Parish ran into another imbroglio. His company filed for bankruptcy in 1935, with $35 million in losses.

To make matters worse, the Justice Department indicted him for misleading shareholders with creative accounting that made the company's assets look much better than they were. At his trial, Parish recycled his congressional testimony.

His case got some help from the competition when it emerged that another rival, Cities Service, had hired a spy to delve into the doings of Missouri-Kansas Pipeline. Whether the spy, a secretary at Parish's company, delivered much usable information is unclear. The jury acquitted him, sympathetic to his suffering under the hands of the shorts. Sloan marvels that Parish "paid no price for his charade."

Summary

- Short sellers are bearish investors who can provide a valuable service highlighting corporate weaknesses, like Enron's. Once, they were shadowy figures who did not advertise themselves. Now they are prominent fixtures on the financial scene whose ideas often deserve a hearing.

- To short a stock, you borrow it and immediately sell it, betting that the price will go down. If that happens as you predict, you buy it back at the lower price (known as covering), return the stock to its owner, and profit from the difference. This is very risky, since sometimes the stock keeps rising. Regular investors may not want to take the chance of shorting, yet paying attention to their targets may be useful as a list to avoid.

- Not every heavily shorted stock is a lemon. Netflix has long been a short sellers' target, but kept churning out good performance through 2010. Despite its lofty valuation, Netflix defied the shorts' pessimism.

- Professional shorts obey a few rules to protect themselves. If a shorted stock rises 25 percent over the price at which it was borrowed, they bail, taking their lumps rather than waiting for further deterioration of their position. They avoid small stocks with market values below $1 billion. When covering needs to occur, these stocks may be harder to find than larger ones.

- Are shorts market manipulators? An academic study concludes they don't tend to act before the market does, a finding that weakens the charges against them. If a lot of funny business were going on, most shorts would be ahead of the market.

- Shorts have had a bad reputation for a long time. Complaints that they were spreading lies to drive down stocks sprouted as soon as shorts first appeared on the Amsterdam exchange in the 1600s. Since then, various attempts to ban the practice have failed. Market crashes in 1907, 1929, 2001, and 2008 made shorts appear especially villainous.

- The best shorts are masters at accounting and also are skillful detectives. An eye for economic trends helps. James Chanos, a celebrated short, has a track record at spotting companies with problems that are priced too high. He was the first to uncover the dubious doings at Enron.

- The financial crisis was a great time for shorts. John Paulson personally made $4 billion by shorting the housing market. David Einhorn correctly predicted the fall of mighty Lehman Brothers.

Chapter 11

Chess Masters: Hedge Funds

Hedge fund mogul Steve Cohen is not the easiest guy to work for. Managers at his SAC Capital know that they can be skewered in an instant. If one loses 5 percent of his peak assets, he can have the rest taken away, according to a *Bloomberg Markets* article by Katherine Burton and Anthony Effinger. Lose 10 percent, and the manager is out the door. In 2008, 12 of Cohen's portfolio managers were fired or resigned. Should a manager or analyst not answer a question to the boss's satisfaction, Cohen likely will ask, "Do you even know how to do this f—ing job?"

Despite or because of this climate of fear, Cohen is one of the best hedge fund operators. Since he started SAC in 1992, Cohen has booked only one unprofitable year, in 2008, when his flagship SAC Capital International fund lost 19 percent. But that negative performance was half what the Standard & Poor's (S&P) 500 lost then. The following year, Cohen bounced back with a 29 percent gain. Over 18 years through 2009, he averaged 30 percent annually.

Cohen is a whip-cracking meany for a reason: a lot of money is at stake. Hedge funds, lightly regulated pools of capital provided by very wealthy people or big institutions, are to the rest of Wall Street what Delta Force is to the U.S. Army. The people who run these financial special ops teams are out for blood, and they have a zealous knack for it.

Hedge funds aim to provide a special genius that can't be had from investing in a boring old mutual fund. The hedge fund industry manages roughly $2 trillion in assets. By many measures, these pools have done better than the S&P 500 over time. Hedge Fund Research, which tracks the industry, finds that it lost 18.3 percent in 2008, close to Cohen's market-beating showing. A study by Yale's Roger Ibbotson of 8,400 hedge funds between 1995 and 2009 shows that the average fund (after fees are subtracted) turned out positive alpha, meaning that part of the return that can't be explained by overall market performance. In other words, their managers had something extra and weren't content to ride the market as do index mutual funds.

The term *hedge fund* is a bit of a misnomer, stemming from the practice of commodity investors' buying or selling futures contracts to offset swings in the price of wheat or whatever. The hedgies' buzzword is *sophisticated,* as in "We provide a sophisticated trading strategy that you won't find elsewhere." Such braggadocio is delivered to potential clients in hushed tones. These funds usually don't tell the world at large what they are doing, and they do not have to. They employ all manner of maneuvers, sometimes shorting heavily, sometimes dabbling in derivatives, sometimes indulging in arbitrage, where managers take advantage of a price difference in two separate markets. Buy-and-hold guys, they are not.

They have a hot-breathed zest for trading, and they trade often. Hedge funds were prime suspects in the May 2010 "flash crash," where the Dow Jones average plunged 600 points in five minutes. They didn't turn out to be the culprits, but. . . . A standard mutual fund set off the cascade, and the hedge crowd joined in to make it worse. A hedge hallmark is the heavy use of borrowed money, or leverage, meant to magnify advances. It can compound losses, as well. But just as airplane pilots don't like to talk about crashes, hedge managers treat losses as bizarre occurrences that happen to others, namely the less sophisticated.

Aside from the supposed brilliance of their managers, these investment groups deliver something humans desire, snob appeal. Hedge funds are like private clubs. There's a special cachet that comes with dropping a subtle financial boast—like "Stevie Cohen runs some of my money"—at a glittering gathering. A person who puts money into hedge funds must be an "accredited investor," which the Securities and Exchange Commission (SEC) defines as having at minimum $1 million in investable assets and $200,000 in annual income for the past two years. The money he contributes to a fund can be tied up for anywhere from a year to three, depending on its rules. Certain mutual funds were launched in recent years seeking to replicate the hedge bunch's returns. These don't have the same membership wealth-and-income restrictions. Several have succeeded at besting the market with high-end strategies.

For their pains, hedge fund managers are very well paid. Cohen owns a sprawling 14-acre estate in Greenwich, Connecticut, that he bought for $14.8 million in 1998. It has a two-hole golf course, a hockey rink, a basketball court, and a fabulous art collection that includes a Picasso, a Van Gogh, and a Monet. At hedge funds, the normal compensation arrangement is "two and twenty," where they slice off 2 percent of assets yearly as a management fee and 20 percent of any profits. Managers keep some of their own money tied up in the funds, so they carry a personal incentive to do well. If a fund drops, managers don't see a cent until assets have returned to their previous level, called a high-water mark.

In the broadest sense, hedge fund advocates say, their fantabulously shrewd and gutsy investing has made the market smarter and more efficient. True, although hundreds of them fail every year, the benchmarks that track the industry's overall performance often neglect to account for the funds that are missing in action. That skews the averages upward, a phenomenon called survivorship bias. The failed funds, one presumes, were not sufficiently sophisticated.

But the hedgies argue, with justice, that at least they were not the villains in the financial crisis. That dubious honor belongs to the likes of old-line Wall Street houses, notably Lehman Brothers. Another traditional Wall Street bastion, Goldman Sachs, did much better than its peers during the crisis and afterward because it deploys typical hedge strategies to a fare-thee-well. Hedge funds certainly use leverage, but they typically confine themselves to borrowing two or three times their equity capital, thus they are less vulnerable to running aground once fate turns against them.

The best of them, along with their cousins, private equity funds, kick the tires. They are very smart about where they put their money. The danger is that they sometimes are too clever for their own good, and reason their way into a tar pit. Diligence and intelligence often work when applied correctly, unblinkered by hubris. Hedge and private-equity (PE) funds have much to teach us about investing, good and bad.

★   ★   ★

PE managers invest for the longer term, measured in years, five or higher; hedge kingpin Cohen tends to hold an investment for no more than 30 days. PE managers, such as Kohlberg Kravis Roberts (KKR), buy entire companies and try to boost their profitability, with the plan to then sell them at a nice gain. The PE gang also charges the two and twenty, although the way they compute the 20 percent is more transparent than is the case with hedge managers.

A PE manager eventually gets to take his 20 percent from the sale of a vassal company, long after the acquisition. With hedge funds, that 20 percent is removed from investment profits based on what managers estimate the value of the assets to be. The worth of arcane derivatives can be anyone's guess. Ordinary investors can partake of PE winnings, sort of, just as they can get a toehold into the hedge world by buying mutual funds that ape hedge funds. Regular folks sup at the PE table, or actually at the children's table nearby, through buying shares in the several PE firms that have gone public. Sadly, these stocks' early record has been uninspiring.

KKR and other PE outfits believe that they, too, have benefited the capitalist system by taking over companies. Originally called leveraged buyout (LBO) funds when they emerged in the 1980s, they have a core principle: some companies are lethargic and need shaking up. When the buyout boys started, they struck fear into Corporate America's corpulent heart. The LBO practitioners were known as raiders. Michael Jensen of Harvard, in his widely known 1989 essay, "Eclipse of the Public Corporation," gave an intellectual shine to the raiders' doings. He argued that corporate shareholders and managers were at odds over how to deploy company finances, but wise LBO artists could do the job better. To the LBO potentates, the heavy leverage they heaped on their conquests served to maintain executives' focus. If the company managers didn't shape up, by firing superfluous workers, selling unneeded assets, and cutting other fat, then the heavy interest payments would do them in.

The results of the buyout brotherhood turned out to be mixed, at best. Steven Kaplan of the University of Chicago researched the performance of PE deals through time and concluded that overall they did better than the stock market by a modest amount.

The most renowned buyout was the titanic battle for RJR Nabisco, which KKR won in 1988 by outbidding and outwitting other hungry acquirers. As chronicled in the book *Barbarians at the Gate*, Henry Kravis, KKR's chief, was ruthless in his quest to capture the tobacco and cookie giant, convinced that he could boost its value once the prize was his. It helped that RJR wanted to be taken over. Jovial Ross Johnson, the CEO of RJR, saw a buyout as his salvation. While profits had surged under his tenure, the stock had stayed in the doldrums. Selling the company would produce a rise in the shares and a nice payday for him, he figured.

Corporate executives are a different breed than those who head hedge and PE funds. Executives, like Johnson, get where they are in part through superior social skills. They enjoy the camaraderie of a long, boozy meal and a sunny day on the golf course. The hedge/PE types are more reserved and calculating. They prefer hunching over spreadsheets to wasting time on fairways. As Johnson rattled on about the magical opportunity he had to sell RJR, his lawyer, Steven Goldstone, thought the CEO was buoyant to the point of naiveté. The book quotes Goldstone's reaction: "God, he believes everyone is his best friend." Later, Johnson had dinner at Kravis's gorgeous Park Avenue apartment in Manhattan. Kravis, "a small, intense man with silvery hair," wouldn't give Johnson a straight answer about who would run the company, post-LBO. The CEO soon found out it wouldn't be Ross Johnson.

KKR won that battle, yet failed to win the war. It overpaid for the maker of Oreo cookies and Camel cigarettes, using several tons of borrowed money. Atop the $26.4 billion it spent for RJR, the LBO firm later had to pump in an additional $1.7 billion to forestall its collapse. KKR took this tarnished trophy public in 1991 at $11.25 a share. By the time it sold off the last pieces of the thing, RJR shares were just below $6. At best, KKR had broken even.

Kravis certainly has scored notable successes in the decades he has been around, such as with insurance brokerage Willis Group, snack food maker Wise Foods, and MTU Aero Engines—which were bought, revamped, and then sold to other acquirers or to the public via stock offerings. He and his cousin, George Roberts, along with colleague Jerome Kohlberg, left Bear Stearns in 1976 to form KKR. (Kohlberg exited KKR in 1987.)

Toys "R" Us is a good example of a buyout that apparently went right. Teaming up with Bain Capital and Vornado Realty Trust, KKR bought the bedraggled toy retailer in 2005. Low-cost competition from the likes of Wal-Mart and Target had the chain reeling. In classic LBO style, KKR moved through its new possession with the subtlety of William Tecumseh Sherman on the road to Atlanta. It installed new managers who promptly shuttered underperforming stores, tied the parent chain more tightly with its Babies "R" Us brand, and slashed costs. The company began to post robust earnings for a change. An internal memorandum placed Toys "R" Us at 1.5 times its purchase price, and KKR teed the chain up for a public offering.

There has been some intermarrying between PE firms and hedge funds of late. Increasingly, PE firms have gotten into hedge funds, seeking their quick returns, and hedgies have branched into private equity, lured by its steadier incomes. Hedge fund operators like Cerberus Management chose to enter the PE lists in spite of the headaches attendant on trying to turn around a sluggish acquisition. Cerberus infamously bought Chrysler, only to watch the automaker partake of the joys of bankruptcy court and a federal bailout.

Edward Lampert's ESL Investments had been a hedge fund that specialized in retail stocks until it bought control of Kmart and then Sears Roebuck, to form Sears Holdings. The merged entity has had a rough go since its 2005 start. While Sears is profitable, questions lingered about its prospects in light of its high debt and the intense competition. "Although Lampert has a good long-term record of generating wealth for shareholders, he's a financier, not a retailer," opined research house Morningstar. Bargain-oriented Kmart has hellacious rivals in entrenched Wal-Mart and Target, while Sears wages hard fights in its two main areas, apparel (where it faces Kohl's and J. C. Penney) and home improvement (where Home Depot and Lowe's reign).

PE players depend on the "exit strategy"—the point when they sell their acquisition to a big company looking for a strategic add-on, or to another buyout shop, or to the public. That last one is hard, given its dependence on the fickle fates that rule the stock market. As the economy struggled to recover in 2010, initial public offerings (IPOs) of stock were down. PE firms, which always had been a minority of IPO volume, found themselves making up half the total new-stock activity—for the simple reason that too few companies were going public. The PE firms raise individual funds with a life of about 10 years. When the time comes around, investors want their money back, with an upside, thank you.

So the PE folks are under pressure to sell. That can be a hit-or-miss proposition, and doesn't always make for the most robust returns. Carlyle Group, the celebrated PE firm with a penchant for hiring political figures (George W. Bush and his father, James Baker, John Major) filed to do an IPO for Vought Aircraft Industries. Then, as the market grew choppy again in mid-2010, Carlyle changed course and sold the unit to Triumph Group. Carlyle likely would have gotten more from a public offering, had a decent IPO environment been available.

A harder question swirling around hedge and PE funds is whether they have helped or hurt the economy in general. Hedge funds may make trading run more swiftly and intelligently, but their quick-buck mentality can go awry. Private equity may make acquired companies leaner and more competitive, yet these deals often come freighted with too much borrowing to weather inevitable economic storms. Long term makes sense if you don't have to trudge for miles with a 200-pound boulder on your back.

★   ★   ★

The father of hedge funds was a Marxist spy. Alfred Winslow Jones had an eclectic early career after graduating from Harvard in the early 1920s. He worked on a tramp steamer, bought exports, crunched numbers for an investment counselor, and served in the State Department. Posted to Berlin in 1930 as a vice consul, he witnessed the chaos enveloping Germany and the rise of the Nazis. He married a girl who was part of a group called the Leninist Organization. He left the diplomatic corps and, under various pseudonyms, embarked on a series of clandestine missions in Europe for the Communists.

His brief marriage to his leftist amour over, he drifted back to the States to pursue a doctorate in sociology, with a thesis aimed at proving the alienation of the American workers from capitalism. After marrying a second time, Jones spent his honeymoon in strife-ridden Spain during its civil war, where he hung out with Dorothy Parker and Ernest Hemingway. Eventually, he came to question his left-wing ideals. His thesis fieldwork, interviewing blue-collar workers, uncovered that they were not anticapitalist after all, a blow to Marxist teachings about class struggles.

Jones became a writer for *Fortune* magazine, conservative publisher Henry Luce's elegant valentine to the free-enterprise system. As a business reporter, he came to believe that classic fundamental analysis of stocks was flawed because, among other reasons, human emotion had a big impact on the market. This early belief in behaviorism was the first of many insights he developed, preceding their formulation in academia. Putting his early career as a financial statistician to work, Jones went on to concoct a long-short strategy, where he'd buy value stocks he expected to pop and short expensive Wall Street darlings with flaws. To augment his results, he borrowed money, often merely double his equity capital, nothing too perilous. He strove to find alpha, the return above and independent from the market's moves as a whole.

Jones dubbed his invention a "hedged portfolio," using $100,000 scraped together from friends as equity capital. The world later dropped the "d" as more financial managers stepped forward to copy Jones. In 1949, his first year, the investment partnership booked a 17.3 percent gain, compared with 10.5 percent for the S&P 500. To limit the tax bite, he originated the 20 percent manager's rake-off of fund profits—capital gains were then and now taxed at a lesser rate than ordinary income. He said he got the idea from Phoenician traders in the ancient world, who claimed a fifth of the profits from voyages. Jones grew moderately wealthy and owned a gracious Connecticut home with a grass tennis court.

From his early days as a Communist spy, Jones believed that secrecy was a wise policy: competitors didn't know what you were doing and the government didn't get too interested in regulating you. He avoided advertising his fund, preferring the discreet tête-à-tête with a rich individual. In the tour-de-force book on hedge funds, *More Money than God*, Sebastian Mallaby describes Jones' capital-raising technique as "word of mouth, sometimes between mouthfuls at the dinner table." Jones, the intelligence op, also recognized the value of getting good, actionable information before others. In the pre-Web era, Jones staffers descended on the SEC to grab important just-issued decisions first so the firm could trade on the news before it became widely known.

The Jones record inspired many to follow him into the hedge world. Michael Steinhardt opened his firm in 1967, using the long-short method, and then began to rapidly trade his positions, seeking an edge, a precursor of today's flash traders. Hungarian immigrant George Soros moved into overseas markets before others cottoned to their potential. Taking a page from Jones's yen for information unknown to the market, Julian Robertson paid to have a new car model tested to see if it was breakdown prone; it was, and Mallaby writes that Robertson cleaned up by shorting the automaker.

Once, Jones described hedging as "a speculative tool used for conservative ends." At the time of his death in 1989 at age 88, he had the financial freedom to indulge in philanthropy, albeit in a nonsplashy manner, founding and funding a group known as the Reverse Peace Corps, where foreigners came to teach the poor in the United States. He kept this low-key, not wanting to invite attention to himself. He shunned taking big risks that could have made him even wealthier. His successors, particularly the super-wealthy ones, embraced risk with swashbuckling gusto.

*   *   *

In 2010, Steve Cohen ranked No. 32 among the 400 richest Americans, with a pie worth $7.3 billion, according to *Forbes*. He had a higher net worth than media magnate Rupert Murdoch, Apple chief Steve Jobs, and eBay founder Pierre Omidyar. Cohen numbered among three other hedge fund grandees making the top 50 of the magazine's Rich List: Soros, John Paulson, and James Simons. Two PE players graced this elite roster, Carl Icahn and Ronald Perelman.

Unlike the clandestine Jones, Cohen and his ilk have little compunction about flaunting their fortunes. Cohen doesn't restrict his luxury surroundings to a grass tennis court. Inside his Connecticut palace is a shark floating in a tank. The beast, jaws wide as it gets ready to feed, is dead and suspended in formaldehyde. This is artwork by Damien Hirst, a trendy Englishman who is fascinated by death and has done pieces involving a dead sheep and a dead cow. Cohen bought this shocking display of offbeat whimsy (or to some, bad taste) for a reported $8 million. Apparently, he views it as an expression of the financial world, or at least his section of it.

Cohen wants everyone to know that he is filthy, stinking rich. He keeps his trading strategy under wraps, but not the personal boodle it has created. In early 2009, he put some of his art on exhibit at Sotheby's in New York, featuring works by such luminaries as Paul Cezanne and Edvard Munch. He is an avid donor to fashionable charities. The Robin Hood Foundation, started by fellow hedge fund star Paul Tudor Jones to fight poverty, is a Cohen favorite. In 2008, according to the Burton-Effinger article, he contributed $8.6 million to the foundation. He sits on its board. A children's wing at New York-Presbyterian Hospital (it got $50 million) and Brown University ($30 million) are some of his bigger beneficiaries.

One way Cohen amassed his wealth was by charging some of the highest fees in the hedge fund industry. To hell with two and twenty. Cohen's investors pay a 3 percent management fee and give him up to half of the profits. Of course, this buys them entrée to SAC's commendable trading record. Cohen couldn't get away with such outrageous tariffs if he did not produce.

Controversy is no stranger to such a successful, hard-nosed guy. His legal struggles with his first (and now ex-) wife were ferocious. In late 2010, SAC got a federal subpoena in connection with an insider-trading probe. The investigation revolved around a former Cohen employee who worked for a research organization that serviced hedge fund clients.

The son of a dress manufacturer, Cohen developed an early fascination with the market by reading the newspaper his father brought home in the evening. He made the transition from the stats-laden sports section to the equally numbers-heavy financial pages. "I was fascinated that these numbers were prices and that they were changing every day," he told Jack Schwager, author of *Stock Market Wizards*.

As a teenager, before there was a Web for stock watching, Cohen hung out at a brokerage and learned the art of reading the tape. "You could see volume coming into a stock and get the sense it was going higher," he said to Schwager. At Wharton, he traded stocks between classes. He joined Gruntal as a junior trader in 1978 and scored big his first day on the job, netting $8,000. Soon, he was regularly churning out six-digit daily returns. The firm in 1985 made him the head of its proprietary trading desk, where he was handling Gruntal's own money, not customers'.

Some of Cohen's success comes from intuition, from his canny ability to read the tape. In 1999, making tall wagers on tech stocks, his biggest fund earned 70 percent after fees. The next year, Cohen felt that the Internet mania had peaked and he got out of tech. In 2000, an awful year for the market, the fund was up 72 percent. *BusinessWeek* in 2003 tried to find what his method was, and concluded that he looks for lower-priced shares with a history of good earnings growth, expectations of more growth ahead, and low debt. Even though Cohen turned over the portfolio a daunting 2.6 times per year then, it's intriguing to know that he has an eye for some of Ben Graham's teachings.

★   ★   ★

While hedge funds weren't the culprits in the financial crisis, they have served up some of the most spectacular wipeouts in recent times.

Anyone, as the saying goes, can hang out a sign and claim to be a hedge fund manager. The supposedly sophisticated investors who put money in them may not really be financially astute, merely rich. In 2005, the founders of Bayou Management, which ran two hedge funds, pleaded guilty to fraud. Despite the handsome profits they reported to gullible investors, the funds never made any money.

Overreaching is a far more prevalent sin than crookedness among hedge operators. Some of these pratfalls are the equivalent of putting all your chips on a snake-eyes roll at the Vegas craps table. The conceptual framework behind such a bet may be dazzling. It also defies common sense. The market, which veteran money manager Ken Fisher calls the Great Humiliator, too often dishes up nasty surprises.

Long Term Capital Management (LTCM) wins the Golden Floogy as the all-time worst hedge fund disaster. The title of the quintessential book detailing its demise captures the firm's hubris nicely, Roger Lowenstein's *When Genius Failed*. The brainiacs at LTCM thought they had divined a way of beating the system. John Meriwether, the former head of bond trading at Salomon Brothers, formed the outfit with other Solly alumni, as well as renowned scholars Robert Merton and Myron Scholes (famed as the coauthor of the Black–Scholes options pricing model).

The firm's quantitative strategy was to pair two securities that should be moving in the same trajectory but weren't—often a newly issued 30-year Treasury bond and one that had launched six months before. The new Treasury usually sold for a higher price than the older "off-the-run" bond. LTCM figured that at some point they would converge, and it sold the new bonds short and bought the off-the-run paper. Because the differences between the two bonds were small, Meriwether and his bunch borrowed heavily to magnify their gains. At one point, they had $125 billion in loans, which was 25 times the equity they held. They also used leverage to invest in exotic derivatives that dealt with how different types of trades interacted. Banks, dazzled by the group's cerebral candlepower and its celestial profitability, happily lent LTCM whatever it wanted.

Then two sure things blew up. In 1998, spreads had widened between Treasuries and riskier bonds, as the result of the previous year's Asian currency crisis. The hedge fund predicted that the spreads would narrow to a more normal width. That didn't happen, and LTCM started losing money. Next came Russia's debt default. Panicked investors did what they usually do during times of upheaval: they scrambled into the safe haven of Treasuries. This meant the spread narrowing that LTCM counted on was not happening. The fund was forced to liquidate its positions, booking excruciating losses. By September, the group had a mere $400 million left in equity and that enormous debt, with a leverage ratio of 250 to one.

As LTCM teetered on the brink of perdition, fears arose that the fund's failure would set off a chain reaction that would destroy the world's financial system. In a preview of the 2008 Lehman Brothers collapse, it turned out that LTCM's investments were deeply entwined in the fabric of many of the largest institutions on earth. The Federal Reserve Bank of New York orchestrated a bailout, not with public money as occurred 10 years later, but with a syndicate of banks and Wall Street houses. They effectively took over LTCM, which a couple of years later was dissolved.

Like LTCM, the geniuses at Amaranth Advisors figured they had the most brilliant model possible. They specialized in energy plays, and made a huge score that emboldened them beyond reason. Initial triumph bred overconfidence. Amaranth, which means "unfading" in Greek, wagered that Hurricane Katrina would devastate the Gulf energy industry. Good call. Natural gas prices blew higher and so did the firm's returns. Listed as the 39th-largest hedge fund in 2005—this in a universe of more than 8,000 then—Amaranth had $7.3 billion in capital at the end of the year. That lovely condition took a bad turn soon after.

With leverage of eight-to-one, Amaranth bet that the price of March gas futures contracts would increase relative to April contracts. The thinking was that prices would keep rising and the spread between the two months would widen. Everything worked fine until September 2006, when an expanding glut of stored gas put pressure on prices. The contracts began to fall frighteningly. The managers ended up liquidating their assets.

At the very least, these hedge fund disasters show that they were resolved within the confines of the financial system. No need for a federal bailout of the hedgies. Apart from LTCM, the hedge funds were small enough to fail. Nevertheless, such problems often spur calls for more regulation of the hedge world.

The Dodd-Frank legislation, passed in 2010 to overhaul Wall Street, required that all hedge funds with more than $150 million in assets be registered with the SEC. The new rule gives investors access to basic information, available on the commission's web site, about a fund's business activities, employees, and disciplinary actions.

There is a long-standing debate over mandatory disclosure of hedgies' positions held, a dictum that mutual funds live under. Even though the disclosures would be made after some time has passed, hedge managers argue that their sacred strategies would be bared for everyone to see, sort of like giving the enemy your battle plan. Predatory investors, the complaint goes, would be able to piece together what cleverness the hedge funds are committing. Following Jones's precedent, the best and the brightest, who populate the hedge habitat, prefer to work under cover of darkness.

Beyond such concerns, one wonders if the lure of these gunslinging firms, with their outsized paychecks, is beneficial for society. Hordes of brilliant young people flock to the employ of hedge and PE funds. What if they instead had headed for the unsexy, lower-paying fields of science, medicine, or engineering? Would the world be better off if Thomas Alva Edison had cast his lot with the plush money temples of Wall Street, rather than set up in the drab confines of a lab in Menlo Park?

★   ★   ★

How can regular investors avail themselves of the financial miracle-working of hedge funds? Well, some hedge operators have opened clones of their pools as mutual funds, within reach of nonmillionaires and promising returns that are not correlated to the market.

Most haven't been around for a long while, so establishing their track records is not easy. They tend to have high fees for mutual funds, averaging around 2 percent yearly, according to Morningstar. Turnover of investments is brisk, meaning they pump up investors' capital gains tax tabs. Hedge manager Clifford Asness moved into mutual funds in 2009, and regularly churns his portfolio at AQR Diversified Arbitrage five times yearly.

Morningstar classifies most of these hedgelike mutual funds in its long-short category, meaning they embrace Alfred Winslow Jones's key maneuver. Quaker Aklos Absolute Strategies, one of the veterans of this breed, had a three-year annual return of 2.7 percent through 2010, far better than the negative 3 percent showing of the S&P 500. In 2008, the Quaker fund lost a mere 3 percent, one twelfth of the S&P's drop. Note, however, that the Quaker fund's returns are not remotely near what Steve Cohen delivered.

Several PE firms have gone public, with good results for their managers, if not for the shareholders. Steve Schwarzman sold stock in his Blackstone Group in 2007, which was fortunate timing. He personally pocketed $2.5 billion from the deal. The share price plummeted from $35 to $4 in early 2009, then trudged up to $17 by winter 2011. Original investors lost half.

The better lesson from hedge managers is to think like they do: be smart and disciplined about investing. And don't take on too much debt, as LTCM did. Hedge and PE managers are the chess masters of the financial realm. They know, as others should, that no one has to be a pawn.

John Castle's Castle

For a big-time PE star, John Castle is a small-scale thinker. His most celebrated deal involved muscling out the Kennedy clan. The rest of his buyouts are obscure. One of the most successful dealmakers, he has a value-oriented approach that is best described as a portrait in miniature.

Let Henry Kravis chase after multizillion-dollar acquisitions like RJR Nabisco. Castle wants to purchase smaller businesses you may never have heard of: United Malt Holdings, Associated Packaging Technologies, Anchor Drilling Fluids.

A tall, sharp-featured man indifferent to the glamorous Wall Street milieu, Castle has a fierce love for research that turns up boring cigar-butt companies, a preference not shared by so many others in private equity, who are drawn to more glamorous properties.

(Continued)

John Castle's Castle *(Continued)*

A propitious opening appeared to Castle when he was leafing through Florida real estate ads in 1995. A rundown oceanfront mansion was for sale in Palm Beach. It had languished on the market for a couple of years. Built in 1923, the Mediterranean-style house had no central air conditioning, tiny bedrooms, few closets, and an elevator in the middle of the living room. The dump carried a $7 million price tag; with all the rehabilitation work it needed, that was too rich for even the rich.

Why the towering price? The owners were besotted by the joint's legacy and their own family name. This was the summer estate of the Kennedy family, the site of Camelot camaraderie. Castle bargained the Kennedys down to $4.9 million. Nowadays, even after the real estate bust, which rocked Florida especially hard, the estate is worth about six times what Castle paid for it.

Castle had a long career at Donaldson Lufkin & Jenrette, an investment firm founded in 1959 with the conviction that top-quality, independent research was rare on the Street, and would prove to be a powerful tool. After years marinating in the DLJ research-rich culture and serving as the house's president, Castle and colleague Leonard Harlan departed in 1987 to form their own PE shop. (Credit Suisse bought DLJ in 2000.) Since then, Castle Harlan has made more than $10 billion in acquisitions and generated a 20 percent annual return.

Castle likes to say that his celebrated peers are too fixed on a limited number of big companies, which are obvious choices. "The Fortune 500 companies have revenues of $3 billion and up, and that leaves you with a limited number to choose from," he contends. At any given juncture, Castle will have 10 companies under his wing, which he and his staffers have intensively vetted.

By Castle's thinking, there are 60,000 companies in the midsized range he prefers. That gives him a range of what every good investor seeks—opportunity.

Summary

- Hedge funds trade stocks and other instruments using supposedly sophisticated strategies, juiced with leverage. They have much to teach us about investing—it pays to be diligent, knowledgeable, and sometimes daring. Most hedge funds beat the market, an achievement that should establish their bona fides. The 2008 market swoon wasn't their fault, and the average hedge fund had half the loss of the S&P 500 that year.

- Hedge funds are lightly regulated pools of money, provided by institutions and wealthy people. To be an accredited investor allowed into the pool, you need $1 million in investable assets and $200,000 in yearly income. Managers have their own capital tied up in their funds, so they possess a personal interest in doing well. They also are well paid, charging 2 percent of assets in fees and 20 percent of the profits.

- PE funds, like Kohlberg Kravis Roberts, are the hedgies' cousins. PE firms buy whole companies, seek to turn them around, then sell them off at a nice markup. Studies show that the overall record of their deals, once known as leveraged buyouts, is mixed. KKR broke even, at best, with its takeover of RJR Nabisco, and has scored well with Toys "R" Us.

- The father of hedge funds, Alfred Winslow Jones, was a former Marxist spy who converted to capitalism and opened shop after World War II. He originated many hedge hallmarks: the strategy of paired long and short sales, the fee structure, and the penchant for secrecy. Icons like Michael Steinhardt, George Soros, and Julian Robertson followed him.

- Hedge fund superstar Steve Cohen, one of the richest Americans, developed an early sense of where stocks were headed, based on trading data. His fat returns permit him to charge very high fees. Cohen turns over his stocks quickly, but sometimes he shows an eye for value names.

- Aside from the vaunted successes, the hedge world also is saddled with some awful wipeouts, many due to managers' hubris—they outsmarted themselves. The worst was Long Term

Capital Management, which fell apart in the late 1990s as it bet wrong on how bond spreads would behave. Along came Russia's default, the spreads widened, and the fund got waxed. The firm's heavy leverage made the situation much worse. LTCM is one of those legendary cautionary tales all investors should heed.

Chapter 12

The Madness of Crowds: Behaviorism

In the 1600s, Dutch investors were crazy about tulips. The good burghers bought up these fragile flowers as if within the petals lay the secrets of life and death. The price of a single tulip could equal that of an Amsterdam house. Tulip mania did not end well for these investors. The flowers wilted, along with many fortunes. How could so many people, a lot of them smart, be so wrong? As Charles Mackay later wrote in his 1841 book, *Memoirs of Extraordinary Popular Delusions and the Madness of Crowds*, "Men . . . think in herds. It has been seen that they go mad in herds, while they only recover their senses slowly, one by one."

Benjamin Graham's character, Mr. Market, the excitable chap enthralled to his emotions, shows how easy it is to behave irrationally—and contrary to your best interests. In the depths of the most recent U.S. bear market, March 2009, people bolted out of stocks, when that was the perfect time to buy because stocks were cheap. A powerful rally ensued, yet many investors were, out of an overabundance of caution, on the sidelines and missed it. They had been burned badly in the slump. Projecting that the future would echo the past, these stricken souls were in no mood to risk more pain by getting back into what had hurt them. And this was despite long-standing evidence that markets move in cycles—up will eventually follow down.

For a long while, the prevailing orthodoxy in financial circles was that investing decisions were sublimely rational. The widely followed efficient market hypothesis (EMH) held that stock prices were determined by available information, meaning that investors were coolly weighing the evidence and trading accordingly. The classic illustration favoring EMH is that, if a $20 bill is lying on the sidewalk, someone will quickly snap it up. That's the rational course of action, right? Hence, we can assume that any spare $20 will get pounced upon. But what if the passersby are distracted by the weather above, or they are nearsighted, or they believe a blog-fed rumor that bills left on sidewalks are poisonous to the touch? In other words, their human limitations might prevent them from snatching that $20 as it nestles invitingly on the concrete.

What seems rational can be very deceiving. In his book, *The Black Swan*, Nassim Taleb spins a parable about a turkey. Experience has taught the bird that every day a friendly human will feed him. He figures that life is a pretty sweet deal, and very predictable. Then comes one day in November when the familiar pattern proves unreliable. Again and again, investors are shocked and surprised to find themselves on the Thanksgiving carving board.

New research has uncovered that, on sunnier days, investors trade more and take more risks; they are more optimistic. Is that smart? Doubtful. Is that human? Very much.

As financial history shows, from the tulip madness to today, human emotions and misperceptions have a large say in driving investing. A whole host of inbred responses governs how people react when they must make a market decision. The long line at a restaurant on the highway may mean that it has great food, correct? But maybe no other restaurants are open nearby. Join the line, and when you finally get a table, you may look forward to lousy service and indigestion.

Economist Terry Burnham has a name for the emotion-driven, irrational, numbskull sector of human mental activity—the "lizard brain." It harks back to the instinctual responses of animals, which we once were and, in many respects, still are. In his book, *Mean Markets and Lizard Brains*, Burnham describes the market's response in the early 1980s when Johns Manville was hit with asbestos litigation. Investors, conjuring up ancestral memories associated with sightings of an onrushing saber-toothed tiger, panicked and dumped the stock. Burnham, though, saw the massive selling as an irrational overreaction, and he bought cheap. The stock's later run-up, once calmer heads prevailed, was a pleasant reward.

A body of math-based techniques, technical analysis, has arisen to quantify market behavior. If stocks bounce around a ceiling, it is a "resistance level," and various outcomes may result. Patterns in trading supposedly augur the market's path. Others think that predicting market actions by math is bosh. There always have been signs that some savants read to explain what stocks are doing—indications that also are questionable. An example is the odd-lot indicator. It holds that betting against small investors, thought to be the dumb money whose timing stinks, is a can't-miss move. (Buying an odd lot means ordering less than 100 shares, which the little guys like to do.) Turns out their track record is not sufficiently consistent to make their behavior a reliable indicator. Odd-lotters were net buyers on just 17 days in the 1980s, when the market soared. Yet, in the 1990s, they were rightly bullish.

It's best to realize that markets are not knowable. Riptides of human quirks and passions buffet them. The great economist John Maynard Keynes, knew this long ago. His biographer, Robert Skidelsky, writes that Keynes "was not prepared to sacrifice realism to mathematics." Keynes himself called economics a "moral science." He warned that the financial world dealt with "motives, expectations, psychological uncertainties. One has to be constantly on guard against treating the material as constant and homogenous."

Since Keynes's time in the 20th century's first half, a new discipline has emerged to explain the emotional side of investing. Called behaviorism, it is mostly a catalog of mistakes to avoid, as opposed to surefire lessons on how to strike it rich on Wall Street. Being astute about dodging bad practices is enormously valuable. As the old sports saying goes, the team that wins the game is the one that makes the fewest errors.

★ ★ ★

The father of behaviorism, Daniel Kahneman, learned early on that human beings are hardly rational, whether in financial matters or other aspects of life. He knew that people sometimes are overconfident in their abilities, see what they want to see, construct patterns divorced from reality, let their last experience distort the perception of what's next, undervalue the truly valuable and overvalue the dross, and mindlessly follow the crowd.

Shortly after Kahneman was born in Tel Aviv, his French parents took him back to Paris. In 1940, when he was six, the Nazis invaded. Jews were required to wear a yellow Star of David and obey a 6 PM curfew. Young Danny was out playing with a Christian friend and realized that he was late. He turned his brown sweater inside out so the star wouldn't show and scampered back home. On a deserted street, he encountered a black-uniformed SS trooper. The soldier scrutinized him closely as the lad hustled past. He beckoned to the boy, and then grabbed him. "I was terrified he would notice the star inside my sweater," Kahneman later recollected.

But instead of harming Danny, the German hugged him and showed him a photo of another young boy, presumably his son, whom he missed. The soldier gave Danny money and sent him on his way. Kahneman credits that episode for steering him toward psychology and for demonstrating the power of emotion in decision making. "I went home more certain than ever that my mother was right," he writes, "that people were endlessly complicated and interesting." The German saw a small boy out after the Jewish curfew and wearing no star, automatically assumed he was a gentile like his own son, and was overcome by a wave of sentiment that clouded the professional suspiciousness Hitler's enforcers prized.

As the Third Reich turned to rounding up Jews for the death camps, Kahneman's family spent much of the war in hiding, a harrowing existence. His father died of diabetes in 1944. With the war over, he and his mother moved to what would soon be Israel. His life on the run in a Europe gone mad had burned into him a deep appreciation for the power of irrationality.

He went on to study psychology at Hebrew University in Jerusalem and at Berkeley in California, where he got a PhD. His first big breakthrough came in the 1960s when teaching training psychology to Israeli military flight instructors. One instructor challenged his assertion, drawn from motivational experiments on pigeons, that punishments were ineffective. The instructor claimed trainees flew better after a dressing down and worse after praise. Kahneman countered that, statistically speaking, the instructor's criticisms had no bearing on trainee performance. Chances are that, whatever a trainee hears, a good or bad performance often was followed by an ordinary one. In statistical terms, that is called regression to the mean. The instructors' behavior had little causal effect.

At Hebrew University, Kahneman struck up a friendship with another psych professor, Amos Tversky, who initially disagreed with him on people's innate irrationality. Tversky felt that humankind was essentially rational when it came to assessing risk. At a famous lunch shortly after they'd met, they hashed out a theory about how people used mental shortcuts in reasoning, sometimes to their own detriment.

These shortcuts, called "judgmental heuristics," are automatic responses that save us time. When our ancestors saw big, fresh paw prints in the dirt, resembling those of a large cat, they knew that danger was near and ran for the caves. Today, these shortcuts can cut in two directions for investors. As Gary Belsky and Thomas Gilovich explain in their book *Why Smart People Make Big Money Mistakes*, a current mental shortcut may make you instinctively shy away from those "who promise Bernard Madoff–like investment returns (a good result for most of us), but it might also tell you to avoid the stock market altogether (a less good result for most people)."

Kahneman and Tversky went on to teach at American universities and collaborated on many seminal studies of behavior. Kahneman eventually landed at Princeton, where today he is an emeritus professor, and Tversky (who died of cancer in 1996) at Stanford. Another influence on Kahneman was an economist named Richard Thaler, who broadened the psychologist's knowledge of economics. Thaler laced his work with anecdotes to demonstrate oddities of financial behavior, such as the tale of a man who would not sell an expensive bottle of wine for $200 but also would not pay $100 to replace it if it broke. Kahneman, who says he never has taken an economics course, went on to win the Nobel Prize for economics in 2002, for his Prospect Theory, which explains how one gauges potential losses and gains.

One of Kahneman and Tversky's most celebrated experiments on the shortfalls of mental shortcuts is the "Linda problem," a test they gave to subjects in the late 1970s about a hypothetical woman by that name. The test subjects were told that Linda is 31, single, very smart, outspoken, cares about discrimination and social justice, and took part in antinuclear demonstrations. Then they were asked to rank a series of statements about her from most to least probable. Which of the following do you think was judged more probable?

Linda is a bank teller.

Linda is a bank teller and is active in the feminist movement.

More than 80 percent of the test takers rated the second statement more likely than the first. The bank teller population is surely larger than the active feminist bank teller population, however. Evidently, information that she was female, outspoken, had liberal views, and protested in demonstrations was enough to skew people's reasoning. The group in the test formed a false pattern based on their limited knowledge of Linda.

Thanks to Kahneman, the field of behavioral economics is a booming one. Several important figures in the Obama administration are devotees of the discipline: Cass Sunstein, coauthor of the behaviorist touchstone *Nudge*, is a White House regulatory adviser; Jeff Liebman is a high official at the Office of Management and Budget; and Austan Goolsbee chairs the Council of Economic Advisers.

The calamitous stock slide during the Great Recession has taught the public once again that the market isn't always a benign, rational place. Knowing about irrationality can make you a better investor, mostly by alerting you to the trap doors in your own mind.

★   ★   ★

One snare concerns how we classify money. Money is the same, no matter where it sits. The $500 you win in the football pool is the same as the $500 you withdraw from the bank ATM. But people don't view it all the same. Thaler came up with a concept called "mental account-ing," which means people put money in different conceptual baskets and treat it differently. The windfall money won from the pool often is seen as less valuable than the money in the checking account, earned on the job. You likely will feel entitled to blow that pool money on something frivolous, but are more parsimonious with your ATM withdrawal.

Similarly, if you put a $200 meal on your credit card, that feels less onerous than shelling out $200 in crisp bills from your wallet. The problem is that the credit card purchase totes up an interest rate charge, perhaps 18 percent if you don't pay it off in a year. Lots of people carry big card balances, even though they have sufficient funds else-where to pay down the acidic card debt. By the same token, several years ago many people took out onerous mortgages to buy houses they really couldn't afford. But they didn't have to put much money down and initially had to pay small interest charges. The big mortgage wasn't "real" money to them. Of course, the housing crunch then left many houses underwater—the loans were higher than the homes' shrunken values, a series of disasters that litter the landscape of America to this day.

There are some safeguards that society has enacted to combat the evils of mental accounting, but not many. One is the payroll deduction for retirement. If employees had to manually transfer part of their pay into their 401(k) accounts every month, a lot less would go into those retirement plans. Further, a 2006 law makes it easier for employers to sign up workers for plans. Once, you had to take the time to opt into a plan. Now, many workers are automatically enrolled and must muster the energy to opt out of a 401(k). That change has helped boost 401(k) participation.

"Availability bias" is a kindred problem, where people make money decisions via mental shortcuts by using information that is closest at hand. When considering buying a stock, you might simply glance at its price and, if the shares don't seem too expensive, buy. Yet the stock may be at a high, and not supported by underlying fundamentals, and is in danger of collapsing. When the market was plummeting in early 2009, many investors bailed since all they could see were falling prices. Experienced investors knew that this was an opportunity.

Belsky tells a story about a money manager after the 1987 Black Monday crash, who got calls from 158 of his clients, almost the entire customer roster. Of those, 156 wanted him to sell. The two others wanted him to buy. Both buyers, the manager said, were over 80. Why did they want him to buy stocks in the wake of the debacle? The broker said, "Because they've seen this before."

Kahneman and Tversky's work shows how people are hurt by their ignorance of odds and their willingness to make false connections. This the two scholars called "neglecting the base rate." Say you flip a nickel 30 times, and 25 of those times the coin comes up heads. What are the odds that the 31st toss will be heads? A lot of folks would reason that heads are on a roll. But the odds actually are 50–50, and the next toss may very well be tails. Roulette players are forever searching for the hot number. Mostly, they are wrong. That's how casinos make money.

The same mistaken thinking applies when picking a mutual fund. If it has had five great years, no divine power will guarantee that the sixth year also will be a winner. Only about a quarter of commodities traders, whether pros or not, make money. Yet the rest keep trying, hoping for that big score. When Hillary Clinton, as a powerful politician's wife in the 1970s, made a killing on pork bellies, rumors were rife that the fix was in for her. She probably was simply lucky. Most are not lucky.

The insurance industry has profited by people's ignorance of the odds. Flight insurance has no reason to be. You also can buy policies targeting specific medical conditions, like cancer. Your existing coverage likely is enough to handle plane crashes and medical problems. Many policyholders shun policies with high deductibles since they don't want a big out-of-pocket expense if they must file a claim. But their premiums then are a lot larger than they should be, and the policyholders often would be better off over time agreeing to the larger deductibles.

★   ★   ★

One of the most insidious traps is "anchoring." Here, you fasten onto a chunk of information and use it as the standard to measure other items against. Sadly, this anchor may well be misleading or even irrelevant in your judging an investment or any other action.

One of your stocks has fallen and you tell yourself that, if it manages to crawl back up to the price you paid for it, you will sell. But your purchase price isn't the best reference point in making a sell decision. The intrinsic value of the stock and its company's prospects are far more important. Maybe you bought at $10 and the intrinsic value is $15; it currently is trading at $5. Recognize that you bought it on the cheap. Selling at still cheaper, $5, makes no sense if the stock is undervalued. Nor does it make sense to sell when it climbs back to the $10 purchase price. Better to be patient and wait for the market to get around to pricing it correctly.

Anchoring also can play hell with what people pay beyond the realm of equities. This is evident in real estate, according to a study by economists Uri Simonsohn and George Loewenstein. Key finding: People who move from a more expensive area to a less expensive one pay higher in rents or home purchases than the going rate in the new town, often getting more house than they need or can afford. Yet people who arrive from cheaper locales pay less in their new rich hometown.

Anchoring can obscure new information that is needed to steer investments wisely. Take Dell, the computer maker. Once upon a time, it was a dominant player in the personal computer world. Then Dell ran into tough competition and never could summon the juice to innovate itself back to being a tech industry champ, as Apple did with the iPod, iPhone, and iPad. As revenue and earnings disappointed, the air went out of Dell stock starting around 2005, when the economy was booming.

Nonetheless, some investors never woke up to Dell's woes. Perhaps they too fondly remember the charming story of how founder Michael Dell began by upgrading computers for other students in his University of Texas dorm room, showing a precocious business moxie and an admirable knowledge of his market. More importantly, they recall how he went on to revolutionize tech retailing by selling custom-built computers directly over the Web, thereby avoiding the need to maintain costly, earnings-sapping retail outlets. Morningstar analyst Paul Larson marvels how lots of investors, anchored in the old view of Dell, never understood that the company's "advantages reached the end of the road. Those who saw the shift and acted appropriately fared much better than those (ahem) who had an outdated view of the company."

Alongside anchoring is "confirmation bias," the tendency to glom onto evidence that supports your viewpoint and disregard what does not. As Michael Metzger of the University of Toronto explains it: "If we've heard that the French are rude to tourists, we may go to France looking for confirmation of that belief and ignore all the contrary experiences we have." You will remember the haughty waiter and tell your friends back home about him, and conveniently forget about the eager concierge, the friendly shopkeeper, and the helpful pedestrian who pointed the way to the Metro.

A Dell devotee might have taken heart in 2007 when Michael Dell reassumed the chief executive post, which he had relinquished three years before to play a more visionary role as chairman and let his No. 2, Kevin Rollins, assume operational control. The sagging stock had a renaissance on the news that the founder had bumped Rollins aside to save the day.

Dell believers, unfortunately, couldn't get past the magical reappearance of the great Michael Dell and memories of his past prowess. They didn't want to see that rival Hewlett-Packard was far superior at customer service and computer consulting, or that Apple had stolen a huge march with cool new products. Sure enough, Dell stock's second honeymoon lasted only a few months. Worsening performance results made it falter again. In the year after the March 2009 market bottom, Dell did rally along with most other stocks, although it trailed H-P; Apple rose double what Dell did.

★   ★   ★

Investors are continually bedeviled by what Thaler calls the "sunk cost" fallacy. If someone has paid good money for a concert ticket but a blizzard is raging outside, he is far more likely to brave the elements to attend than would a person who got the ticket for free. While the money already has been spent, the payer figures he should get what he shelled out for, even if he risks the physical and financial costs of injury or death. Hal Arkis and Catherine Bloomer's study of Ohio University theatergoers shows that patrons who got discounts are far less likely to appear for performances than those who paid full price. A gremlin in the brains of the full-price crowd insists that they not be wasteful, even if the reviews all say a play reeks.

Equally insidious is "loss aversion." People hate losses more than they enjoy gains. In fact, research indicates they are twice as likely to fear losses as covet gains. In a Kahneman experiment, subjects were given a choice based on a coin toss. Lose the toss and you had to pay $5. Win the toss and you could claim the entire jackpot. But Kahneman then asked: How big must the jackpot be to entice you to play? The average answer was $10. So they insisted on winnings of double the potential loss before they would take the risk.

The upshot of this is questionable investing practices, like holding onto losers (for surely they will come back) too long and selling winners (quick, before the market turns) too soon. A massive study of 10,000 trading accounts from 1987 to 1993 by Brad M. Barber (University of California, Davis) and Terrance Odean (Berkeley) explored how investors are far more likely to sell winners than to unload losers—and the consequences that followed. This tendency stunts wealth accumulation in the long term. Investors may squirrel away the bulk of their holdings in supposedly safe bonds or even low-returning money market funds (ignoring the out-of-sight-out-of-mind threat that inflation may slam these investments). But the stocks they sold outran those they kept by 3.4 percentage points over the next 12 months. The investors did the exact opposite of what they should have done. In panics, investors flee stocks—whether winners or losers—at the worst possible time, and are reluctant to return to equities once the market rises again. Hey, the rally could be a head fake and everything will be a loser for a long, long time.

Coupled with that tendency is the "endowment effect," whereby you value something that belongs to you far more than something that belongs to others. Thaler randomly handed out coffee mugs to a class of Cornell students, items that were for sale in the campus store for $6 apiece new. Some students received the mugs, some didn't. All got to examine the mugs. Then Thaler asked the mug nonowners what they would pay for one and the mug owners what price they would accept. The owners did not want to sell below $5.25, while the nonowner wouldn't go above $2.75. The owners clearly valued their mugs at twice the price as potential buyers did.

The endowment effect plays out in pricing houses. Real estate brokers have a tough time with sellers who believe their palace is worth far more than the market rate. And even though many employers routinely match a worker's 401(k) contributions, which is free money, workers who don't participate in the retirement programs don't seem to care. Some may not be properly informed about the match, some may not be able to afford to contribute, but many simply value the money they have in their bank accounts more than the money stashed away for the far future. Belsky and Golovich point out that retailers use the endowment effect with money-back-guaranteed trial periods for merchandise. Once that flat-screen TV is gracing the rec room, it has become part of the house and psychologically hard for consumers to return.

★   ★   ★

Memories are short. Investors too seldom bring history to bear when making decisions. Fund manager William Smead contends that they can only remember back two years: "It's a classic 'what have you done for me lately'" approach that animates people's thinking, he laments.

In March 2009, Bank of America stock was priced at around $3 per share, as if the company were about to go bankrupt. The year before, when it was widely hailed as a financial colossus that churned out good earnings, the stock had changed hands for $45. The horrible blowback from the financial crisis, multibillion-dollar losses, a radically sliced dividend, the troubled merger with stricken Merrill Lynch, the outcry over allegations that investors hadn't been fully informed about Merrill's condition—all led to the bank stock's drubbing. News of Bank of America's myriad travails was constant on TV and the Web. Few focused on B of A's strengths, such as its extensive branch network and global reach. A year after the low point, the stock had advanced to $20. Those who had bought the bank's shares when the news was bleakest would have enjoyed an almost sevenfold increase.

Behaviorists call this phenomenon, of weighing what just happened higher than events from further back in time, "recency." Unlike the two old investors in 1987 who told Belsky's money manager to buy because they knew how market crashes turned out, most are influenced by the here and now. They extrapolate present trends into the future, and cast aside evidence showing that markets revert to the mean. They swallow canards like: "It's different this time." That is hardly ever the case.

The contagion of recent news doesn't affect only individual investors, often derided as the chumps of the financial world. In May 2009, hard on the heels of the market's worst point, with fear still jangling the air, forecasters surveyed by the Philadelphia Federal Reserve concluded that the economy would grow at merely a 1 percent rate by year-end. Well, it was five times that figure. A long market bull run or a sustained upward swing in real estate prices convince people that these wonderful times can go on forever. Painful market slumps and housing crashes make them more leery than they should be. That's why during the big rally following the March 2009 market low, investors continued to pull money from stock mutual funds and put it into bond funds, which seemed safer.

Jason Zweig, in his book *Your Money and Your Brain*, recounts how investors surveyed in December 1999, after five straight years of market advances, figured that the next 12 months would bring an 18.4 percent rise. Instead, stocks crumbled. Then, following three years of losses, the market bottomed in late 2002. Cautious investors, singed by experience, predicted a 6.3 percent rise for 2003. They were wrong: stocks rocketed up by a third. Zweig observes: "Their reliance on the recent past caused investors to get the future exactly backwards."

★   ★   ★

Humans are social animals. In prehistoric times, they banded together for safety and for the advantage of group effort. They first cooperated in hunting and gathering, and later on tilling the fields and building towns. The practical reality was, is, and always will be that many hands make the load lighter. As part of that, conformity became a powerful force, a badge of group identity. In the hit TV comedy *Modern Family*, Jay's stepson, Manny, who is from South America, plans to go to his first day of his new U.S. school in the garb of his homeland, complete with sombrero. Jay persuades the boy that this is a bad idea—to avoid ridicule, he should dress like his classmates.

Broadly speaking, conformity to group norms is positive for society. Philosopher John Locke called this the social contract. It teaches us that violence is not an appropriate response to frustration, that we should not zoom through red lights, and that refusing to bathe is bad.

But devotion to groupthink can have a baleful effect, especially in investing, where out-of-control trends can decimate your future. There's a big difference between going to see *Iron Man 2* in summer 2010 (everybody else was) and buying Internet stocks in early 2000 (ditto). Herd behavior is what Charles Mackay called the "madness of crowds." If everybody in the village thinks that the strange old lady at the end of the lane is a witch, she soon will be sitting on a bonfire. If everyone in the village wants to invest in Pets.com, the inevitable outcome will be harrowingly widespread. They all will be a lot poorer.

Hot stocks and hot mutual funds get popular initially because they have nice returns, and then from a second-stage booster phase: because excitement spreads through the crowd. Such faddish zeal has trashed the old advice about buying and holding. In 1970, the average holding period for a fund was 16 years; lately, it's four. Zweig tells the cautionary tale of Firsthand Technology Value fund, which raked in investor dollars during the late 1990s, thanks to spectacular showings like 1999's 190 percent gain. Then came the reckoning. The worst off were the hapless saps who piled into the Firsthand fund in 1999 and 2000, at the very end of its run. From tech stocks' high-water mark in early 2000 to 10 years later, the S&P 500 had lost a fraction of 1 percent annually, the Nasdaq Composite (a benchmark for tech issues) was down 5.6 percent, and the Firsthand fund was off a spine-tingling 12.3 percent.

News drives the herd. The psychologist Paul Andreassen did an experiment testing the old saw that the more information you have about a stock, the better trader you will be. He divided subjects into investment groups that did mock trades based on real stocks. One group was fed bona fide news about the stocks, the other group was left in the dark. The better-informed group did less well, mainly due to their higher trading volume as they vainly chased the latest news.

Few believe that they are following the herd blindly or making any kind of stupid mistake. Why? They have an overweening respect for their own abilities. In a 1981 poll of motorists, Swedish researcher Ola Svenson founds that 90 percent ranked their driving abilities as better than average, a statistical impossibility. Unlike Lake Woebegone, all children can't be above average. The upside of big egos and solid self-confidence is that these motivate people to start new businesses, create new inventions, delve into medical mysteries. Then comes the downside.

The downside is that some folks, investors in particular, fancy that they know more than they do, and pay a vicious price for their delusions. Belsky and Gilovich deride home sellers who handle their own sales, trying to avoid a broker's 6 percent commission. Distressingly often, these Fizzbo types (that's FSBO, or For Sale by Owner) emerge as object lessons for their ignorance of the market, their overpricing of their houses, and their lack of sales contacts. They save the commission, but manage to unload their places for less than an agent would have gotten them.

Just as bad, ego-inflated investors tend not to learn from their mistakes. According to Harvard psychologist Ellen Langer, people often view their successes as owing to their innate abilities, and chalk up their defeats to bad luck or other forces beyond their control. She calls this "heads I win, tails it's chance." In the early 1970s, Baruch Fischhoff, now at Carnegie Mellon, had his students predict what would happen during Richard Nixon's upcoming trip to China. Afterward, many recollected their predictions in altered form, to make themselves appear smarter.

Female investors won't be astonished to hear that men are guiltier of overconfidence. In their 2001 paper, "Boys Will Be Boys: Gender, Overconfidence and Common Stock Investment," Barber and Odean surveyed investing behavior in 35,000 households and reported that men traded stocks 50 percent more often than women, which also increased the males' trading costs. Net returns for men were 0.94 percentage points lower than for women.

This gender difference has been persistent over time. Vanguard, the fund giant, scrutinized the 2.7 million people with individual retirement accounts at the company during 2008 and 2009. Men were far more likely to dump their holdings at market lows. What's more, men more eagerly forged ahead with investing moves, despite their lack of knowledge, which they were loath to admit. Women, more risk averse, were more open to admitting what they didn't know.

Neuroscience plays a role in how we invest. One brain region, called the nucleus accumbens, is important in risk taking. This area is involved in feelings of reward, whether through food or sex or financial gain. Brain scans performed by Stanford's Brian Knutson show we are more excited at the possibility of a reward than actually getting the payoff. Hungry people get a bigger rush from the prospect of eating a juicy steak than from finally digging into one. This can have a socially beneficial result. Excitement over an upcoming reward allows us to plan for this to make it happen, rather than seeking immediate gratification by right now gobbling the cookies close at hand. So long-term fortunes can get made.

Alas, neurons don't rule always. Plenty of investors grab the short term at the expense of the long term and fail to appreciate the culinary superiority of steak over cookies. This all, of course, is in the mind. In Benjamin Graham's assessment, it was as absurd as it was expected that "Mr. Market lets his enthusiasm or his fears run away with him."

Summary

- A new discipline, called behaviorism, demonstrates that emotions and human fallibility are large factors in investing decisions—contrary to the efficient market hypothesis, with its foundation on a belief in the rational investor. Behaviorism offers a list of mistakes that fallible, irrational humans often commit. The father of behavioral economics, Daniel Kahneman, developed many theories in the field. The first is that people use mental shortcuts to make judgments, and that can lead to blunders.
- Cognitive traps are abundant in investing. One is "mental accounting," where we classify money into different strata, and thus treat it differently. Although we have ample bank funds, we will not tap them to pay off high-interest credit card balances. With "availability bias," we take the shortcut of employing the most readily accessible information, such as a stock's price, to make a buy decision, not bothering to dig into its fundamentals.
- Ignoring the odds and making false connections, a phenomenon called "neglecting the base rate," is a pernicious pitfall. A five-year

winning streak for a mutual fund doesn't mean that a sixth good year is guaranteed. "Anchoring" involves using outdated or wrong information to measure value. Someone may invest in Dell, the computer maker and market laggard, by fondly recalling its glory days. A similar snare is "confirmation bias," where you fasten onto information backing your viewpoint and ignore contradictory evidence.

- The "sunk cost" fallacy makes us do things if we've already paid for them, even if doing them is a bad idea. With "loss aversion," we hate losses twice as much as we covet gains. We then go on to hold losers long after we should and sell winners too soon. Under the "endowment effect," you value more what belongs to you than what others own. So you may ask too much for your home, at far over the market's going rate.

- "Recency" fosters the illusion that what just occurred is most important in making plans. That's why, after the market roared up from its March 2009 low, many investors withdrew from stock funds. They remembered the 2008–2009 free-fall vividly.

- "Herd behavior" leads you to invest in dubious stuff like Internet stocks, circa 1999. Group excitement is a powerful motivator, the belief that if everyone is doing something, that something must be good. Who cares about deeper analysis? In fact, the more bulletin-style news that people get about a stock, the less wisely they tend to invest in it.

- Overconfidence is epidemic among investors, especially men. People think they can sell their houses solo, saving a broker's commission, and end up getting lower prices. Plus, hubris prevents folks from learning from their own mistakes.

Conclusion

Out of the Shadows

To many people, investing is a shadow world, unknowable, dangerous, best shunned. The Wall Street that existed before the 1929 crash was indeed such a stygian place, where clans of professionals labored to fleece the uninitiated. Many of the shady practices that Wall Street employed pre-1929 are now illegal, but snares still exist.

Benjamin Graham first shined a light into this dark place. In the midst of the Depression, which had savaged his own personal wealth, he wrote a masterpiece that still allows ordinary investors to navigate the financial terrain with confidence and skill. Since Graham's day, there has been an explosion of financial information that anyone with an Internet connection can access. Incisive magazines and books devoted to investing are legion. Successful investing doesn't require a fancy MBA from an expensive university. It does require intelligence and diligence.

Investing success does not come in one flavor. Many strategies must be explored to get to that blessed state where you can say, "I've got plenty of money to sustain me, thank God." Modern-day investors confront far more choices than Graham had to contend with. That translates to far more opportunities, and more pitfalls.

The new approaches to investing that have sprung up each have devoted adherents. The trick is to be sufficiently flexible to dip into any or all of them, but by the same token, to know their limitations.

Graham's greatest idea was security analysis for the masses. His second greatest creation was value investing, the quest for good, cheap stocks that the market may have overlooked and eventually would rediscover.

Over time, studies show, value stocks do better than growth stocks. Putting all your chips into value plays, however, can stunt your portfolio's performance. Some stocks are cheap because they are lousy. Plus, the market is cyclical: growth stocks have spells when they outrun value shares; thus, it pays not to be overweight in value then. The problem with growth is that, while these stocks can soar, after a while some have a tendency to crash. Witness the dot-com bubble of the early 2000s.

Followers of Jeremy Siegel believe that equities are the best means of building wealth over time. And that is true, except when nasty Black Swan events occur, as happened twice in the century's first 10 years, called the Lost Decade. Among stocks, a rancorous debate rages over the wisdom of investing in index funds, which track the broad market. Index investing has a coterie of acolytes, who take comfort that most actively managed mutual funds fail to beat the S&P 500. Their conclusion may be too narrow. The challenge is to find the active funds that do excel.

Another investment movement is centered on the necessity of owning foreign securities. With half the world's market value now outside the United States, putting money overseas makes sense, particularly in fast-expanding emerging economies. Trouble is, some of these plays are prone to self-immolation, as we saw in 1997 and 1998.

Bonds offer excellent ballast for your holdings, and also have spawned several new varieties that present higher risks and rewards than ever before. The ups and downs of junk bonds and mortgage-backed securities illustrate the point. In some years, bonds outdo stocks. Bonds did well for much of the 2000s, although they flagged in late 2010 as Treasuries lost popularity.

Real estate, whether classic homeownership or commercially oriented investments such as real estate investment trusts (REITs), have come to the fore as much-heralded asset classes. Spiraling ownership of houses, aided by too-easy lending standards, rested on the shibboleth that home prices always rise. The housing bust, which precipitated the worldwide financial crisis, gave the lie to that. REITs, available only in recent decades and trading like stock, offer a more liquid option. Yet as with homeowning, the key is to avoid trusts with excessive debt. In real estate investing, debt is like food—although vital to make the body function, too much of it causes serious problems.

Once the province of the megabucks crowd, alternative investments like commodities and currencies became more and more important in the 1990s and 2000s, and now are open to ordinary investors. Big money can be made here, its advocates say. This is a siren song best resisted, as these creatures often are much too volatile for those without deep pockets. Still, decent mutual funds do exist to give you exposure to these areas, which usually do not correlate with the stock market.

How do all the pieces—stocks, bonds, commodities, real estate, and so on—fit together? A whole industry devoted to financial planning has taken shape to answer that question. Diversification of assets is an ideal that is surprisingly hard to realize. Even statistically sophisticated models of asset allocations, like Monte Carlo simulations, can fall short because they don't factor in the possibility of extreme events. The world has experienced two such huge debacles in the space of 10 years. Not encouraging.

Aside from consulting planners, average investors can get some decent ideas by riding in the slipstream of pros. Short sellers have arrived on the scene as a force. The best ones show remarkable prescience and grit. Jim Chanos, for instance, unveiled Enron's sham accounting—a finding that at first was greeted as heresy and later hailed as genius. The practice of shorting is not for the faint of heart or light of wallet. At the very least, stocks that are heavily shorted may serve as warnings signs of what to avoid or dump.

Hedge funds, such as Chanos's, are where a lot of the finance-intellectual firepower is housed nowadays. While most investors can't afford to put money in a hedge fund, new mutual funds have opened that try to replicate the hedgies' exploits. How the best of these pros invest is instructive to everybody else: The top hedge managers are resilient and well-informed, hallmarks of investing accomplishment.

One investment discipline that has achieved a special standing since its arrival in the 1950s is behaviorism, the method of explaining how human emotions drive markets. Many an elegant market theory has smashed onto the rocks of people's inability to act rationally. Thinkers ranging from Ben Graham to Charles Mackay have long recognized that emotional reactions have a strong influence on the fate of investments. Individual investors can watch for, and maybe overcome, their own inclinations to react irrationally when hearing about market turbulence.

Anticipating what is coming next is hard. The power to predict correctly does not reside in mere mortals. Investing success contains a strong element of luck. That said, alertness and nimbleness are virtues that give good investors a leg up, and a means to thwart fickle fortune.

In 2002, amid the ruins left by the tech bust and the Enron scandal, Apple had a market value of a few billion, less than the cash on its balance sheet, and a has-been's reputation. Google was a private company with a few hundred employees and a seemingly faddish product. The two companies' prospects provoked yawns. By 2010, the two had a combined value of $490 billion. Just 19 nations had economies larger than that. Those investors with the wit to get in early on Apple and Google touched the stars.

My advice: read everything. Watch for trends and opportunities. Which investments appeal to you? What conditions do they thrive in? Ask questions. Talk to people. Ponder.

Graham once listed two criteria for investing success: "One, you have to think correctly; and secondly, you have to think independently."

Bibliography

Some of the books cited have been published in many editions. I have chosen a recent, readily available one of each. Some of the sources are available online. I have indicated where to find them.

PROLOGUE   **The Rosetta Stone**

Fisher, Irving. *The Nature of Capital and Income* London: Macmillan, 1906.

Graham, Benjamin. *The Intelligent Investor,* rev. ed. New York: Collins Business, 2003.

Graham, Benjamin. "The New Speculation in Common Stock," *The Analysts Journal,* June 1958.

Graham, Benjamin, and David L. Dodd. *Security Analysis: Principles and Technique,* 6th ed. New York: McGraw Hill, 2009.

Keynes, John Maynard. *The General Theory of Employment, Interest and Money.* New York: Classic Books America, 2009.

Loeb, Gerald M. *The Battle for Investment Survival.* Hoboken, NJ: John Wiley & Sons, 2007.

Lowe, Janet. *Benjamin Graham on Value Investing.* New York: Penguin Books, 1994.

Smith, Adam. *The Wealth of Nations: Books 1–3.* New York: Penguin Classics, 1999.

Smith, Adam. *The Wealth of Nations: Books 4–5.* New York: Penguin Classics, 1999.

Stewart, Jon. *The Daily Show* interview with Jim Cramer, Comedy Central, March 12, 2009. Available at: www.thedailyshow.com.

Taleb, Nassim Nicholas. *The Black Swan: The Impact of the Highly Improbable,* 2nd ed. New York: Random House, 2010.

CHAPTER 1   Tarnished Gems: Value Investing

Cramer, Jim. "Cramer Rewrites 'Follow These Five Tenets toward a Fortune.'" www.TheStreet.com, January 21, 2000.

Dreman, David. *Contrarian Investment Strategies: The Next Generation.* New York: Simon & Schuster, 1998.

Dreman, David. "Jim Cramer: Wrong!" *Forbes,* February 21, 2000. Available at: www.forbes.com.

Greenblatt, Joel. *The Little Book that Beats the Market.* Hoboken, NJ: John Wiley & Sons, 2010.

Lowe, Janet. *Warren Buffett Speaks: Wit and Wisdom from the World's Greatest Investor.* Hoboken, NJ: John Wiley & Sons, 2007.

Lowenstein, Roger. *Buffett: The Making of an American Capitalist.* New York: Random House, 1995.

Matthews, Jeff. *Pilgrimage to Warren Buffett's Omaha.* New York: McGraw-Hill, 2009.

Rogers John W., Jr. "Premature Burial." *Forbes,* April 24, 2006. Available at: www.forbes.com.

Schloss, Walter. "The Superinvestors of Graham-and-Doddsville." Speech delivered at Columbia University, 1984.

Young, Lauren. "Mr. Rogers' Neighborhood." *SmartMoney,* March 2002.

CHAPTER 2   Eternal Equities: Stocks Do Best?

Arnott, Robert. "Bonds: Why Bother?" *Journal of Indexes,* May/June 2009.

Arnott, Robert. "Was It Really a Lost Decade?" Research Affiliates, *Fundamental Index Newsletter,* January 2010.

Bennett, Rob. "Jeremy Siegel Is a Dangerous Individual," www.passionsaving.com.

Blodget, Henry. "Jeremy Siegel, Wrong." *The Business Insider,* February 25, 2009. Available at: www.businessinsider.com/.

Crowther, Samuel. "Everybody Ought to Be Rich." *Ladies Home Journal,* 1929.

"The Death of Equities." *BusinessWeek,* August 13, 1979.

Evans, Sir Harold. *They Made America: Two Centuries of Innovators from the Steam Engine to the Search Engine.* New York: Little Brown and Company, 2004.

Fisher, Ken. *The Ten Roads to Riches: The Ways the Wealthy Got There (and how you can too!)*. Hoboken, NJ: John Wiley & Sons, 2009.

Fisher, Ken. "We're Too Gloomy." *Forbes*, January 28, 2008. Available at: www.forbes.com.

Glassman, James, and Kevin Hassett. *Dow 36,000: The New Strategy for Profiting from the Coming Rise in the Stock Market*. New York: Three Rivers Press, 2000.

Greenblatt, Joel. *The Little Book that Beats the Market*. Hoboken, NJ: John Wiley & Sons, 2010.

Hall, Alvin D. *Getting Started in Stocks*, 3rd ed. Hoboken, NJ: John Wiley & Sons, 1997.

Hulbert, Mark. "Now the Long Run Looks Riskier, Too." *New York Times*, March 28, 2009.

Katsenelson, Vitally. "Jeremy Siegel Is Brilliant, Uplifting, and Just Plain Wrong!" http://ContrarianEdge.com.

Rouwenhorst, K. Geert. "The Origins of Mutual Funds." December 12, 2004. Yale ICF Working Paper No. 04–48. Available at: SSRN: http://ssrn.com/abstract=636146.

Shiller, Robert J. *Irrational Exuberance*, 2nd ed. New York: Broadway Books, 2005.

Siegel, Jeremy J. *Stocks for the Long Run: The Definitive Guide to Financial Market Returns and Long-Term Investment Strategies*, 4th ed. New York: McGraw-Hill, 2008.

Smith, Edgar Lawrence. *Common Stocks as Long Term Investments*. New York: Macmillan, 1928.

Stovall, Sam. *The Seven Rules of Wall Street: Crash-Tested Investment Strategies that Beat the Market*. New York: McGraw-Hill, 2009.

Zweig, Jason. "Does Stock Market Data Really Go Back 200 Years?" *Wall Street Journal*, July 11, 2009.

CHAPTER 3　On Autopilot: Indexes

Arnott, Robert D., Jason C. Hsu, John M. West. *The Fundamental Index: A Better Way to Invest*. Hoboken, NJ: John Wiley & Sons, 2008.

Bogle, John C. *John Bogle on Investing: The First 50 Years*. New York: McGraw-Hill, 2001.

Bogle, John C. *The Battle for the Soul of Capitalism: How the Financial System Undermined Social Ideals, Damaged Trust in the Markets, Robbed Investors of Trillions—and What to Do about It*. New Haven, CT: Yale University Press, 2005.

Bogle, John C. *The Economic Role of the Investment Company*. Thesis, Princeton University, 1950.

Fama, Eugene F., and Kenneth R. French, "Luck versus Skill in the Cross Section of Mutual Fund Returns," December 14, 2009. Tuck School of Business

Working Paper No. 2009–56; Chicago Booth School of Business Research Paper; *Journal of Finance*. Available at: SSRN: http://ssrn.com/abstract=1356021.

Ferri, Richard A. *The ETF Book: All You Need to Know About Exchange-Traded Funds*. Hoboken, NJ: John Wiley & Sons, 2008.

Fox, Justin. *The Myth of the Rational Market*. New York: HarperCollins, 2009.

Greenspan, Alan. "The Challenge of Central Banking in a Democratic Society," speech to the American Enterprise Institute, December 5, 1996. Available at: www.federalreserve.gov/boarddocs/speeches/1996.

"Index Funds—An Idea Whose Time Has Come." *Fortune*, 1976.

Malkiel, Burton. *A Random Walk Down Wall Street*. New York: W.W. Norton & Company, 1973.

Samuelson, Paul. "Challenge to Judgment." *Journal of Portfolio Management*, Fall 1974.

Seyhun, H. Nejat. *Stock Market Extremes and Portfolio Performance*, study commissioned by Towneley Capital Management, 1994. Available at: www.towneley.com.

Shiller, Robert J. Web site. Available at: www.econ.yale.edu/~shiller/.

Zweig, Jason. "Will '12b-1' Fees Ever Stop Bugging Investors?" *Wall Street Journal*, December 19, 2009.

CHAPTER 4   From Mild to Wild: Bonds Take Wing

Altman, Edward I., and Scott A. Nammacher. *Investing in Junk Bonds: Inside the High Yield Debt Market*. Beard Books, 2002.

Bruck, Connie. *The Predators' Ball*. New York: Penguin Books, 1988.

Cohen, Marilyn, and Chris Malburg. *Bonds Now!* Hoboken, NJ: John Wiley & Sons, 2010.

Condon, Bernard. "Back in the Game." *Forbes*, September 17, 2007.

"The Death of Equities." *BusinessWeek*, August 13, 1979.

Fitzgerald, F. Scott. *The Great Gatsby*. New York: Scribner, 2004 edition.

Gross, William H. *Investment Outlook* (monthly, PIMCO).

Keene, Thomas R., and Susanne Walker. "Pimco's Gross Buys Treasuries Amid Deflation Concern." Bloomberg.com, September 29, 2009.

Lewis, Michael. *Liar's Poker*. New York: W.W. Norton, 1989.

Mack, Consuelo. *WealthTrack* interview with Robert Rodriguez, Public Television, November 27, 2009. Available at: www.wealthtrack.com/.

Mamudi, Sam. "Pimco's Gross Unwinds Mortgage Positions." MarketWatch, October 20, 2009. Available at: www.marketwatch.com/.

Nocera, Joseph. *A Piece of the Action: How the Middle Class Joined the Money Class*. New York: Simon & Schuster, 1994.

Sjoblon, Miriam. "Schwab YieldPlus Continues Its Monumental Slide." Morningstar.com, January 27, 2009.

Thorp, Edward O. *Beat the Dealer*. New York: Vintage Books, 1966.

TreasuryDirect. Web site. Accessed at: www.treasurydirect.gov/.

Zuckerman, Gregory. "A Bond Star's Plays Turn Riskier." *Wall Street Journal*, August 23, 2006.

CHAPTER 5   The Fast Lane: Growth Investing

AQR Capital Management. "The Case for Momentum Investing." Summer 2009.

Birger, Jon. "They Call Them Flippers." *Money*, April 2005.

Birinyi, Laszlo Jr. "Murphy's Mouse Click." *Forbes*, November 26, 2007.

Elkind, Peter. "The Hidden Face of Janus." *Fortune*, January 22, 2001.

Forrest Gump, 1994 film, DVD edition, 2001.

Korn, Donald Jay. "Real Estate Revisited." *Financial Planning*, November 2010.

Tom Murcko, "What Is the Difference between Gambling and Investing?" InvestorGuide.com. Available at: www.investorguide.com/gambling-vs-investing.

One, Two, Three, 1961 film, DVD edition, 2003.

Paton, James. "A New Life on the Ranch." *Rocky Mountain News*, July 22, 2006.

Porttnoy, Brian. "For Now, We'd Steer Clear of Janus Fund." Morningstar.com, September 3, 2003.

Nocera, Joseph. "The Quantitative, Data-Based, Risk-Massaging Road to Riches." *New York Times*, June 5, 2005.

Schiller, Robert J. "Irrational Exuberance, Part 2." *Money*, February 2005.

Train, John. *Money Masters of Our Time*. New York: HarperBusiness, 2000.

Young, Kathryn. "This Mutual Fund Is a Good Option for Moderate Large-Growth Exposure." Morningstar.com, October 15, 2010.

CHAPTER 6   Over There: Foreign Investing

Christy, John H., and Susan Kitchens. "Casting a Wider Net." *Forbes*, July 26, 2004.

Condon, Bernard. "An Investment Legend's Advice." *Forbes*, February 4, 2004.

Fingleton, Eamonn. *Blindside: Why Japan Is Still on Track to Overtake the U.S. by the Year 2000*. New York: Houghton Mifflin, 1995.

Friedman, Thomas L. *The World Is Flat: A Brief History of the 21st Century*. New York: Farrar, Straus and Giroux, 2005.

Grantham, Jeremy. *GMO Quarterly Letter*, Fall 2010.

Herrmann, Robert L. *Sir John Templeton: Supporting Scientific Research for Spiritual Discoveries*. Radnor, PA: Templeton Foundation Press, 2004.

Krugman, Paul R., and Maurice Obstfeld, *Internation Economics: Theory and Policy*, 8th ed. Boston: Prentice Hall, 2008.

Light, Larry. "Emerging-Market Rally Spurs Unease." *Wall Street Journal*, October 30, 2009.

Norton, Leslie P. "China's Sure Bet." *Barron's*, November 8, 2010.

Powell, Bill. "Chanos vs. China." *Fortune*, December 6, 2010.

Rein, Shaun. "How to Invest in China." *Forbes*, July 20, 2010.

Ricardo, David. *On the Principles of Political Economy and Taxation*. London: Cambridge University Press, 1973 edition.

Ruddy, Christopher. "Sir John Templeton Reveals the Future of the Stock Market, Real Estate, and Life." *Financial Intelligence Report*, January 1, 2005.

Templeton, Lauren, and Scott Phillips. *Investing the Templeton Way*. New York: McGraw Hill, 2008.

CHAPTER 7   Un-Real Estate: Property's Pull

The Apprentice with Donald Trump, NBC-TV. Available at: www.nbc.com/the-apprentice/.

Donsky, Paul. "Zombie Subdivisions." *Atlanta Journal-Constitution*, August 9, 2009.

Fitch, Stephane. "The Everything REITs." *Forbes*, June 20, 2005.

Goldfarb, Alexander. "The Future of GGP—Anything but Clear and Simple." Sandler O'Neill & Partners, LP Research Paper, January 11, 2010.

Heavens, Alan J. "On the House: Next Loss Could Be Their House." *Philadelphia Inquirer*, August 30, 2009. Available at: www.philly.com/inquirer/.

Heavens, Alan J. "A Foreclosure on Hold as a Couple Holds On." *Philadelphia Inquirer*, September 2, 2009. Available at: www.philly.com/inquirer/.

It's a Wonderful Life, 1946 film. 60th anniversary edition DVD, 2006.

Lewis, Michael. *Liar's Poker*. New York: W.W. Norton, 1989.

Lewis, Sinclair. *Babbitt*. New York: Prometheus Books, 2002.

Light, Larry, and Joseph Weber. "The Donald's Trump Card." *BusinessWeek*, March 22, 1992.

Light, Larry. "Trump Tries to Pull a Houdini." *BusinessWeek*, November 29, 1993.

McMahan, John. *Property Development*, 2nd ed. New York: McGraw Hill, 1989.

The Money Pit, 1986 film. DVD edition, 2003.

Mr. Blandings Builds His Dream House, 1948 film. DVD edition, 2004.

O'Brien, Timothy L. *TrumpNation: The Art of Being the Donald*. New York: Warner Business Books, 2005.

Poniewozik, James. "Biggest Global Real Estate Boom of All Time." *Time*, June 13, 2005.

Slater, Robert. *No Such Thing as Over-exposure.* Upper Saddle River, NJ: Prentice Hall, 2005.

Slatin, Peter. "A Conversation with Martin Cohen." *Forbes/Slatin Real Estate Report,* July 2009.

Trump Donald J., with Tony Schwartz. *The Art of the Deal.* New York: Warner Books, 1987.

Trump, Donald J., with Kate Boner. *Trump: The Art of the Comeback.* New York: Random House, 1997.

Tully, Sean. "The New Kind of the Real Estate Boom." *Fortune,* April 18, 2005.

Woolley, Suzanne. "The New World of Real Estate." *BusinessWeek,* September 22, 1997.

CHAPTER 8   Not Just for the Rich: Alternatives

Cheng, Jonathan. "Traders Follow Rush to Forex." *Wall Street Journal,* December 16, 2010.

Dempster, Natalie, and Juan Carlos Artigas. "Gold as a Tactical Inflation Hedge and Long-Term Strategic Asset." *World Gold Council,* July 2009. Available at: www.gold.org.

Ferguson, Niall. *The Ascent of Money: A Financial History of the World.* New York: Penguin Press, 2008.

Fisher, Daniel. "Commodities." *Forbes,* May 22, 2006.

Fox, Justin. "The Dollar in Danger." *Time,* November 16, 2009.

Graham, Benjamin. *The Intelligent Investor,* rev. ed. New York: Collins Business, 2003.

Grant, James. *Money of the Mind.* New York: Farrar, Straus and Giroux, 1992.

Grant, James. "Tears to My Eyes." *Grant's Interest Rate Observer,* October 2, 2009.

Hosenball, Mark, Rich Thomas, and Eleanor Clift. "Hillary's Adventures in Cattle Futures Land." *Newsweek,* April 11, 1994.

Jastram, Roy W. *The Golden Constant: The English and American Experience 1560–2007.* Hoboken, NJ: John Wiley & Sons, 1977.

Keynes, John Maynard. *A Tract on Monetary Reform.* Amherst, NY: Prometheus Books, 2000 edition.

Lauricella, Tom, and Dave Kansas. "Currency Trading Soars." *Wall Street Journal,* September 1, 2010.

Pilon, Mary. "Is Art the Next Boom Investment?" *Wall Street Journal,* May 22, 2010.

Plevin, Liam, Carolyn Cui, and Scott Kilman. "Commodity Prices Surge." *Wall Street Journal,* November 8, 2010.

Samuelson, Robert J. "Let's Shoot the Speculators!" *Newsweek,* July 7–14, 2008.

Schwartz, Nelson D. "Uncertainty Restores Glitter to an Old Refuge, Gold." *New York Times,* June 12, 2010.

Ocean's Eleven, 2001 film. DVD edition, 2007.

CHAPTER 9   Spreading It Around: Asset Allocation

Brandon, E. Denby, and H. Oliver Welch. *The History of Financial Planning: The Transformation of Financial Services.* Hoboken, NJ: John Wiley & Sons, 2009)

Brinson, Gary P., L. Randolph Hood, and Gilbert L. Beebower. "Determinants of Portfolio Performance." *Financial Analysts Journal*, July/August 1986.

ESPlannerBASIC. Web site. Available at: https://basic.esplanner.com/.

Fabrikant, Geraldine. "Big University Funds Report Steep Investment Losses." *New York Times*, September 23, 2009.

Gibson, Roger C. *Asset Allocation: Balancing Financial Risk*, 3rd ed. New York: McGraw-Hill, 2000.

Ibbotson, Roger. "The Importance of Asset Allocation." *Financial Analysts Journal*, March/April 2010. Available at: www.cfapubs.org.

Jahnke, William. "The Asset Allocation Hoax." *Journal of Financial Planning*, February 1997.

MarketRiders. Web site. Available at: www.marketriders.com/.

Markowitz, Harry M. *Portfolio Selection: Efficient Diversification of Investments.* Cambridge, MA: Blackwell, 1991.

McKeown, Kim, and Mike Nowak. "Actuaries Urge More Long-Term Planning and Sophisticated Tools to Address Retirement Risks." Report of the Society of Actuaries and Actuarial Foundation, December 2009.

Powell, Robert. "Retirement-Planning Tools Are Risky Business." MarketWatch, January 8, 2010. Available at:
www.marketwatch.com/story/retirement-plan-tools-are-risky-business-2010–01–08.

Twain, Mark. *Pudd'nhead Wilson.* New York: Pocket Books, 2004.

Williams, John Burr. *The Theory of Investment Value.* Fraser Publishing Library, Contrary Opinion Library, 1997.

CHAPTER 10   Looking for the Bad: Short Selling

Chanos, James. "Ten Lessons from the Financial Crisis that Investors Will Soon Forget (if they haven't already)." Virginia Value Investing Conference, University of Virginia, October 22, 2009. Available at: www.scribd.com/doc/22490530/Jim-Chanos-Presentation-at-Darden-22-Oct-2009.

Einhorn, David. *Fooling Some of the People All of the Time.* Hoboken, NJ: John Wiley & Sons, 2008.

Engelberg, Joseph, and Adam Reed. "How Are Shorts Informed? Short Sellers, News, and Information Processing" Social Science Research Network. November 19, 2010. Available at:
http://papers.ssrn.com/sol3/papers.cfm?abstract_id=1535337.

Ferguson, Niall. *The Ascent of Money: A Financial History of the World.* New York: Penguin Press, 2008.

Fuld, Richard S. Jr. Prepared Testimony before the House Committee on Oversight and Government Reform, October 6, 2008.

Lewis, Michael. *The Big Short: Inside the Doomsday Machine.* New York: W.W. Norton, 2010.

Liang, Jonathan R. "The Bear that Roared." *Barron's*, January 28, 2002.

McLean, Bethany. "Is Enron Over-priced?" *Fortune*, March 5, 2001.

Pozen, Robert. *Too Big to Save? How to Fix the U.S. Financial System.* Hoboken, NJ: John Wiley & Sons, 2010.

Sherman, Gabriel. "The Catastrophe Capitalist." *New York*, December 7, 2008.

Sloan, Robert. *Don't Blame the Shorts: Why Short Sellers Are Always Blamed for Market Crashes and How History Is Repeating Itself.* New York: McGraw-Hill, 2010.

Weil, Jonathan. "Energy Traders Cite Gains, but Some Math Is Missing." *Wall Street Journal*, September 20, 2000.

Zuckerman, Gregory. *The Greatest Trade Ever: The Behind-the-Scenes Story of How John Paulson Defied Wall Street and Made Financial History.* New York: Crown, 2009.

CHAPTER 11   Chess Masters: Hedge Funds

Burrough, Bryan, and John Helyar. *Barbarians at the Gate: The Fall of RJR Nabisco.* New York: HarperBusiness, 2008.

Burton, Katherine, and Anthony Effinger. "Steve Cohen's Trade Secrets." *Bloomberg Markets*, April 2010.

Burton Katherine, and Jenny Strasburg. "Amaranth's $6.6 Billion Slide Began with Trader's Bid to Quit." *Bloomberg News*, December 6, 2005. Available at: http://papers.ssrn.com/.

Fishman, Steve. "Divorced, Never Separated." *New York*, August 5, 2010.

"The 400 Richest Americans." *Forbes*, 2010. Available at: www.forbes.com/.

Ibbotson, Roger G., Peng Chen, and Kevin X. Zhu. "The ABCs of Hedge Funds: Alphas, Betas, and Costs." Yale School of Management, March 30, 2010. Available at: http://papers.ssrn.com/.

Jensen, Michael C. "Eclipse of the Public Corporation." *Harvard Business Review*, September–October 1989. Available at: http://papers.ssrn.com/.

Kishan, Saijel. "Hedge Funds Lost Record 18.3% on Misjudged Markets (Update 3)." *Bloomberg News*, January 8, 2009. Available at: http://papers.ssrn.com/.

Lowenstein, Roger. *When Genius Failed: The Rise and Fall of Long-Term Capital Management.* New York: Random House, 2001.

Mallaby, Sebastian. *More Money Than God: Hedge Funds and the Making of a New Elite.* New York: Penguin Books, 2010.

Mamudi, Sam. "Safe Haven: Mutual Funds that Act Like Hedge Funds." *Wall Street Journal*, May 1–2, 2010.

Patterson, Scott. "A Hedge-Fund King Is Forced to Regroup." *Wall Street Journal*, May 23, 2009.

Schwager, Jack D. *Stock Market Wizards: Interviews with America's Top Stock Traders.* New York: HarperBusiness, 2003.

Story, Louise. "For Private Equity, Try a Very Public Disaster." *New York Times*, August 9, 2009.

Vickers, Marcia. "The Most Powerful Trader on Wall Street You've Never Heard Of." *BusinessWeek*, July 21, 2003.

CHAPTER 12   The Madness of Crowds: Behaviorism

Andreassen, Paul. "On the Social Psychology of the Stock Market." *Journal of Personality and Social Psychology*, 1987.

Barber, Brad M., and Terrance Odean. "Boys Will Be Boys: Gender Overconfidence and Common Stock Investment." *Quarterly Journal of Economics*, 2001.

Belsky, Gary, and Thomas Gilovich. *Why Smart People Make Big Money Mistakes . . . and How to Correct Them.* New York: Simon & Schuster, 1999, 2009.

Burnham, Terry. *Mean Markets and Lizard Brains: How to Profit from the New Science of Irrationality.* Hoboken, NJ: John Wiley & Sons, 2005, 2008.

Kahneman, Daniel, and Amos Tversky. "Choices, Values and Frames." *American Psychologist* 39(4), 1984.

Langer, Ellen. "The Illusion of Control." *Journal of Personality and Social Psychology*, August 1975.

Mackay, Charles. *Memoirs of Extraordinary Popular Delusions and the Madness of Crowds.* Hoboken, NJ: John Wiley & Sons, 1996 edition.

Skidelsky, Robert. *Keynes: The Return of the Master.* Philadelphia: Perseus Books Group, 2009.

Swenson, Ola. "Are We All Less Risky and More Skillful Than Our Fellow Drivers?" *Acta Psychologica*, 1981. Available at:
http://heatherlench.com/wp-content/uploads/2008/07/svenson.pdf.

Tversky, Amos, and Daniel Kahneman. "Extensional versus Intuition Reasoning: Conjunction Fallacy in Probability Judgement." *Psychological Review* 90, 1983.

Zweig, Jason. *Your Money and Your Brain: How the New Science of Neuroeconomics Can Help Make You Rich.* New York: Simon & Schuster, 2007.

About the Author

Larry Light is a veteran financial journalist who has written and edited stories at *Business Week, Forbes*, and the *Wall Street Journal*, winning many journalism awards. He covered national politics for *Congressional Quarterly*, then segued to business coverage for *Newsday*.

He is the author of several mystery novels, including the Karen Glick series set on Wall Street (Dorchester) and *Ladykiller* (Ocean-view), which he coauthored with his wife, Meredith Anthony. Larry has served two terms as the executive vice president of Mystery Writers of America. He also holds the rank of Lieutenant Colonel in the U.S. Army Reserve.

Larry and his wife live on Manhattan's Upper East Side.

Index